American Airlines, US Airways
and the Creation of the World's Largest Airline

ALSO BY TED REED

Carl Furillo, Brooklyn Dodgers All-Star (2011)

American Airlines, US Airways and the Creation of the World's Largest Airline

Ted Reed *and* Dan Reed

McFarland & Company, Inc., Publishers

Jefferson, North Carolina

LIBRARY OF CONGRESS CATALOGUING-IN-PUBLICATION DATA

Reed, Ted, 1948 April 2–
American Airlines, US Airways and the creation
of the world's largest airline / Ted Reed and Dan Reed.
p.   cm.
Includes bibliographical references and index.

ISBN 978-0-7864-7783-8 (softcover : acid free paper) ∞
ISBN 978-1-4766-1775-6 (ebook)

1. American Airlines—History.   2. US Airways—History.
3. Airlines—Mergers—United States.   4. Airlines—United States—
Management.   5. Aeronautics, Commercial—United States—
History.   I. Reed, Dan, 1957–   II. Title.
HE9803.A44R44 2014   387.706'573—dc23   2014036292

BRITISH LIBRARY CATALOGUING DATA ARE AVAILABLE

Front cover: Tailfins of planes from American Airlines
and US Airways (courtesy American Airlines)

Printed in the United States of America

McFarland & Company, Inc., Publishers
Box 611, Jefferson, North Carolina 28640
www.mcfarlandpub.com

To Alexandra,
for love and support
—T.R.

To Janet,
my constant support and love,
whom I don't deserve.
—D.R.

Table of Contents

Preface
by Ted Reed

I joined the *Miami Herald* in 1988 and, in 1989, two months after the start of the Eastern Airlines strike, I was assigned to the airline beat. This was because nobody else wanted it. Since that time, I have remained on the airline beat almost continuously, writing for two newspapers, the *Herald* and the *Charlotte Observer;* for two web sites, *Forbes* and *TheStreet*; and for an airline, US Airways, in the year before it merged with America West.

Two things struck me as I wrote this book. First, the airline industry, like most institutions, is really a small club. Many of the people I engaged with for this book were people I knew in Miami 20 years ago. These include Dave Bates, who was the media spokesman for the Allied Pilots Association and who would sometimes come to the *Herald*'s newsroom to talk; Mark Richard, who was attorney for the flight attendants at Eastern; and Bob Crandall, whom I frequently interviewed in Miami, I think because American did so well in Miami after he decided to purchase Eastern's Latin American routes.

Also, while covering American in Miami, I came to know Terry Maxon of the *Dallas Morning News,* who repeatedly helped me to understand recent developments at American for this book, and Dan Reed, who worked at the time for the *Fort Worth Star-Telegram*. Dan became my co-writer for this book. He wrote five chapters on American, and we jointly wrote the first chapter on Bob Crandall. I should add that Dan and I are not related.

I was also struck because the modern U.S. airline industry developed so recently that every one of its principal architects is still living. Ed Colony was the main person in shaping US Airways. America West was Ed Beauvais' idea. Crandall remade American in his own image. Stephen Wolf built United: when he arrived there, United did not have a single European route. Frank Lorenzo laid the foundation for a successful Continental and, additionally, did more than anyone else to create the airline industry we know today. I spoke with all of them, although my interviews with Stephen Wolf occurred before I started to work specifically on this book.

The key figures who shaped Delta, JetBlue and Southwest are also still living. And obviously, Doug Parker is going to be viewed as a main player in the airline industry's development.

1

I want to thank everybody who agreed to be interviewed, as well as several others. Our principal proofreaders were Dave Carpenter, Scott Hamilton, Gabriela Reed (we *are* related) and John Yurechko. Jeff Siner did all of the photo work. Our primary airline contacts, who helped to arrange interviews and secure photographs, were Michelle Mohr at US Airways, Mike Trevino at American and Chip Wilson at Weber Shandwick. I would also like to thank Rick Thames, executive editor of the *Charlotte Observer*, who allowed me to use photos and to quote from my stories in the *Observer*, and Bill Inman, editor-in-chief of *TheStreet*, who allowed me to quote from my stories on our site.

I would particularly like to thank David Castelveter. He encouraged US Airways to hire me, and then became my boss; he helped me track down people from US Airways for this book and he provided some wonderful reminiscences of his time there. However, he never once let me go home early on Friday. One other thing about the airline industry: I spent 30 years working for newspapers and one year working for an airline, and my two best bosses, David Castelveter and Terri Pope, were both at the airline.

Finally, I want to mention that in my life I have come to fully understand just two things, baseball and airlines, and now I have written books about both of them. I realize that this leaves me with limited options going forward.

Introduction

This is the story of three airlines—American, America West and US Airways—which came together in 2013 to form the world's biggest airline. It is also the story of the U.S. airline industry, a consolidation story almost from its start, as hundreds of small companies failed or got acquired or merged. Ultimately, American, Delta and United, already among the industry leaders in the years just after World War II, ended up as the big three survivors—evidence perhaps that the best way to get ahead in the airline business was to start out ahead in the airline business. Nevertheless, once-dominant carriers, including Eastern Airlines and Pan American World Airways, failed to survive deregulation. Multiple causes explain the failures, but in the end Eastern succumbed to intense labor conflict while Pan Am could not assemble a domestic route system, even as competitors who already had domestic route systems added international flying. By contrast with Eastern and Pan Am, the three airlines that came together late in 2013 as the new American Airlines all played their hands well—even though all three endured bankruptcies and one, US Airways, went through two bankruptcies in three years.

American is generally considered to have started in Dallas in 1934, when accountant C.R. Smith and entrepreneur E.L. Cord decided to put together 82 airline companies, which Cord had accumulated, under the name American Airlines. What most distinguished American for the next six decades was superior management by CEOs Smith, Al Casey and Bob Crandall. American was early to fly trans-continental routes. It always seemed to be in the forefront in industry innovations, from aircraft acquisition to computer reservations systems to frequent flier programs. When deregulation came, American built hubs in the right places, Dallas and Chicago and New York, and Crandall acquired the Miami hub in 1989. As other early airlines like Braniff, Eastern and TWA faltered, American filled in the gaps they left or acquired their best assets. Unfortunately, after doing so, American paid too much to acquire the near-empty hulk of TWA just before the September 11, 2001, terrorist attacks. It also derived little benefit from the acquisitions of AirCal in 1986 and Reno Air in 1999. American's Achilles' heel was airline acquisitions. It never did well with them.

US Airways started in Pittsburgh in 1939 as All American Aviation Inc., with the idea of picking up bags of mail suspended from steel poles, without having to waste time landing and departing. If American was an airline that grew internally and generally shunned acquisitions, All American Aviation—which should not be confused with American Airlines—was the opposite. It changed its name four times and it grew through mergers. Its longest serving CEO, Ed Colodny, presided over four mergers and considered half a dozen more. In 1996 the board of directors brought in Stephen Wolf, who had already presided over two airline mergers and had also built United into a world-class airline, to engineer one more merger. Wolf turned USAir into US Airways and built its European service, but an attempt to merge with United failed. In 2005 another merger-hungry executive, Doug Parker, stepped in. By then it was clear that Allegheny–USAir–US Airways was in many ways the ultimate consolidation airline. Off this platform, Parker engineered the final major merger, not only for US Airways but also, perhaps, for the U.S. airline industry.

America West Airlines started in Phoenix in 1981 and flew its first flight in 1983. It was one of the few post-deregulation startups not to shut down. After deregulation, the key to starting an airline was to have a good hub. In Phoenix, America West had an adequate hub, one that enabled it to survive until a 2005 merger with US Airways and to retain its Tempe headquarters until the 2013 merger with American. Probably its most important contribution to commercial aviation was to nurture a management team, headed by Parker, that chased mergers for eight years. After it succeeded in securing a merger with US Airways, that team created a strong airline out of two weak ones—helped by a controversial seniority ruling that divided pilots and kept their wages at the bottom of the industry for eight years. This created the foundation that enabled a successful run at American.

The story of the American–US Airways merger is nevertheless a story of a labor movement success. The airline industry remained a stronghold of the union movement during five decades when labor's influence declined in most other industries. Labor's involvement and advocacy contributed to the airline industry's spectacular safety record, as U.S. commercial air travel became the safest transportation system in the history of the world, and to the creation of middle-class lifestyles for tens of thousands of workers. When the balance of power tipped too heavily to the unions, contributing to crushing cost structures, airlines collectively turned to the bankruptcy courts in the years following the 2001 terrorist attacks. Bankruptcy court provided a unique forum in which a single judge held sufficient power to efficiently resolve problems.

In seeking the last great airline merger, Parker's team convinced the unions at another airline, American, that their members would be beneficiaries, and labor leaders emerged as key partners. It represented a complete reversal of the strategy of the early airline bankruptcies, in which airlines fought fierce battles with their unions, and where once-dominant carriers such as Braniff, Eastern and Pan Am withered and died.

1

Uncle Ed Builds an Airline

In September 1957 Ed Colodny, a 31-year-old lawyer schooled in the complexities of a regulated airline industry, climbed the stairs to Allegheny Airlines' second-floor headquarters in Hangar 12 at Washington's National Airport. Colodny took his seat in a small, windowless, eight-by-ten-foot office. "The corporate offices were on the second floor of what was then the maintenance facility of the airline," Colodny recalled. "To describe my office as modest would be an overstatement. But it was all I needed at the time."[1] Colodny had just been hired as assistant to the president of Allegheny, in which position he would serve as the airline's first corporate attorney.

Allegheny was just 18 years old. It had started out as All American Aviation, which, like most early U.S. airlines, was originally created to transport mail, one more way government funding nurtured an experimental technology that eventually grew in unimagined ways. This is not to say that in every case, subsidized experimentation pans out. All American Aviation's unique, cutting-edge concept involved airborne airplanes picking up mailbags suspended from cables in isolated sites in the Allegheny Mountains of western Pennsylvania. It seemed like a good idea at the time. In an introduction to the May 1989 edition of USAir's inflight magazine, Colodny recounted some of the key events of 1939, including the early days of other new technologies such as television, the first helicopter and nylon stockings: "With pluck, luck and perseverance, USAir survived the early years and became part of America's postwar aviation system," he wrote.[2]

All American's first official flight took place on May 12, 1939: A winch reeled in mail pouches suspended between two steel poles in Latrobe, Pennsylvania. Within a year, All American was providing mail service to 54 Allegheny region cities. In 1940, founder Richard Du Pont applied to regulators for permanent certification to operate 6 multi-stop routes, providing service to 244 communities in 7 states and converging on Pittsburgh.[3] In the early years, All American struggled financially. In 1948, the Civil Aeronautics Board, which regulated the airline industry, issuing route authorities when it believed air service was appropriate, allowed the carrier to enhance its business by adding a new component: passengers. All American was awarded the rights to operate flights on 6 feeder lines in 7 states and the District of Columbia. That year, it moved its offices to Hangar 12, which it leased from the Federal Aviation Administration. By

1948, the foundation for what would eventually become US Airways was well established. The airline had a Pittsburgh hub, a headquarters at Washington National and a history of financial problems. In 1953, the name was changed to Allegheny Airlines. Allegheny underwent two more name changes as it became the only local-service airline from the 1950s to survive into the 21st century, thanks largely to the expansion Colodny oversaw during his 34 years at the company.

Colodny will forever be remembered as US Airways' longest-serving and, in many ways, most accomplished leader. He was in charge from 1975 to 1991, guiding it from regulation through deregulation and overseeing the purchase of four competitors. During this transitional phase for the nation's airline industry, Allegheny was among the most successful participants, at least among the dozen or so smaller "local service" airlines. At the time, the airline industry consisted of 12 major trunk airlines—American, Braniff, Continental, Delta, Eastern, National, Northeast, Northwest, Pan Am, TWA,

Ed Colodny ran USAir for 16 years. He presided over four mergers, preserved a paternalistic culture and became known as "Uncle Ed" (courtesy Ed Colodny).

At All American Aviation, Stinson SR-10F Reliant aircraft snatched the mail from portable pickup stations, starting in 1939 (courtesy American Airlines).

United and Western, which served bigger cities and longer routes—and the dozen local service airlines including Allegheny, Lake Central, Mohawk and Piedmont, which served small cities.

Although the U.S. airline industry has consistently been characterized by intense competition, it is worth noting that the list of the dozen carriers that started out on top includes the names of the three carriers—American, Delta and United—that, six decades later, ended up as the three global U.S. airlines, an indication that perhaps the best way to get ahead in the airline business was to start out ahead in the airline business. Of course, survival was a struggle for the big carriers as well as the small ones. Pan Am, easily the biggest and best of the trunk airlines, fell by the wayside. The anomalies include the tiny percentage of successful startup carriers such as America West and Southwest. As for Allegheny, it underwent two more name changes as it became the only local service airline from the 1950s to remain viable into the 21st century, thanks largely to the expansion Colodny oversaw.

Colodny's management style emphasized a high regard for the airline's employees.

"They're the ones who run the airline," he said. "People like myself don't fly airplanes, maintain airplanes, check luggage, or take care of passengers. The rank and file do that. Without them, you don't have anything."[4] Although cyclical layoffs were not uncommon, many employees were unionized and the postwar American economy was generally expanding, assuring wage and benefit growth, fueled partially by the tendency to extend USAir's more generous wage and benefit packages to employees at the airlines Colodny acquired. Eventually high costs would get the airline into trouble, but by then Colodny would be gone. During his tenure, he was widely known by the nickname "Uncle Ed" and was generally well-liked. Colodny "led the airline because he was always available," said John Goglia, who joined Allegheny as a mechanic in Boston in 1966 and stayed for 29 years, eventually leaving to join the National Transportation Safety Board. "He was a visible and reachable leader who was always around the property."[5] David Castelveter, who during 28 years at the airline rose from a part-time baggage handler in Pittsburgh to managing director of corporate communications and investor relations, called Colodny "the guy who put us in the big leagues." Castelveter recalled the day in the late 1970s when Allegheny extended its western service to Phoenix. "When we went to Phoenix, that was big time," he said. "Before that, the furthest west we flew was to Nashville."[6]

Born in Burlington, Vermont, the son of a grocer, on June 7, 1926, Colodny graduated from the University of Rochester and, in 1951, from Harvard Law School. (Years later, from 2001 to 2002, he served 13 months as the University of Vermont's interim president, helping the school through a troubled period.) During his military service, Colodny spent three years in the army's Judge Advocate General's Corps, which handles military legal cases. In 1954, after retiring from the military, he became a staff lawyer for the CAB. In a regulated industry, "you couldn't fly anywhere without a certificate of public convenience," Colodny said. "I was a CAB trial lawyer, assigned to represent the public interest in cases where airlines applied to fly new routes. They had to show that there was sufficient economic justification and, if it was a competitive route, that it could support the competition. The theory was that limited competition should be allowed in the industry: that led ultimately to deregulation."[7]

In one case, involving an effort to start a helicopter service in Chicago, Colodny needed to interview Mayor Richard J. Daley. "That caused a ripple," he said. "Nobody was willing to ask the mayor anything. But he answered my questions."[8] In another case, four airlines—Allegheny, Lake Central, Mohawk and North Central (Colodny reeled off the names 55 years later)—all wanted the right to fly between Detroit and Erie, Pennsylvania. "When we finally came up with a recommendation for the Board, we recommended having two carriers, Allegheny and Mohawk, in the market, since they served different 'beyond' cities," Colodny said. "Afterwards, both airlines started providing flights, and at one time there were 12 flights a day between Detroit and Erie, even though the market could support only two or three. So the board investigated to see if one should come out, then decided not to do that, and ultimately there was no service at all."[9] Perhaps this incident shows everything that is wrong with government regulation of industry, or perhaps it shows that even more regulation was needed. Probably the most important consequence of the case was that Allegheny president Leslie Barnes met Colodny and later hired him away from the CAB.

Allegheny served 8 states and about 50 communities, including small cities such as Altoona, Bradford, Erie, Harrisburg, Jamestown, Lancaster, Redding and Williamsport. It wanted to grow, and Colodny led various efforts to convince the CAB to relax restrictions on local service airlines. Over time, Allegheny acquired more routes and more aircraft. In 1963, it moved its maintenance, engineering and flight operations functions from Hangar 12 to Pittsburgh. It grew through mergers, encouraged by the CAB, which had decided that mergers represented a path to reduced subsidies. In 1968, Allegheny merged with Indianapolis-based Lake Central Airlines. "Lake Central was the easiest merger, a friendly deal with few problems," Colodny said.[10] In 1972, Allegheny merged with Utica, New York–based Mohawk Airlines. "Mohawk was in trouble and the banks forced it into a merger," he said. "It worked out fairly easily."[11]

At the time, two young entrepreneurs, Frank Lorenzo and partner Bob Carney, were looking at troubled airlines with the thought of acquiring one. "The first airline we looked at was Mohawk and, in fact, we received the Mohawk board approval for a deal we had proposed," Lorenzo said. "But they took a long and difficult pilot strike and we became very concerned about the solvency of the company after the strike. So we recommended they consider a merger with Allegheny Airlines, and we went after Texas International instead."[12] In 1972, the potential for labor unrest associated with the merger led the CAB to adopt the Allegheny-Mohawk Labor Protection Provisions, which became the standard protocol for labor integration in the airline mergers that followed. Allegheny-Mohawk required that seniority integration be "fair and equitable" and provided for mediation and arbitration to resolve disputes. It also mandated financial reimbursement for employees whose jobs were lost, whose compensation was reduced or whose relocation was required. Half a century later, when American merged with US Airways, U.S. District Court Judge Roslyn Silver looked to Allegheny-Mohawk to ascertain how the newer labor protection provisions in the 2008 McCaskill-Bond Act might be interpreted.

Like most established carriers, Allegheny opposed deregulation. "We thought the major carriers had so much more strength and muscle than we did that they would take over whatever strong pieces we had and we wouldn't be able to compete very well with them, both because of marketing and sheer size," Colodny said. "The only airline that favored it was United, because they were already the biggest airline in the country and they had a hard time getting route authorities from the CAB."[13] Despite industry opposition, Congress approved the Airline Deregulation Act of 1978, encouraged by broad consumer support and the expectation that deregulation would lead to lower fares. That perception proved accurate. Following deregulation, Allegheny and most

The durable DC-9 was an important part of the fleet at Allegheny Airlines (courtesy American Airlines).

other airlines re-evaluated their business models. "We recognized that if we were going to expand and take advantage of it, we had to be selective and careful, modernize our fleet and be sure we could finance our growth properly," Colodny said. "I used to use the analogy 'Just because they took the lid off the cookie jar doesn't mean we have to get a bellyache.'"[14]

"We had already started to develop a Pittsburgh hub," he said. "Deregulation allowed us to greatly expand to the West Coast, Texas and Florida."[15] One casualty of the carrier's expansionism was the Allegheny name, which was changed to USAir in October 1979. Route expansion continued and, in the mid–1980s, Colodny began a push to expand through ever larger mergers. USAir bought Pacific Southwest Airlines, better known as PSA, in 1987. "PSA wanted to do it," Colodny said. "But from a cultural standpoint, there were differences, and when we took the smile off the PSA planes, there were screams up and down the West Coast."[16] During the 1980s, Colodny also engaged in merger discussions with Continental, Eastern, Northwest and United. "We saw we had to bulk up or we would not go anywhere," he said. "We came close with Continental."[17]

Mike Flores, son of the famous Associated Press reporter Ike Flores, joined USAir in 1982 as a Boston-based flight attendant. Two decades later, he would become president of the US Airways chapter of the Association of Flight Attendants. At first he thought he might become a reporter like his dad, who during the 1960s was among the handful of U.S. reporters who, working in Havana, covered Fidel Castro's ascension and early days in power. Mike Flores attended the University of Florida at a time when, following the glamorization of the investigative reporters who had brought an end to the Nixon administration, everybody wanted to be a newspaper reporter. "My father discouraged me from that line of work because at the time everyone was majoring in journalism," Flores said. "There weren't going to be enough jobs."[18] In any case, Flores found another rewarding pursuit at college: playing golf. He even had a golf scholarship.

After graduating in 1979, he played on golf tours for several years, but eventually he ran out of money and took a job with USAir.

Colodny at the time was continuing to expand the airline. "Colodny was forward-thinking," Flores said. "He realized that there was an opportunity to make Allegheny into a major carrier so he changed the name and positioned it to be a carrier that was sustainable, broadening the route structure into Florida and the West. He realized that the only way to do this was to buy new airplanes. When I got hired, they had just ordered the 737–300."[19] USAir became the first airline to take delivery of the 737–300 when Boeing delivered that aircraft on November 28, 1984. Two days later, Southwest took delivery of its first 737–300: as a result, airplane buffs sometimes differ on which carrier was the launch customer. US Airways began using 737–300s to fly from Pittsburgh to the West Coast. "It was a single-aisle plane flying all the way to the West Coast, and nobody liked that, but at least it had the capability." Flores said.[20]

In the late 1980s, as the potential survivors of the first stage of deregulation began to emerge, various Wall Street investors hovered over the industry. They included Carl Icahn, who acquired TWA in 1985 and, the next year, set his sights on USAir. "Icahn started calling me," Colodny said. "He wanted to put TWA and USAir together. He used to get on the phone and we'd go on for 30 or 40 minutes at a time. He would say we pay employees too much, we have to cut employee costs, and if we merged with TWA he could force us to take the same wage cuts TWA had put on their employees. I told him that, in that case, he would have a lot of very unhappy employees providing very bad service. So we weren't interested in doing that. We were making good money and we had no basis to seek concessionary labor agreements."[21]

The fourth and best-remembered USAir merger came in 1987 with North Carolina–based Piedmont Airlines. It was a merger that Icahn tried to stop: on the day when the boards of USAir and Piedmont were scheduled to meet to approve the deal, he sent Colodny a letter in which he offered to buy USAir for $1.65 billion. As it turned out, TWA had already acquired about 9 percent of USAir's shares. "We turned down his proposal and went to court in Pittsburgh to enjoin him from acquiring more stock," Colodny said. "We got an injunction, and afterwards there was a picture of me in the *Pittsburgh Post-Gazette* with a big smile on my face. After that, I received, from the employees of USAir, a scroll that is twelve feet long and three feet wide, with thousands of signatures thanking me for keeping Icahn away from the company. I always prized that. It reflected that our culture at the company as we grew was still to honor the role of the people who made the airline work. The culture of sharing was very strong, it was a time when we were able to do that, and I was always pleased that our employees recognized it."[22]

After the brief interruption, the Piedmont merger went ahead. Today, it is often cited as an example of an extreme case of corporate culture clash. As Jerry Orr, the longtime director of Charlotte Douglas International Airport, once said: "When you buy somebody, you ought to save the good parts and throw away the bad parts, but

USAir did the opposite."[23] USAir was the more corporate, button-down company, while Piedmont was Southern and genteel, with a customer focus. Nevertheless, Colodny said the merger was not so bad, despite the challenges of merging two successful airlines. "There was a very proud group of employees and managers at Piedmont," he said. "They had built a wonderful airline and they weren't anxious to lose their identity. As with many things, there was emotional resistance, and they thought USAir people were imposing USAir operating policies on their systems.[24]

"But it did come together," Colodny said. "When we merged with Piedmont, we doubled the size of the airline and Charlotte became a wonderful hub." A favorable aspect, recalled Mike Flores, was that Colodny and Piedmont founder Tom Davis shared the belief that an airline's most important asset was its employees. "Ed Colodny was extremely employee-friendly," Flores said. "He could meet a flight attendant one time and five years later he would know their name. Tom Davis was the same way. He and Ed Colodny were cut from the same cloth. Tom Davis was a Southern gentleman and Ed Colodny was a Northern lawyer, but they both understood you had to make friends with your employees."[25] In spite of the commonalities between Colodny and Davis, some leadership conflicts simmered, particularly in the case of Piedmont CEO Bill Howard. A few years before the buyout, USAir had sought a friendly merger. "It fell apart largely over the issue of leadership," Colodny said. "I was willing to let Bill be CEO first for a couple of years, but then, at 65, he would retire and become chairman and I would take over as CEO. But he claimed he had a deal with his board to be CEO until he was 67. I said 'I am sorry, I can't buy that deal' and we walked away from each other." When USAir finally acquired Piedmont, Howard left. Recalled Colodny: "I would not say we parted on lovey-dovey terms."[26]

Another problem with the Piedmont merger was that wages rose faster than had been anticipated, a result of negotiations with the International Association of Machinists (IAM), which represent the fleet service workers and mechanics at the two airlines. Because USAir had higher wages than Piedmont, it negotiated a gradual phase-in of its contract for Piedmont pilots and flight attendants. But the IAM insisted on an immediate phase-in. "It was a very frustrating negotiation," Colodny said. "After months of negotiating, we were getting nowhere and the Piedmont operation was starting to deteriorate. The decision was made that we couldn't negotiate with the IAM any longer, so we finally conceded on pay parity."[27] Management also conceded on another issue, agreeing to continue to have mechanics push back airplanes, as they did at USAir, even though lower-paid fleet service workers performed the work at Piedmont. Once the concession on pay parity was made for IAM members, "we had to go back and give pilots and flight attendants immediate pay parity," Colodny said. "Our labor costs did not ramp up as gradually as we had planned, and so we had a much different scenario than we had envisioned from day one of the operational merger."[28] By contrast, at PSA the USAir contracts were phased in over time. Lake Central and Mohawk came in at Allegheny levels, but those levels were below the industry average at the time.

Ed Colodny (right) and David Castelveter at 2011 Wright Memorial Dinner in Washington, D.C. In 1990 Colodny won the Wright Brothers Memorial Trophy, which honors significant public service to U.S. aviation (courtesy David Castelveter).

Although USAir had been largely successful throughout the 1980s, things began to change in 1989, and not just because of the Piedmont merger. "We ran into some difficulties," Colodny said. "We started having some losses." The events presaged the future of the airline industry over the next two decades, during which high costs regularly outran management's ability to raise revenues. A seminal event was the Eastern Airlines bankruptcy in March 1989. Operating under bankruptcy court protection, Eastern began to aggressively reduce fares in markets including East Coast to Florida, which USAir also served. Meanwhile, in 1990 oil prices surged from around $17 a barrel in July to $36 a barrel in August and $40 in October, reflecting fears surrounding the Iraqi invasion of Kuwait. "The industry had never made a lot of money," Colodny said. "Even in the first ten years after deregulation, on operating revenue of $381 billion, the profit was $1.6 billion, a margin of less than one half of one percent. We were a money tube: A lot of money came in, a lot went out and very little stuck."[29]

But the industry still appealed to investors, including Warren Buffett. In 1989, hedge fund manager Michael Steinhardt had acquired about 6 percent of USAir and appeared poised to launch a hostile takeover bid. After a friend suggested that he talk with Buffett about protecting the airline from Steinhardt, Colodny went to Omaha, where he and CFO William Loftus joined Buffett for lunch at Gorat's Steakhouse, a Buffett favorite. "We spent a couple of hours talking about the airline, a very friendly casual conversation, and I had a great T-bone steak," Colodny said. "At the end of the discussion, Warren indicated he was interested in making an investment. We set up a small team to meet with his folks, and two weeks later we had an agreement to sell him convertible preferred stock at 9.25 percent. After we made the deal, Michael Steinhardt went away. We never had any real problems with him."[30]

Buffett bought $358 million worth of debt at 9.25 percent, convertible in two years to USAir stock at $60 a share, up from the trading price of $52. The shares represented about 12 percent of the company. Buffett and his close associate Charlie Munger subsequently served a few years on the USAir board of directors. The shares never appreciated, and Buffett never converted. "He wrote down his investment at one point, and he cashed out as soon as he was able," Colodny said. "I think at the end of the day he got all his dividends paid and his principal back."[31] Nevertheless, Buffett famously decried his investment in USAir in various forums, calling it the worst investment he ever made, despite his respect for Colodny. At the 2013 annual meeting of Berkshire Hathaway, he said, "Investors have poured their money into airlines and airline manufacturers for 100 years with terrible results," and he called the industry "a death trap for investors."[32]

In 1991, Colodny turned 65 and company policy dictated that he retire. Colodny had managed his succession by putting two younger executives, Randy Malin and Seth Schofield, on fast tracks where they could in effect compete for the top job. Malin was polished, a strong public speaker, and had become executive vice president of marketing. Schofield, more plainspoken, had rapport with the unions. Eventually Colodny chose Schofield. Unfortunately, Schofield inherited a franchise that was beginning to show cracks. The losses had led to the start of concessionary bargaining with the unions. "I left him with that," Colodny said. "He came in at a very difficult time in the industry." Moreover, Southwest's arrival in Baltimore, a USAir hub, was just two years away. Very quickly, Colodny said, "Seth was in the hot seat."[33]

2

Call Me Butch

Between 1989 and 1994, USAir experienced the worst five years in its history, not because of the carrier's financial performance, although this deteriorated, but rather because of an unprecedented series of fatal crashes. The airline's spirit suffered immensely. It was not that individuals felt they could have prevented the crashes—in nearly every case they could not have—but rather because airline corporate cultures tightly bind people and airline crashes produce a sense that the airline somehow has failed. In 1994 the phrase "five for five" emerged, recalling the five crashes in five years and further damaging the airline's self-image. Among employees, "everybody was sickened" by the successive crashes, recalled David Castelveter, who was Phoenix sales manager at the time and who worked on the airline's family support team following three of the crashes. "It was not just that our company had a crash and some of the victims were our fellow employees, but also because for many of us in sales the victims were people who flew as a result of our efforts. So we were sickened by the loss of life and we were fearful for the outcome for our company. At the time, having a crash was a sign of doom for the organization. You were considered to be unsafe and maybe people wouldn't want to fly you. And you kept asking 'Why is this happening?' I remember saying that to myself: 'How could this keep happening?' and 'Where does it stop?' You start asking yourself all kinds of questions about why it's happening and what's being done to stop it."[1]

Concern over the crashes came to dominate the CEO tenure of Seth Schofield, a popular executive who had worked his way up through the ranks and who successfully maintained the employee-friendly environment that Colodny had created. Amazingly, Schofield managed to become chairman and CEO of a major airline and later a director of four companies—US Steel, Marathon Petroleum, PNC Bank and Calgon Carbon, where he became board chairman—even though he never received a college degree. Many knew him as Butch, his nickname. "Schofield was a good man," said longtime pilot James Ray. "He was the last CEO we had who cared about his employees. He worked his way up from the ramp to the board room. He was one of us. He wasn't a bean courter. He was an airline guy."[2] Schofield was, however, "surrounded by incompetent people,"[3] Ray said. Added Mike Flores: "Schofield was seen as a blue-collar guy, not as a member of the Wall Street club. He never tried to change that."[4]

Schofield was born August 22, 1939, in Stafford Springs, Connecticut. A few months after graduating from Stafford Springs High School in 1957, he joined Allegheny as a ramp agent, the start of a 39-year-career at the airline during which there were few jobs he didn't hold. As an agent, he loaded bags and sold tickets and boarded aircraft at Washington National Airport. In 1960, the CAB authorized Allegheny to fly in New England, which provided Schofield with a chance to return home, overseeing the opening of airport facilities around the region. He became interim customer service manager at Hartford's Bradley Airport at 21 and ascended on the customer service side, eventually overseeing customer service integration in the mergers with Lake Central in 1968 and Mohawk in 1972. Young Schofield showed promise, so in 1975 the airline sent him to a Harvard Business School six-month

Seth Schofield worked his way up from ramp agent to CEO. "He wasn't a bean counter. He was an airline guy" (courtesy American Airlines).

executive management program. After graduating, Schofield moved to the Pittsburgh-based operations side, ultimately rising to executive vice president of operations, overseeing flight operations, maintenance, engineering, customer service and labor relations. Working in so many jobs and at various locations, Schofield came to know most of the employees at the airline. He moved to the Washington headquarters to become executive vice president of operations and vice chairman of the board in 1989.

Schofield acknowledged that he inherited an airline with problems. "We acquired PSA and Piedmont, and that was a handful, doing two mergers back to back," he said. "PSA was smaller, but it had a different culture than we did. Piedmont was almost equal size, and there were some issues, [including] seniority integration and labor issues, that we had to work our way through."[5] Additionally, "We ran into a recession in 1991 with the beginning of the Gulf War," he said. "We had just kind of gotten the three airlines put together and we were beginning to get some momentum going, improving the quality of customer service, and then with the recession, we had to do a really difficult, heart-wrenching personnel reduction. That took a very serious toll on the employees and on the service."[6]

Schofield oversaw a series of critical deals. In 1992, he acquired the Trump Shuttle and accompanying slots and gates at Boston, Washington and LaGuardia, as well as the former Continental terminal building at LaGuardia. In 1992, he paid TWA $50 million to buy a Philadelphia-London route. The following year, British Airways paid $300 million for a 20 percent stake in USAir as well as a lopsided code-share agreement in which it received most of the revenue from USAir flights to London. Schofield was criticized, but the investment was essential as USAir, facing about $2 billion in debt, was continuing to lose money and beginning to hear bankruptcy chatter.

As Schofield negotiated concessions, the IAM balked. In October 1992 it took 8,300 mechanics out on a six-day strike. Other than a 1969 strike by Piedmont pilots, the strike was the only one in the history of USAir, Allegheny, America West, Piedmont and PSA. "We were asking employees for concessions on pay and work rules," Schofield said. "I had gotten the pilots and the flight attendants and a couple of Teamster locals (representing fleet workers in four cities) to go along. It was going to be short-term and we were going to pay them back over a period of time. I had a good relationship with the IAM, but they would not concede and I could not give up the concessions I had already obtained from the other unions. So I had no choice. I took a strike. The IAM probably did not believe that we would take a strike, but when they realized how serious we were, they realized that there was no choice. In the meantime, we ran a good airline while they were out."[7]

USAir planes, including a Boeing 737, gather at the terminal at Pittsburgh International Airport (courtesy US Airways).

Essentially, Schofield continued to run the airline the way Colodny had, with a high regard for employees. "From Les Barnes to Colodny to me, we always had very good labor relations," Schofield said. "All three of us were always, in the final analysis, very engaged in the process and in the final agreements. I like to view myself as a person who always thought of the shareholders and the customers but never forgot the employees. I never forgot my roots and where I came from. I treated everybody with the respect I would have liked to have had when I came up through the ranks. I always tried to handle power in a thoughtful way."[8]

Schofield's common touch made a big impression on Castelveter. In 1980 Castelveter, who had also started out working on the ramp for Allegheny, got his first management job as a baggage claims representative. People whose bags had been lost or damaged would call his office, seeking to arrange settlements. But the airline had to search for 30 days before it could reach a settlement. This made for a lot of phone calls. Often, in the passengers' memories, the number and value of their lost possessions would increase over time. They never decreased, but they often increased. "People would call and say 'I forgot to mention, I also had this or that in there,'" Castelveter said. "By the end of the day, you needed a break. So I would leave the office and go sit in the main corridor of the airport and watch the passengers go back and forth. One day as I was leaving the office, Seth walked in. He had been walking by with some people, going into a conference room. I was a young kid, fresh out of college, in my first job in management and I was in awe of the leaders of the airline. He said 'How are you?' I said 'Good.' He said 'It's good to meet you,' and I said 'Thanks, Mr. Schofield.' He said 'Call me Butch.' I never forgot that, that somebody of his stature would talk that way to a low-level person like I was."[9]

Despite Schofield's warm heart, history could not be turned back. The unraveling of the USAir model, which relied heavily on charging high fares for short-hop Northeast routes, can be said to have begun on September 19, 1993, the day Southwest began service to Baltimore. Late that same year, Continental began its Continental Lite low-fare operation, focused on Greensboro, North Carolina, about 100 miles from the Charlotte hub. At the same time, American, Delta and United were adding capacity. "They created an imbalance between capacity and demand," Schofield said. "There was a lot of discounting going on." Did Schofield face a plague of locusts? "I would describe it as a challenge we got through together," he said. "Ultimately, things got turned around and in the last year I was there we made some money. Things were looking up, not just for USAir but also for the airline industry in general. We went through a bad time and came out of it quite well."[10]

Nevertheless, the crashes sapped the spirit of the airline. "We were criticized because we had five accidents in a short period of time," Schofield said. "It should be remembered that in the final analysis by the NTSB, we were not responsible for three of those in a way that would be described as being negligent or irresponsible."[11] Still, the crashes "emotionally tugged at every employee group,"[12] recalled John Goglia.

Goglia, who joined Allegheny Airlines in 1966 as a mechanic in Boston, eventually emerged as one of the airline industry's leading safety advocates. At USAir, he served for 20 years as the International Association of Machinists' safety representative on accident investigation teams; while on that job, he investigated all five of the USAir crashes. Later, in 1995, he became the first airframe and power plant mechanic to be appointed to the National Transportation Safety Board, where he served two terms, departing in 2004. While on the board, Goglia drew attention to airport safety issues, to the significance of the maintenance process and to the need to respond to the needs of victims and their families—including the need for timely, accurate information.

The first of the five U.S. crashes occurred on September 20, 1989, when Flight 5050, a Boeing 737–400 departing from New York LaGuardia for Charlotte, attempted to take off in stormy, wet weather—although many other departures had been canceled. The captain was relatively inexperienced, with just 140 hours as a captain, and he allowed the first officer to make the takeoff, a policy violation given that the first officer's level of experience was also limited. The plane overran the runway and ending up submerged in the East River. The incident resulted in 21 injuries and two deaths. The NTSB determined that the probable cause was "the captain's failure to exercise his command authority in a timely manner to reject the takeoff or take sufficient control to continue the takeoff, which was initiated with a mistrimmed rudder.... Also causal was the captain's failure to detect the mistrimmed rudder before the takeoff was attempted."[13]

According to Goglia,

> The airplane sat on the gate for five or six hours, waiting to take off in the heavy rain. During that time, the crew and the refuelers and a whole bunch of people were on and off the plane and somewhere along the line, the rudder got pushed in one direction. We suspected it was someone who came into the cockpit and sat down in the jump seat and inadvertently hit the rudder with their foot. The same crew had flown the plane into LaGuardia, and they did their en route checklist, so when they were ready to take off they did an abbreviated checklist and they didn't check the rudder.[14]

The second crash occurred at Los Angeles International Airport on February 1, 1991, when Flight 1493, a Boeing 737–300 coming from Columbus, Ohio, attempted to land and collided on the runway with SkyWest Flight 5569, a 19-seat Fairchild Metroliner. The 34 fatalities included all 10 passengers and 2 crew members on the SkyWest plane as well as 20 passengers and 2 crew members on the 737. Most of the Boeing fatalities resulted from asphyxiation, as passengers were unable to use all of the emergency exits. "The SkyWest flight was positioned on the same runway awaiting clearance for takeoff," said the NTSB report. The board concluded that the probable cause of the crash was "the failure of the Los Angeles air traffic facility management to implement procedures that provide redundancy standards, [and] the failure of the FAA air traffic service to provide adequate policy direction and oversight to its air traffic control facility managers." Those failures, the

NTSB said, "led to the failure of the local controller to maintain an awareness of the traffic situation, culminating in the inappropriate clearances and subsequent collision."[15]

Goglia added:

The runway was 12,000 feet long and the controller let the SkyWest plane take off from the intersection of a taxiway with the runway. In the crush of business, with all the airplanes coming in, she forgot that the SkyWest plane was out in the middle of the runway and she cleared USAir to land. It was about 6 p.m. and the USAir plane was landing into the sun and the pilots had problems seeing the ground because of the sunlight in their eyes, so the little plane went unnoticed. A couple of other unique things happened too. [In reviewing the accident,] the NTSB sent in a helicopter to make the approach at the same time of day, and they couldn't see the rotating light that flashes on top of the [SkyWest] fuselage because the tail obscured it. If there would have been any hope of seeing something, it would have been that light, but the tail blocked it out. Not only that, but also the [Sky-West] airplane was right on the center line of the runway, where the runway lights are, so you couldn't distinguish the lights on that airplane even if you could see them. So all of the visual cues in the system were negated by chance—you are talking about an explosion of bad luck.[16]

At the time of the Los Angeles crash, Castelveter recalled, USAir had little experience in handling crashes or in dealing with the families of the victims. "The people who worked at Los Angeles airport were there with the families," he recalled:

Annette Murphy, who was regional sales director in Los Angeles, went to the area where the families were assembled and she recognized that the people who were assigned to family support had no experience with it. So she made the decision to use the sales people. They had a lot of experience dealing with people; they had their jobs because they were personable and had interpersonal skills, and also they had expense accounts—not that we were going to spend frivolously, but we had the authority to spend when we needed to, which the airport people didn't have. So we were assigned to the families from the beginning, sometimes for weeks on end, to help them with whatever they needed, whatever we could do. We were there until the deceased was buried, and sometimes for several days after that.[17]

The third crash occurred at LaGuardia on March 22, 1992, when USAir Flight 405, a Fokker F28, sought to take off for Cleveland but crashed into Flushing Bay, just beyond the runway. Of the 51 passengers, 27 were killed including the captain and one of the flight attendants. The NTSB blamed inadequate de-icing procedures. "Ice contamination on the wings resulted in an aerodynamic stall and loss of control after liftoff," the agency said in its report, which noted that a de-icing fluid widely used at the time was effective for only 15 minutes. "The probable causes of this accident were the failure of the airline industry and the FAA to provide flight crews with procedures, requirements and criteria compatible with departure delays in conditions conducive to airframe icing and the decision by the flight crew to take off without positive assurance that the airplane's wings were free of ice accumulation after 35 minutes of exposure to precipitation following de-icing," the board said. The NTSB also cited "inadequate coordination between the flight crew that led to a takeoff rotation at a lower than prescribed airspeed."[18]

Goglia said that although snow was pouring down, it was pouring down in such a way that the wind kept the front of the aircraft clean, so that the pilot could clearly see the nose through the windshield, creating the sense that conditions were not as bad as they actually were. Additionally, the airplane was right at the end of a 30-minute interval since being de-iced, which would have triggered the next de-icing. "The mechanics said it was clean so the airplane went out and slowly taxied to the end of the runway," Goglia said. "There was a requirement for a 30-minute [interval], but you don't hit a time clock when you push off, so it was probably a minute or two over, and one of the wings was contaminated by ice. As soon as the pilot lifted off—almost anything will lift off the ground—he immediately lost control. The plane tipped over and ran off the end of the runway. After this accident, there were many changes in procedures: the ground procedures changed and the de-icing fluid that airlines used was also changed."[19]

The fourth incident on July 2, 1994, involved Flight 1016, a DC-9 from Columbia, South Carolina, to Charlotte, which crashed as a result of wind shear as it attempted to land at Charlotte Douglas International Airport. Thirty-seven passengers were killed; the flight crew and two passengers survived. The NTSB determined that the probable causes of the accident were the flight crew's decision "to continue an approach into severe convective activity that was conducive to a microburst," as well as its failures "to recognize a wind shear situation in a timely manner [and] to establish and maintain the proper airplane attitude and thrust setting necessary to escape the wind shear." The pilots' failures, the NTSB said, resulted from air traffic control's failure to provide them with "real-time adverse weather and wind shear hazard information." The combination of mistakes "led to an encounter with and the failure to escape from a microburst-induced wind shear that was produced by a rapidly developing thunderstorm located at the approach end of runway 18R."[20] The agency said contributing factors were inadequate air traffic control procedures, the control tower supervisor's failure to ensure controllers were fully aware of conditions, shortcomings in USAir's procedures, and the failure of USAir to equip the aircraft with a wind shear warning system.

Goglia commented, "The NTSB blamed the pilot, who may have been one degree below where he should have been, but it should not have been pilot error. At the time those pilots entered into that wind shear, there was nothing they could do. They started landing in a clear sky but ran into wind shear, a violent downdraft, when they were only 200 feet above the ground, so there was no margin for error and no recovery possible."[21] The FAA had Charlotte Douglas on the list of airports that should have had Doppler radar, Goglia said, but funding was short and so "year after year, it was put on the back shelf. It wasn't only Charlotte, it was other airports too, where we had the technology that could make a difference and we didn't install it in time."[22]

Castelveter recalled working in the Charlotte airport with the family support team:

We would hear that a family member was arriving at the airport and we would get on the airplane as soon as it arrived and get the family members off first, and escort them to the club and begin working with them to get them to the hotel, to get them whatever they needed. I remember that one of the sales representatives had a breakdown, a meltdown, going to the gate to meet a plane. She fell to the ground and started crying. She had been doing it for several days and she hit the point where her system didn't want to deal with it anymore. With one of the passengers, I had to go to his funeral in Phoenix, knowing it was my company that killed him. I had to stand there with his family, his wife, his kids and his friends, all the while knowing it was my company that killed him.[23]

The fifth crash came just two months later on September 8, 1994, and was the worst in the airline's history. A total of 132 people were killed after Flight 427, a Boeing 737 flying from Chicago to Pittsburgh, crashed while attempting to land. The cause, it turned out, was rudder malfunction. Because of the vast difficulty in pinpointing the cause of the crash, the NTSB did not issue its report until four and a half years later. The board concluded that the probable cause of the accident "was a loss of control of the airplane resulting from the movement of the rudder surface to its blowdown limit. The rudder surface most likely deflected in a direction opposite to that commanded by the pilots as a result of a jam of the main rudder power control unit servo

Rescue workers search for bodies after the July 3, 1994, crash of US Airways Flight 1016 in Charlotte (John D. Simmons, courtesy *Charlotte Observer*).

23

valve secondary slide."[24](A servo or servomechanism is an automatic device that detects errors and corrects them.) The board's report was "focused on Boeing 737 rudder malfunctions, including rudder reversals; the adequacy of the 737 rudder system design; unusual attitude training for air carrier pilots; and flight data recorder (FDR) parameters."

Goglia said that in its investigation, the board learned of a rudder failure mode that Boeing had not anticipated. As a result, he said, the probable cause of the 1991 Colorado Springs crash involving United Airlines Flight 585 had to be changed, and Boeing had to spend $1 billion or more to make alterations on every 737 that was still in service. "I am convinced that we prevented other crashes with those findings," Goglia noted. "There would have been at least one more and maybe we wouldn't have figured it out even then. It was a tribute to everybody involved in the process, including Boeing, who resisted at first, but once the cause was determined they went back and did the right thing."[25]

On the day of the crash, which occurred soon after 7 p.m. the entire US Airways sales and customer service staff were gathered in the gym at Robert Morris University, just outside Pittsburgh. Schofield and top marketing executives were previewing "Business Select," a new product that enabled flight attendants to flip a lever to convert coach seats into first class seats when loads warranted. It was to be used on departures in 16 cities. "It was a very joyful day," recalled Castelveter, then district sales manager in Phoenix, who attended the meeting. "We were announcing a new product that the marketing people sold us so strongly that you left there saying 'I have a new product to sell and it's a good one.'" That afternoon, Castelveter flew back to Phoenix. As he landed, he noticed lights flashing outside the plane and wondered about the reason. The plane pulled to the gate, the door opened, and the customer service manager boarded. "Would David Castelveter come forward first?" he said. He quietly told Castelveter that a crash had occurred in Pittsburgh and that a return flight was waiting. "There I was, returning from a wonderful event after a long flight and when we land they say 'You just had another crash,'" Castelveter said. "I had to fly back, sitting on a plane for four hours, thinking 'We had another one. What are we going to do now?'"[26]

By this time, even though only the two LaGuardia crashes could be said to have resulted directly from the actions of US Airways pilots, most employees were shell-shocked. "The pilots mobilized to pick apart the whole organization, to see what they could do differently," Goglia said. "The pilot community started to do work after the first one, then more on the second and third, getting things under control, making improvements." In 1994, Schofield brought in Robert Oaks, who had been an air force fighter pilot and had risen to become a four-star general, commander of the United States Air Forces in Europe, to be senior vice president in charge of safety. "He was the first person I ever worked closely with that there was no question why he was a general," Goglia said. "The man was competent, he got things done, and if you worked around him you needed to perform."[27] Oaks became senior vice president of flight operations before retiring in 2000 to become a missionary leader for the Mormon Church.

But the changes were permanent, Goglia added. "US Airways made the commitment to make wholesale changes in the operation, and they brought in people from the outside who could cut through the territorial and bureaucratic processes that live in any large organization to effect those changes." As an example, Goglia said that if mistakes had occurred in implementing an aircraft maintenance safety procedure, the initial reaction had been to blame the person who made the mistake and get rid of the person, when the real problem was with the procedure itself. "General Oaks would say 'Fix the procedure,'" Goglia said.[28] Before Stephen Wolf joined the carrier as CEO in 1996, he and longtime associate Larry Nagin reviewed the crashes to determine if somehow the carrier was fundamentally flawed but found no common link or corporate fault, Nagin once recalled.

By 1995, Schofield was ready to retire. "I had indicated to the board that I wanted to retire at 55," he said. "I had other things I wanted to do, something different. I had been head of operations from the mid–1970s through when I retired and it was 24 hours a day, and that takes a toll on you. So they formed a search committee at my request, the search committee looked at a number of candidates, and it was felt that Steven Wolf was an individual with experience, who was well thought of."[29] Wolf joined the airline in 1996, while Schofield began a successful second career outside of commercial aviation.

3

Teaching an Eagle to Fly

The 1920s were an era of wild entrepreneurship in the aviation world, not unlike the high-tech boom decades later in the 1990s. Anyone who could put together enough cash to buy an airplane immediately began experimenting with ways to make money at it. Early pilots put on local air shows, doing what seemed to most people of the day to be impossible, as they swooped and dived and rolled their wood-and-cloth bi-winged craft just feet above the earth at breathtaking speeds approaching 100 mph. They also charged daring thrill-seekers—and many a young boy dreaming of becoming a pilot—for joy rides. Since most planes of the day were U.S. Army Air Corps bi-wings sold as surplus after World War I, using them as a means of commercial transportation wasn't really feasible. They were, however, ideal for carrying small amounts of urgent cargo between cities too distant for single-day delivery by rail. The U.S. Post Office Department, which had operated its own small fleet of "air mail" planes beginning in 1918, was kicked out of the flight operations business by the Kelly Act in 1926. From that day forward, air mail would be shipped via contract carriers on specific routes awarded by the Post Office.

One of those early contract carriers was a St. Louis–based startup company called Robertson Aircraft. Its pilots included a young aviator named Charles Lindbergh. On April 15, 1926, Lindbergh, then an obscure, skinny 24-year-old, loaded mail into a DH-4 biplane operated by Robertson and flew it from St. Louis to Chicago. Lindbergh didn't stick around Robertson very long. He spent most of the next year preparing for a somewhat longer flight. On May 20, 1927, he took off on the first unrefueled transatlantic flight from New York's Long Island to Paris. Robertson was one of many small carriers that contributed a branch to American's family tree, so years later American's official history dated itself to Lindbergh's flight with Robertson. But that's a stretch. Lindbergh himself never claimed to have flown for American, or even for one of American's predecessor companies. Rather, he considered himself to be instrumental to the establishment of Transcontinental and Western Airlines in the late 1920s and 1930s. Indeed, throughout much of the '30s, TWA, which became Trans World Airlines after World War II, was known as the Lindbergh Line after some smart advertising man determined that well-heeled Americans who could afford to travel by air during the Depression were concerned about the safety of airlines (appropriately so, given the high number of crashes, many of them fatal, in those days). "Lucky Lindy" was the most celebrated name in aviation, in no small part because, unlike so many of his contemporaries, he didn't die in a crash despite having his fair share of them. So the thinking was that linking TWA to Lindbergh's reputation would ease potential customers' safety concerns and attract them to TWA flights over those of other fledgling airlines, including American.

In fact, literally hundreds of fledgling aviation companies sprang up all around the nation to carry the mail, barnstorm, and put on flying demonstrations. Some began experimenting with the technologies and methods that we know today as crop dusting. That's how Delta Air Lines got its start in Monroe, Louisiana, in the early '20s. Others began tinkering with engine technologies and aircraft designs, marketing approaches, and financial formulas that might be combined to make carrying passengers for hire a profitable undertaking. One such startup was Texas Air Transport, a Fort Worth–based offshoot of a regional bus company, which began flying in 1928. Owner A.P. Barrett, who was involved in a number of enterprises in the Dallas–Fort Worth area, quickly determined that the aviation business was different enough from his bus company that it needed to be managed separately, and by someone who was more concerned about finances and profits than aeronautical design and engine improvements. In early 1929, he transferred a bright young accountant from one of his Dallas companies to Fort Worth and put him in charge of the aviation firm, which upon the acquisition of several smaller aviation outfits in the area had been renamed Southern Air Transport.

Cyrus Rowlett "C.R." Smith was an up-by-the-bootstraps kid from the small farming community of Minerva, Texas. Smith earned his accounting degree from the University of Texas despite not having graduated from high school. He had never been in an airplane before being named general manager of SAT. But it didn't take him long to figure out that the flying business was not then—and might never be—very profitable, even though it was great fun and probably would become an important business. Smith also quickly determined that SAT was not going to survive long unless drastic action was taken. It was too thinly capitalized, and its operating scale was too small to support the relatively high cost of flying people in addition to cargo and mail. So Smith negotiated the sale of SAT to a fledgling airline holding company named the Aviation Company, commonly called AVCO, where he stayed on as general manager. In 1932, AVCO came under the control of industrialist E.L. Cord, who was building an empire that included some 150 companies, most of them in transportation.[1]

Cord, who as a dashing young man had gained international fame as a race car driver, owned controlling stakes in the Auburn, Cord, Duisenberg and Checker automobile companies. Cord's empire also included Lycoming Engines, Stinson Aircraft and New York Shipbuilding, as well as AVCO. Working with Smith as both the general manager and chief financier of the airline group within AVCO, Cord negotiated joint branding and operating agreements with dozens of small airlines (including Robertson)

A young C.R. Smith poses with an American Airways Lockheed Orion 9-D in 1933. The carrier was renamed American Airlines in 1934 (courtesy American Airlines).

based all around the nation. They operated under the single name "American Airways." They all took their orders from Smith, who almost immediately began urging Cord to go all-in and buy the disparate member companies of American Airways outright. Cord listened, and by 1934, he had fully acquired 82 airline companies and placed them all under Smith's command. In 1934, the company's name was changed to American Airlines because Congress banned existing airlines from bidding for mail contracts following a flawed, exclusionary bidding process four years earlier. In response, most airlines changed their names so they could rebid.

Cord, who had high society tastes and great disdain for what he considered backwater places such as Fort Worth, moved the airline's headquarters in 1931 to Chicago, and a few years later to New York, where they would remain for nearly 40 years before returning to Fort Worth. In 1933, Cord, dogged by threats that his children would be kidnapped, moved to England, leaving Smith fully in charge of all his aviation interests. When he returned to America in 1936, Cord quickly came under attack from federal lawyers over alleged improprieties in the trading of Checker Cab stock. A year later a frustrated Cord sold all of his transportation-related companies. AVCO became an independent, publicly traded company, with Smith, now known universally by American's employees as "Mr. C.R.," as CEO and chairman.

Smith pioneered many airline industry innovations and operating procedures. For instance, he effectively co-designed the famed Douglas DC-3 during a famously long phone call with Douglas Aircraft's founder, Donald Douglas. Douglas had built the experimental DC-1, and then the operational DC-2, in response to urging from TWA. But the plane lacked sufficient seating capacity and range to be operated profitably. American wanted to begin long-distance and cross-country flying because Smith recognized the significant demand from the financial and entertainment industries for a faster, better option for travel between New York and Los Angeles, and between New York and important regional finance centers in the middle of the country. Smith wanted to buy the Boeing 247 monoplane, which was already in production. But Bill Boeing refused to sell 247s to any airline until United, which at the time was still a Boeing subsidiary, had received all 60 that it had ordered. Reluctantly, Smith ordered 15 copies of the Douglas DC-2. With four more seats than the Boeing 247, and more advanced engines that gave it greater speed and range, the new, extraordinarily sturdy DC-2 was a better plane than the 247. However, it rapidly became apparent that the DC-2 had too many technical bugs and too little capacity to fly profitably on a consistent basis.

That prompted Smith to call Donald Douglas with a detailed proposal to build a stretched, re-engined version of the DC-2 that could carry more passengers longer distances in greater comfort. An accountant by training, Smith didn't just dream up that idea entirely on his own. Rather, he came up with the big-picture concepts, and spent hours with Bill Littlewood, American's chief engineer, working through ways to produce a plane with a fighting chance of being a market winner. By the time Smith called Douglas, he had a clear idea of what he wanted. With the economy stalled by the Depression, Douglas initially had no interest in risking capital on what he considered Smith's blind faith that a market for long-distance air travel actually existed—especially not so soon after production of the DC-2 had begun. The pair stayed on the phone for several hours. Several times Douglas threatened to hang up. Smith refused, gambling that Douglas' well-known gentlemanly manners would prevent him from making good on those threats. Eventually Smith convinced Douglas to at least explore the possibility, in part by promising to order 20 of the new planes for the then-staggering price of $4 million if Douglas would actually build them.[2]

Less than two years later, the "Douglas Sleeper Transport" or "DST" was flying. Smith never signed a contract to buy the DST. But his reputation was such that, even in those early days, others took him at his word. In Douglas' eyes, Smith's promise to spend a record $200,000 each on 20 airplanes was better than any contract. A slight problem was that American at the time had almost no cash. It was 1934, near the low point of the Depression. Smith, using contacts from his years in Texas, began working the Franklin Roosevelt administration. His chief contact was Amon Carter, the powerful Fort Worth newspaper publisher, oilman and mayor. Carter was one of Roosevelt's biggest financial boosters and friends. Another old friend from Texas was Jesse Jones, whom Roosevelt had put in charge of the Reconstruction Finance Corp. Smith turned those contacts into a $4.5 million loan from the RFC, the proceeds of which went mostly to pay for the DST.

Oddly, while Smith focused most of his thinking on the DST, believing that sleeping berths would be great revenue-generators because of their appeal to well-heeled transcontinental flyers, it was the daytime version of the DST that wound up becoming the most important piston engine plane ever designed and flown—the DC-3. It carried 21 people in unprecedented comfort. Inflight meals were served on china. Passengers used real silverware (not silver plate) and drank expensive wines poured into crystal stems by white-gloved, attractive and impeccably attentive "stewardesses." Nearly every airline put in big orders for the DC-3 and began earning profits as soon as they could get them in the air. But the start of World War II ended the relatively short run of the DC-3 as the premier commercial airplane. Douglas switched to making cargo and other specialty versions of the plane for the military. Later, General Dwight Eisenhower credited the military version, the C47, as one of the most important tools in the Allied Powers' victory in the war because of its unmatched load-carrying ability, its range and its renowned durability even after taking battle damage.

Smith's skills also included marketing and managing. In 1934, he broke all the rules of aviation marketing by talking directly to the public about safety. The industry's safety performance in those days was horrendous. American's planes were still made mostly of wood and cloth, and were powered by enormously heavy and chronically unreliable cast-iron piston engines. Pilot training had not been standardized. The rules governing how and where planes could fly were only beginning to be worked out, and the preferred method for doing so was trial and error. The errors often had unfortunate consequences. So Smith took the bull by the horns. In 1934, he placed ads in newspapers around the nation asking, "Why Dodge This Question: Afraid to Fly?" The ads discussed frankly the safety challenges as well as the advancements that had been made to ensure passenger safety and comfort. Those ads went a long way toward convincing those Americans who could afford to fly that getting on board an airliner wasn't quite as risky as they had believed. Passenger traffic began to pick up nicely, not only on American but on all airlines.

Smith also worked with New York mayor Fiorello LaGuardia to plan and open LaGuardia Airport. New York was then served by Newark Airport, across the river. The feisty mayor, determined that his city should have its own airport, once refused to get off a TWA airliner at Newark because his ticket said New York. The airline eventually flew him to the Brooklyn naval air station. Smith saw the huge market opportunity that awaited the carrier that could best serve the nation's largest city and financial hub, and he recognized that the half-dozen or so airfields used prior to LaGuardia's opening were too far away to be convenient for busy New York business people. When LaGuardia approached him about signing on as the first user of a new airport that would be built on the edge of Flushing Bay in Queens—just across the East River from Manhattan—Smith jumped at the chance. He got deeply involved in the airport plan-

C.R. Smith typed thousands of his terse-yet-clear instructions, notes of encouragement, stern upbraidings and sometimes humorous comments on his old Underwood manual typewriter (courtesy American Airlines).

Brigadier General C.R. Smith (left; later a major general) and President Franklin D. Roosevelt tour the Air Transport Command's operations in 1944. At the start of the war, Roosevelt asked Smith to build an efficient airline for the U.S. Army (courtesy American Airlines).

ning process in hopes of securing for American every advantage possible at what he believed would become the nation's most important airport.

In the late 1950s, Smith was one of the first to recognize that the coming jet age not only would improve airlines' operational and financial performance and customer service, but also that the first carrier to fly jets would gain a vast marketing advantage. American and Pan Am competed to be first. After Pan Am committed to buying four-engine DC-8s from Douglas Aircraft for use on its international and transcontinental routes, Smith convinced Boeing to speed up production of its new 707, another four-engine jet that it was offering as a direct competitor. But Pan Am also bought 707s, and it began 707 service in October 1958. American followed in January 1959. At both airlines, the early version 707s were so underpowered that 1,700 pounds of water had to be injected into the engines to get the planes off the ground. The water cooled the engines enough so that the turbines could spin faster and produce the necessary takeoff thrust.

Smith's informal, highly personal management style also was instrumental in creating American's reputation for operational excellence and innovation. He supposedly knew the name of every employee—and the names of many of their spouses and children—up until his first retirement in 1968. His brief, even terse, notes of instruction and encouragement—which he typed himself on his trusty Underwood manual typewriter—remain to this day a lesson in how senior executives can communicate with employees to achieve specific results and enhance employee morale. Many retirees from the C.R. Smith era at American cherished notes from C.R. that they'd received so much they framed them or put them into scrapbooks. Little escaped Smith's notice during his four decades at the helm, yet somehow he never got a reputation for being a micro-manager, in part because he believed in surrounding himself with lots of talented managers, training them and then getting out of the way. That's not to say he accepted shoddy performance. Smith dismissed plenty of executives over his career, including some who went on to have outstanding careers at other carriers and travel companies.

Another American innovation was the airport club. In the 1930s, Smith saw that his many famous customers and friends from the entertainment world couldn't get through crowded airports without being mobbed for autographs, and that his buddies in the business world couldn't find a quiet place to work while awaiting their flights. It wasn't unusual at all for Smith to leave his office in Manhattan and drive out to LaGuardia to personally welcome arriving movie stars. He even made a habit of traveling as the personal escort of the wife of one close friend, President Franklin Roosevelt. Eleanor Roosevelt's celebrity made traveling by public conveyance difficult in the days before private government aircraft were used by First Ladies. Smith's relationship with President Roosevelt also led him to leave American during World War II to run the Air Transport Command, the division of the U.S. Army Air Corps that was responsible for the massive airlift of men and materials across the Atlantic and throughout the Pacific. After the war, Smith returned to the helm at American.

Smith's abilities included an uncanny ability to discover and groom outstanding young managers. This was so much the case that from 1930 onward, American was known as the airline industry's best breeding ground for airline executives. Yet Smith's biggest failure at American was his inability to adequately prepare American for the day he would no longer be there. At the time he retired, it was widely assumed that his replacement would be Marion Sadler, American's vice president and general manager. Sadler was a one-time high school teacher who joined American as a ramp agent in Dallas in 1941. He quickly moved up to become a salesman in Buffalo, New York. In the early 1950s, Sadler composed a sales manual that was eventually adopted by the airline as its primary sales training text. In 1955, he was promoted to director of passenger sales at the airline's headquarters in New York. In 1959, he was promoted to vice president and general manager. Popular with employees, Sadler effectively ran the airline for the next eight years, and he was named president in 1964.[3] His presidency coincided with a strong economy: airlines' financial performances reached a peak and American was the top performer, with its profit reaching $52.1 million in 1966. Also, like other big airlines, American placed an order for Boeing's new bump-nosed behemoth international jet, the nearly 400-passenger 747.

Everything seemed to be going well under Sadler's presidency. So it's easy to understand the shock wave that rocked American in the summer of 1967, when Smith announced that the company's new vice chairman—and as such, the new CEO-in-waiting—would be George Spater, American's respected but low-key, academically minded general counsel. No one understood what C.R. was doing. A few days later the company disclosed that Sadler had undergone cancer surgery. It was made to seem that Sadler had informed Smith of his diagnosis before Smith promoted Spater. However, neither man ever spoke publicly of the matter, so it remains unclear to this day whether Smith chose Spater to lead the company over Sadler because of Sadler's cancer or for some other reason. It is possible that over the years the two strong-willed, popular leaders had clashed enough that Smith had grown too annoyed with Sadler to make him the crown prince. Or perhaps Smith was not specifically aware of Sadler's cancer but was sufficiently concerned about his obviously declining general health that he didn't want to risk putting his beloved American under the control of a leader who seemed headed for health battles.

In the summer of 1967, at the dinner concluding American's annual marketing planning conference for the airline's officers, Smith rose to deliver what everyone assumed would be a routine speech. Instead, he announced that both he and Sadler would be retiring at year's end. Then he sat down. He could not yet say so publicly, but Smith knew at the time that President Lyndon Johnson was about to name him to be secretary of commerce. There was a long, stunned silence in the room. Eventually several executives rose to offer profuse praise for both men. Rounds of standing ovations followed. But the sense of shock did not go away. Not only was American losing its heroic founding father figure, it was losing the much-beloved executive who everyone had thought would be C.R.'s perfect replacement. And in their place the airline would get the competent but uninspiring, even reticent, George Spater. He fit no one's expectations for the man to replace the beloved and legendary "Mr. C.R."[4]

Johnson, a fellow Texan and longtime friend, asked Smith for help during the troubled days near the end of his first full term. The Vietnam War was hugely controversial and the nation's economy was beginning to show worrisome cracks. Johnson saw Smith as the sort of business-savvy, well-connected, no-nonsense leader he needed to handle the economy so he could devote most of his time to managing the war and implementing his Great Society social reforms. Smith became secretary of commerce late in 1967. But very shortly thereafter, in April 1968, Johnson decided not to run for re-election. Smith cleaned out his desk around Thanksgiving 1968 and eased quietly into what he thought would be a serene retirement.

For his part, Spater was a top-shelf transportation lawyer, but he lacked the executive skills to run American Airlines, especially in a troubled economy. The year 1968 was a watershed year for the nation and a tough one for the airline industry. American's profits fell in both 1968 and 1969. The airline then lost $26.4 million in 1970 before reporting minuscule profits of $3 million and $5.6 million in 1971 and 1972. The bottom fell out in 1973 with a then-record loss of $48 million. The general problem was that American, like its rivals, had signed up to buy widebody jets during the high times of the mid–1960s, only to receive them and put them into service during the down-cycle years of the late '60s and early '70s. As a result, too many seats on too many expensive airplanes were being flown around empty because too few people could buy tickets. Things got so bad that American removed about ten rows of seats from its widebody cross-country flights and installed electric pianos and standup bars. Quite out of desperation it created the world's first flying piano bars. The innovation led to lots of grand stories of jetsetters singing and drinking and laughing their way across the continent. But it did not lead to airline profitability.

Spater was ill-suited to the task of stopping the downward spiral. Otto Becker, a long-time American marketing executive who retired in 1980, recalled Spater as "a very bright guy and ... a very capable lawyer. He just was not an executive. He was not a manager."[5] Nor did he look like one. In an era when the fashion of strong men who needed visual aid was to wear bold, black, horn-rimmed glasses, Spater wore wire rims. In an industry in which drinking and flirting were not only accepted but expected from executives, Spater did neither. He didn't smoke at a time when it seemed every other employee did. He didn't tell jokes. In short, he was the antithesis of C.R. Smith. And his weaknesses became painfully obvious thanks to a series of scandals that took place at American during his watch.

Juan Homs, a flashy young Spaniard who'd made his mark as head of promotions at Pan Am, had been hired by Sadler in 1966 to design, edit and publish an inflight magazine for American similar to the ones that both Pan Am and United published. *American Way* was a hit with readers and the airline's accounting department. It quickly began to produce impressive revenues, especially given the very modest resources spent producing the magazine. Unfortunately, Homs' methods were something less than reputable. As the head of promotions and marketing, whenever Homs negotiated deals with suppliers he required that the supplier pay him a personal kickback, usually equal to five percent of the total deal. After Homs refused to pay restitution, Spater not only fired him, he went to the FBI and to U.S. Attorney Whitney North Seymour, Jr. Homs was hauled before a federal grand jury, but before he could be indicted he fled to his native Spain.

Meanwhile, Spater followed up by asking every officer of American to describe in writing what gifts or money worth more than $100 they had received from Homs over the years. When American's senior vice president of marketing, Walter Rauscher, disclosed that he had borrowed $14,000 from Homs in the past, Spater turned his report over to the U.S. Attorney's Office. Rauscher was indicted and upon the advice of his personal attorney pleaded guilty. Then in 1971, Spater was told that his vice chairman, Jack Mullins, was discovered also to have taken kickbacks. An internal investigation found no evidence of kickbacks, but the *Wall Street Journal* published a story accusing Mullins of using company money to buy a car and carpet for his house. The story included Spater's strong denial of the accusations, but the story only added to the growing perception that American's management was full of crooks.[6]

To top it off, during the 1972 presidential campaign a Chicago lawyer named Herbert Kalmbach working for the now-infamous CREEP—the Committee to Re-Elect the President—approached Spater with a "request" that American ante up a large donation to Richard Nixon's re-election effort. Kalmbach was not only Nixon's personal attorney; he had also done legal work over the years for United Airlines. It seemed likely that United already was onboard with CREEP. If American didn't join the team, it could expect to get zero support from a second Nixon administration in route authority and rate cases pending at the Civil Aeronautics Board. So Spater gave in, and American made an illegal $100,000 contribution to Nixon's campaign. Following the election, in the spring of 1973, Dave Frailey, head of American's public relations team, got a tip from a reporter that Ralph Nader's Public Citizen organization was seeking to get the Nixon campaign's records on improper corporate contributions made public. The tipster told Frailey that American's contribution was on the list. At the time, the Watergate story was boiling and the country was repulsed by the improprieties.

Informed of the tip, Spater ordered Frailey set up two news conferences, one in Washington and one in New York, where he came clean before Public Citizen. The news media broke the story. If Spater expected American to be given credit for telling on itself, he was extraordinarily naive. The media and the public were outraged and tore into both the airline and the man. "Spater took a lot of heat for that," Frailey said, "but he was far from the only head of a major corporation who made such a contribution."[7] In fact, within a few weeks it was revealed that more than 100 large U.S. corporations had made such illegal contribution to the Nixon re-election effort. Spater, however, was done. He had violated his own high standards of ethical behavior, then in a fit of guilt ratted himself—and American—out. Had he waited for the news to be reported and understood in the context of widespread strongarming of U.S. corporations by a corrupt president and his team, perhaps American would have been spared the public's ire. But in light of the previous internal corruption scandals at American on his watch, it became clear Spater had to go. He did the airline's board a favor and resigned in September 1973.

Then came another surprise. American's father figure, C.R. Smith, had been retired for four-and-a-half years, and had been gone from American for five-and-a-half years when Francis H. "Hooks" Burr, a Boston attorney who was the longest-serving non-executive board member in American's history, called him and told him that Spater was out. Burr's call was more than just a courtesy. He told Smith that the board needed to move fast to put a trusted and tough leader in charge of a rapidly failing American. But the board had no one in mind, not even a list of candidates. In effect, Burr, and later the full board, begged C.R. to return on an interim basis so the board could take the time to conduct a proper search for a permanent CEO. Once back in place, Smith was an aggressive, demanding CEO despite knowing that he would not be around for long. When American president George Warde, a long-time aircraft maintenance and operations manager whom Spater had promoted to the no. 2 job in 1971, presented a proposed budget for 1974 that included a projected loss, Smith fired him. American had lost money under Smith in many years, but he'd never begun a year with a budget that had just assumed a loss was inevitable. And he was not going to accept such a notion for what he was certain would be his very last year in business.[8]

4

Al Casey's Five Big Decisions

Al Casey was a Bostonian through and through: gregarious, clever, Harvard-educated, tough, hard-working, and hard-partying. A clear-thinking, keep-it-simple kind of guy. Indeed, the only box not checked on his Boston pedigree was "Democrat." Casey was that rarity of rarities, a Boston Republican. He was also successful in business and widely liked and admired. After a stint in the army, Casey spent the first half of his business career climbing the managerial ranks in the railroad industry. Then in 1963 members of the often fractious Chandler family, who collectively owned a majority stake in Times Mirror Co., parent of the *Los Angeles Times,* recruited Casey to be their CEO because of his combination of financial and people skills. For 11 years, Casey managed both to build Times Mirror into a powerful media company through the acquisition of TV and radio stations and skillful financial maneuvering, and to keep the warring factions of Chandlers from destroying one another as well as the company. But by late 1973 even Casey's resources for dealing with the Chandlers had been exhausted. He was tired of dealing with them, and they with him. Since his contract was coming up for renegotiation in 1974, Casey began scouting around for a new opportunity.

A headhunter brought his name to the attention of the American board, which intrigued board member Hooks Burr and surprised fellow board member James Aston. Burr didn't know Casey, but he was well aware of Casey's reputation. Burr was deeply involved in fund-raising for his alma mater, Harvard, on the East Coast, while Casey was Harvard's leading fund-raiser on the West Coast. Aston, meanwhile, didn't have to check up on Casey. As a member of Times Mirror's board, he was a strong supporter of Casey's effort to run the newspaper company for the benefit of all shareholders, not just the Chandlers. After American's board spent several months considering and rejecting several other candidates, Casey's name came up for earnest consideration. Within a few weeks, Casey had met with and impressed every board member. He also impressed C.R. Smith.[1] During a three-month transition period after Casey was named president, Smith stayed away from the office and out of Casey's hair. Then Smith re-retired.

When C.R. Smith walked into a room, he quickly won it over with charm, wit, playful humor and wisdom. That made him popular with the troops at American. When Al Casey walked into a room, he took it by storm. During his early years at

American, he always stood on top. To make sure everyone knew that, he literally took a sledgehammer with him to work one day at the airline's headquarters on Third Avenue in Manhattan. And he put it to use, personally knocking down the wall that for years had separated the CEO's office from the president's. Casey's message was clear. He was in charge, and there was no number two. "I didn't know who I could trust," Casey explained years later.[2] He didn't know much about airlines, and he didn't know which executives he'd inherited were, in his words, "worth a damn" and which ones weren't. But everyone at the company expected him to name a "real" airline guy to manage the airline while he focused on finances. "So I fooled 'em," he said. "I named myself president."[3] In so doing he forced himself to learn, quickly, the many ins and outs and peculiarities of the complex airline business. He also tore through the leadership ranks, firing or demoting a dozen vice presidents in his first 18 months on the job. He immediately set about changing what had been American's spendthrift financial culture by putting the airline on a spending diet.

When Casey arrived, American had just $75 million in cash and short-term investments, along with $587 million in debt. But his experience at Times Mirror had taught him that having both lots of cash and a tight budget allowed a company to grow. American, Casey determined, needed to grow to survive, and to grow it needed more cash. So he made every decision with an eye toward saving or accumulating cash. Despite having joined American during the first Arab oil embargo, at a time when American was saddled with an aging fleet of 237 gas-guzzlers, Casey was able to build the carrier's cash to $115 million by the end of 1974 and to cut its debt nearly 20 percent to $474 million. American also reported a profit of $20.4 million. That's not a lot, but it is important to remember that in the fall of 1973, George Warde's proposed budget for 1974 had projected a loss. By late 1974, Casey was ready to make his first big strategic move. He ordered 21 of Boeing's new, popular and versatile 727 tri-jets. They were, by the standards of the day, highly fuel-efficient. And the order gave both employees and investors reason to believe in Casey, and in American's future.

Still, American wasn't out of the woods. The concept of deregulation was moving ahead in Washington. Of all of the nation's airlines, American was most threatened by the potential switch to unfettered competition. Its historic route system, heavily concentrated in the Northeast and the Ohio Valley region with lonely outposts in Los Angeles, San Francisco and Dallas—and no rights to fly to Europe or Asia—would be a big disadvantage. So would its large number of old, inefficient and ill-sized Boeing 707s. In short, deregulation would require a complete makeover of the company—and a whole lot more cash and financial flexibility than American had or could hope to have in the next few years. So American fought hard against deregulation. But, as Casey expected from the outset, it was a losing battle. Only at the very end of the fight in Washington did American finally switch sides and reluctantly endorse the passage of the Airline Deregulation Act of 1978. Nevertheless, between 1974 and deregulation's implementation in 1979, virtually every significant decision made by American and

Casey was made with at least one eye on the possibility of deregulation. After his retirement, Casey explained that even if deregulation had not come to the airline industry, the decisions American made during that time would have put it in a better position to compete.[4]

In addition to his many incremental financial and budgeting decisions that gradually led to an improved balance sheet, Casey made five monumentally important decisions during his 11 years as CEO. Each one required him to act based on intuition and his finely honed business instincts. That's not to say he didn't study the data. But in each case, the data did not, and could not, lead him all the way to the conclusion he eventually reached.

The first of those big decisions came during his first weeks at the airline. With the Arab oil embargo both pushing prices up and triggering a jet fuel shortage, Casey made the then-shocking decision to ground half of American's 16 Boeing 747s (eventually all 16 were sold). Passengers loved the spacious 747. So did employees. But accountants and route planners hated it. Except for a few flights to the Caribbean, Mexico and Canada, American did not fly international routes in those days. And the 747, which seated nearly 400 passengers, simply was too big to operate profitably on domestic routes. There wasn't enough passenger demand to support buying, fueling and staffing such a large plane. Indeed, American determined it could operate the 747 profitably on only one of its routes, New York to Los Angeles, and even then only in the summer, and only if it operated just two flights each way a day. There was abundant evidence that more total passengers would buy seats if the carrier offered multiple flights on smaller planes.[5] Casey's decision to dump the 747s went against conventional wisdom and consumer preference, but it nevertheless was the right move.

Al Casey was hired as American CEO in 1973. His first assignment was to prevent the airline's financial collapse (courtesy American Airlines).

Five years later Casey made a similar decision to ground American's antiquated 707s. Nine planes were grounded immediately. By October 1981, all 67, including 7 freighters, would be gone. Together those 67 planes represented 27 percent of American's passenger capacity and 100 percent of its dedicated freighter capacity. Most everyone in the industry—and on Wall Street—was shocked. Yes, the old 707s were especially inefficient in an era of high fuel costs and recession. But wiping out that much capacity in short order threatened to strangle the airline's revenue genera-

Al Casey (left) visits the flight deck of an American 707. In 1980, he made the decision to ground all 67 of American's 707s (courtesy American Airlines).

tion capabilities. Neither the numbers nor airline industry convention supported the decision. A team of bright young MBAs working at American, including Bob Crandall, Don Carty, Stephen Wolf and Tom Plaskett—all of whom went on to become CEOs of U.S. airlines—were involved in the study that led to the grounding of the 707s. Even though the numbers did not fully support the decision, Casey—at the strong urging of Crandall, on whom Casey came to rely most heavily—grounded them anyway. History proved it was the right decision. The 707s would have been not only an extremely poor fit for the route network American was beginning to build under deregulation, but also an impediment to every subsequent marketing, financial and route planning decision for the next decade.[6]

Casey's third critical decision at American also came early on. He knew better than to fall into the trap of believing that American's small, surprising profit in 1974 meant the company was turning itself around. He publicly warned shareholders and Wall Street that 1975 would be a tougher year. Privately, he grew deeply concerned about American's shortage of cash, high fuel prices and a rapidly weakening U.S. economy, all of which were amplifying the cyclicality of the industry in general and American in particular. Casey gave Plaskett, who had succeeded Crandall as finance chief, the task of studying the positive and negative aspects of merging with Pan Am. In early 1976, days after American announced a $20.5 million loss for 1975, Plaskett gave Casey the thumbs up. He urged the boss to buy Pan Am and wipe out the Pan Am name.[7] Combining American's strong domestic network with Pan Am's world-leading international network made all sorts of sense. So Casey called Pan Am chairman Bill Seawell to launch merger talks.

As the talks progressed, American learned that Pan Am was in significantly worse financial shape than American. Casey got cold feet. Ultimately he backed out before ever reaching a final deal, and began looking for other merger partners. For a time he considered merging with Ryder Corporation, the Miami-based truck leasing firm. Then he held talks with both Transamerica and American General, two of the nation's largest insurance companies. Casey was attracted by their deep pockets, which could help American ride out the airline industry's frequent and bleak down cycles. But the insurers balked, fearing that the big chunks of cash that airlines can generate in good years would not be enough to offset the cash drain they'd represent in bad years. Thus, with no other avenues left to pursue, Casey decided in 1976 that if American was to survive, it would have to do it on its own. "I said, 'Screw it! We'll sell the hotels and fix the damn thing ourselves,'" he explained years later, adding that at the time he was far from certain American really could be fixed.[8] Still, selling the money-losing Americana hotels chain generated cash needed for acquiring new planes and upgrading American's Sabre computer reservations system. And it got rid of a big distraction and helped refocus management more intently on airline operations and marketing.

Casey's fourth enormous decision came in 1978. Though the core company of what eventually evolved into American Airlines had gotten its start in Fort Worth, Smith had moved American's headquarters to Chicago and then to New York. Over its four decades in Manhattan, American culturally became very much a New York airline. It did, however, keep a presence in Fort Worth, where it maintained a telephone reservations center and other facilities. It also had a decent operational presence at Dallas' Love Field and, briefly, at Great Southwest International Airport/Amon Carter Field (the first, failed attempt by Dallas and Fort Worth to jointly operate a major airport). The new Dallas/Fort Worth Airport opened in 1974 adjacent to the old Great Southwest Airport, which closed the day DFW opened. American, Braniff, Delta and Texas International all had decent-sized operations at the new airport. In fact, American was only the third-largest carrier in DFW's early days.

Four years after the airport opened, representatives from DFW visited Casey in New York, ostensibly to discuss building a new, bigger reservations center. But during that visit, DFW board chairman Henry Stuart, a prominent Dallas business and civic leader who'd known Casey for years through previous business dealings, brought up a sensitive subject. Everyone in the Dallas- and Fort Worth–area business circles believed that it was American's destiny to one day come back home. In fact, a few of them, including Stuart, knew that George Spater briefly had studied relocating American's headquarters to North Texas in 1972 before the idea got swamped by the events that led to Spater's forced retirement. So Stuart asked Casey if he was ready to make the move. It wasn't the first time Stuart had asked that question. Previously Casey had always laughed and jokingly dismissed the question as unserious. American, he would always say, would never think of leaving New York.

This time, however, Casey didn't laugh. Rather, he asked what the cities and DFW might offer to induce American to return. A month later, Casey had a formal proposal from North Texas sitting on his desk. He assigned Plaskett, who'd become senior vice president of finance, to study whether to move to the DFW area or Chicago or to remain in New York. Plaskett, Crandall and several other senior American executives had frequently discussed leaving New York for Texas. But Casey told Plaskett to focus solely on the numbers and to ignore sentiment and strategic concerns. Plaskett came back with a report supporting the headquarters move. As far as he knows, the report was never read by anyone other than Casey and American's board members. Casey took up every copy of the report after the board presentation and burned them.

Deciding to move American back to Fort Worth was one of the toughest decisions Casey ever made, at least in terms of the personal heat he took for it. He'd served on the board of advisers that steered New York out of bankruptcy only a few years earlier. He and his wife were leading figures in New York's highest business and social circles. Mayor Ed Koch felt betrayed and launched scathing public and personal attacks on Casey, who was mercilessly criticized by the New York media. And New York's political leaders made a bold, mean-spirited effort to block American's move by influencing a key official at the Internal Revenue Service to rule that American's new headquarters building could not be built with money from the sale of bonds by DFW's board. In fact, if not for a last-minute delay engineered by U.S. Representative Jim Wright of Fort Worth, who at the time was House majority leader, the deal would have been scuttled. The IRS ruling did take effect, but not until the American-DFW bonds deal was closed. Never again has an airline facility not directly related to flight operations been financed with bond money raised by a U.S. airport authority.[9]

American's headquarters officially moved to the DFW area in August of 1979. At first it was located in temporary quarters in a vacant industrial facility in Grand Prairie. Subsequently, it was moved into a glistening, modernistic low-rise facility hidden in the woods just south of DFW, on property owned by the airport and within the Fort Worth city limits. In the 1990s, the fast-growing airline ran out of space in that building, which was turned over to its Sabre computer reservations system subsidiary for use as its headquarters. American's corporate flag was replanted about a half-mile east, on Amon Carter Boulevard—a road created by paving over what had been the main runway at the old Great Southwest Airport, which was being redeveloped as an office park. Though Casey always maintained that the move to Texas was undertaken strictly for financial reasons, even he eventually admitted that the move's significance went far beyond the few million dollars a year in operating savings on which Plaskett's report had focused.[10] Moving the headquarters contributed heavily to the change in the way American's executives and its people thought about their company and their industry. The dynamic team of young Turks who came to work at American in the Casey years likely would have been just as aggressive had the headquarters remained in Manhattan. But their horizons would have been different, and it's likely that some of their decisions would have been different. It now seems clear that the move back home to Texas gave Casey and his team a sense of commercial and intellectual freedom, and the ability to think in new and very different ways about what their airline could become.

Despite the high stakes involved in each of those four big decisions, Casey's fifth decision of enormous import clearly was the most critical—and most momentous. Casey met Bob Crandall the day he was named president and CEO-designee in February 1974. A week earlier Casey had read a note from C.R. Smith in which the old man rendered his assessment of senior executives Casey would be inheriting. On Crandall, C.R. had written: "One of the brightest young financial men I've ever met. Formerly with TWA. Entirely competent."[11] That was all Casey knew about Crandall, but he was intrigued and wanted to learn a lot more about him and to do it quickly. So upon their first meeting in the office, Casey asked Crandall, who was CFO at the time, to come to the apartment in New York City where the company had arranged for its new CEO to live during his transition period from the West Coast. Casey wanted a thorough briefing on the airline's financial condition.

Crandall showed up that night on time, armed with a thick notebook to go over with his new boss. But there was more on the relentlessly ambitious Crandall's mind than just getting the new boss up to speed on American's finances and formal plans. It was his first opportunity to make an impression, and he made sure it was a good one. "Bob was running for office from day one," said Plaskett, whom Crandall had hired one month before Casey's arrival at American.[12] There was never a moment's doubt from that point on that Crandall wanted someday to be Casey's replacement. Ultimately, the competition that emerged between Crandall and Donald Lloyd-Jones, American's senior vice president for operations, became the stuff of legend not only within American but all around the industry and into the broader business world, mostly for the extraordinary intellectual power, industry savvy and energy each man brought to the fight.

Upon his arrival, Casey set about building the four-man team of senior vice presidents he wanted to report directly to him. Lloyd-Jones, who held a Ph.D. in economics from Columbia University, was a highly regarded and respected industry veteran who had basically run the airline during the otherwise leaderless Spater years. During his stint as interim CEO, C.R. Smith was highly impressed by Lloyd-Jones, who'd joined American in 1957 as a staff economist. Casey, too, immediately took a liking to Lloyd-Jones, who had a mastery of the airline business and an ability to get things done. Gene Overbeck, who'd become general counsel upon Spater's ascension to CEO, also quickly proved himself in Casey's eyes to be an excellent administrator in addition to being a good aviation lawyer. Casey made him senior vice president of administration, which meant he effectively ran the headquarters operation in addition to legal affairs. Crandall, who had been hired by George Warde shortly before Spater's departure and Smith's return, continued as CFO.

For a time, Casey, who had so colorfully used a sledgehammer to consolidate the CEO and president positions, took on a third assignment for himself. He personally ran American's marketing department for about six months, primarily as a way of learning the airline business but also to buy himself time to find someone to lead the marketing team permanently. In that role, Casey quickly discovered that there was no one currently in American's marketing department with the skills he thought necessary to handle such a critical job. So he engaged an executive search firm and began bringing outside candidates in for interviews. There were a number of impressive candidates. But Casey began noticing something during the interview sessions, which typically included group interviews with all of American's senior vice presidents. "Crandall asked better questions," Casey explained years later. "He'd never worked in marketing a day in his life, but I could tell from the questions he asked that he instinctively knew more about airline marketing than any of the candidates we'd brought in."[13]

Casey eventually decided that either Crandall or Lloyd-Jones would do a better job than anyone he'd brought in for interviews. He chose Crandall, not because Lloyd-Jones wasn't bright enough but because Crandall was brighter. Besides, Lloyd-Jones would continue to run operations and, as such, would lead by far the largest group of employees and manage by far the largest budget. In effect, by moving Crandall from finance to marketing, Casey set up another competition between the two to become his eventual successor. If that wasn't immediately obvious to others, Casey took steps in 1976 to make it so. Lloyd-Jones had been named to the American board during the dark days of Spater's demise and had retained his board seat under both Smith and Casey. Indeed, he was the only senior executive at American to ever hold a board seat other than the CEO himself—until Casey gave a board seat to Crandall. Their competition could not fairly be described as mean. The two remained reasonably collegial and professional over the next four years. But their fight was the intellectual and managerial equivalent of a cold war. Casey sometimes grew so exasperated with his two stallions' fierce competition—with each other and for his attention and approval—that he would complain to Plaskett, Overbeck and other senior executives that he was fed up with both of them. They squabbled over strategy. They fought over budget allocations. They fought over route planning. They fought over technology matters. They fought over American's management of and response to critical issues in Washington, such as legislative efforts to deregulate the airline business.

Their preferred weapon was the memo, a weapon that Casey, who preferred one-on-one communications with his direct reports, loathed. Crandall would write long memos complaining about Lloyd-Jones' and his staff's actions and positions. Lloyd-Jones would respond with similarly long, complaint-filled memos about Crandall and his team's actions and plans. Sometimes their fight would spill out into pitched battles between their respective staffs. But because Casey eschewed the sort of giant, marathon senior staff meetings for which Crandall later became famous, Lloyd-Jones and Crandall rarely engaged in sharp face-to-face arguments in front of other senior American executives. Only Casey witnessed the battle in an up-close and personal way. Casey later said that two factors swung his decision in Crandall's favor. Lloyd-Jones was effective enough as a communicator to get people he managed to do what he wanted. But Crandall was a master communicator who could use any number of approaches not only to get his people to do what he wanted but also to get them to think and perform far beyond expectations. And Crandall, relying on his communications skills, was able to assemble an extraordinary team of young, intelligent and aggressive managers who, with Crandall alternately inspiring them and driving them relentlessly, literally changed the airline industry. Lloyd-Jones never assembled anything close to such a team.[14] Understandably, Lloyd-Jones was disappointed when in 1980 Casey named Crandall as American's president, a promotion that meant he almost certainly would follow Casey as CEO. The gentlemanly, amiable Lloyd-Jones remained at American for another year, serving faithfully under Crandall until the time seemed right for him to slip away quietly and with dignity.

After he named Crandall president, Casey remained at American for another four years before retiring. During that time, he continued to play the key role of respected corporate don during a period when Crandall, known for his withering profanity, unrestrained aggressiveness and ruthless competitiveness, had not yet rounded off nearly enough of his rough edges to have survived long in the top job. Crandall's ascension, though likely, was never a certainty. In fact, he almost talked himself out of it in an infamous February 1982 phone call with Howard Putnam, CEO of Braniff, American's Dallas-based rival. Braniff was headquartered at DFW and still operated more flights at the time than did American, but was suffering enormous losses. When Putman complained to Crandall about American's ongoing expansion at DFW, Crandall—exasperated by Putnam's inability to see what Crandall thought was the obvious solution to both airlines' problems there—screamed over the phone to Putnam that if Braniff raised its fares, American would do the same. Putnam, who recorded his phone calls, turned the tape over to the Justice Department, which sought to make Crandall the prime example of airline industry eagerness to collude on prices.[15] The call got Crandall an embarrassing slap on the wrist from the U.S. Department of Justice, which originally sought his ouster and perhaps his indictment on attempted price-fixing charges. And it nearly got him fired. Casey had only 10 minutes' advance notice from the Justice Department that it was going after Crandall. Before that, he had not even known of Crandall's conversation with Putnam. Years later, Casey admitted that he seriously considered firing Crandall on the spot, but decided that he was so good that it was in American's best interests to keep him and fight the DOJ.[16]

After leaving American, Casey came out of retirement several times to take on high-profile financial salvage operations for the government. He served as U.S. postmaster general long enough to reorganize the Postal Service and save it from one of its periodic brushes with financial collapse. And he served as head of the Resolution Trust Corporation, which was charged with straightening out the mess from the savings and loan industry's scandals and near-collapse in the late 1980s. He died in 2004 at age 84.

Business historians regard Crandall as the man who saved American and built it into the world's biggest—and arguably best, for a time at least—airline. But Casey played an important role in the turnaround and ascendance for which Crandall gets, and perhaps deserves, most of the credit. Casey made decisions that kept American alive at a time when the carrier was near collapse. And he oversaw the building of one of the most talented and successful management teams ever assembled at any company—not just among airlines—in U.S. business history. He may forever be known primarily as the man who chose Bob Crandall to lead American to the pinnacle of the global airline industry, but it should also be remembered that Al Casey did what even the legendary C.R. Smith had failed to do. He made sure American was left in capable hands upon his departure.

5

Our Son of a Bitch

Bob Crandall has been a bigger-than-life figure in the airline industry for nearly four decades, so imposing that 15 years after he stepped down as CEO of AMR in 1998 he remains one of the industry's biggest stars. The best known description of Crandall, which gained widespread use in the 1990s, was: "He's a son of a bitch, but he's our son of a bitch." The origin of the description is unclear. Some credit a Transport Workers Union official. *Dallas Morning News* reporter Terry Maxon said he was told by a pilot in the 1990s, "First, we said he was our guy. Then we said he was a son of a bitch, but he was our son of a bitch. Then we dropped the last part of the sentence."[1] In any case, Crandall is one of those executives whose personality became the personality of the company he ran. American "became, like Crandall, supremely confident," Dan Reed has written. Once Crandall took over, American "began acquiring a reputation for managerial excellence and arrogance. That perceived arrogance stems from their profound sense of 'rightness.' They have a rock-solid faith that their disciplined study of the facts and their methodical number-crunching always leads them to make the correct decisions. That attitude—which permeates every office cubicle, airport ticket counter and cockpit at American—is pure Crandall."[2]

For reporters, Crandall was generally a pleasure to cover because he was so sure of himself and so quotable. However, when he was unhappy or when he disdained a reporter, he saw no need to be diplomatic about it. When Ted Reed covered American for the *Miami Herald,* Crandall once called him into a small office, closed the door, and proceeded to yell at him for 20 minutes about a story that used the word "concessions" in regard to pilot contract negotiations. Crandall's general theme was that he was seeking only costs that were competitive with those of other airlines, and considered "concessions" an inflammatory term. After that one blistering assault, Crandall always treated Ted Reed courteously during the seven years that Ted covered American in Miami.

Dan Reed got the Crandall treatment a half dozen times, especially in the first few years after he began covering the airline industry in 1984 for the *Star-Telegram* in American's hometown, Fort Worth. It typically would begin after a probing question posed from the point of view of one of American's or Crandall's critics or opponents. Crandall would ask to go off the record, with the tape recorder turned off. Then he would launch into a profanity-laced attack, using a unique piercing/snarling/growling voice that a lifetime of smoking allowed him to conjure up whenever he needed to use it for affect. Dan Reed's 1987 reporting about then-record-setting fines imposed on American by the FAA for improper maintenance record-keeping practices led to an unofficial—but very real—three-month-long American advertising boycott of the *Star-Telegram*. Dan did not learn of the boycott until long after it was over, because his publisher did not want him to be influenced by it. Over time, Dan developed a congenial relationship with Crandall, whom he covered for 14 years. Extrapolating from years of Crandall stories swapped by reporters, it is apparent that while Crandall never had to summon up fake anger in his various encounters—with reporters, underlings, competitors, bureaucrats or even elected officials—it seemed that he sometimes made the tactical decision to let his anger show. It was one of the ways he tested people. If the target of such an outburst survived relatively intact, and was able to defend his or her views in a creditable way, Crandall thereafter generally treated them with professional courtesy at a minimum, and sometimes even with respect.

Born December 6, 1935, in Westerly, Rhode Island, Crandall attended William and Mary College, then earned a BS from the University of Rhode Island and, in 1960, an MBA from the Wharton School of the University of Pennsylvania. He worked for Eastman Kodak and for Hallmark before joining TWA in 1966 as assistant treasurer, rising to become vice president of data processing and later, vice president and controller. During those early years in management, Crandall developed a reputation for intense focus on cost controls and a keen appreciation for the revenue-enhancing power of computers. He was distressed when TWA selected Ed Meyer to be president and left in 1973 to become Bloomingdale's senior vice president and treasurer. But he didn't like that. "The fact is I liked the airline industry and I hated the goddamn retail business," he said. "They really thought it was a big event when they moved men's underwear from the first floor to the third floor."[3] Crandall spent just six months at Bloomingdale's before his return to the airline business at age 37, when he became chief financial officer for American. At the time the carrier, then based in New York, was in retrenchment mode, hemorrhaging money and rapidly losing ground in the industry. It was embroiled in a heated labor dispute with its pilots over a rule known as the "Hard 75"—a reference to the number of hours the airline could require its pilots to fly each month. On his first day, "I walked into the lobby and took the elevator up to the fourth floor," Crandall said. "I got off and there was Donald Lloyd-Jones (senior vice president of operations). He said, 'I hope you understand how screwed up this place really is.'"[4]

One of Crandall's top priorities was to beef up American's huge computer reservations and data management system, known as Sabre. Crandall had first seen the power of computerized data management while working in Hallmark's data processing department. Using computers and operations research techniques, Hallmark was able to determine which cards were in demand and to systematically upgrade the price of the cards offered in Hallmark shops. Crandall reasoned that the same methods could apply to the pricing of airline seats, and he oversaw development of computer methods that would enable American to offer discounts at times when seats were selling slowly. The concept eventually led to the development of sophisticated yield-management approaches now widely used in both the airline and hotel industries. However, the tools were not at hand in 1973.

American's marketing executives had resisted upgrading Sabre, arguing that more sophisticated reservations capabilities were not needed. Neglected and under-financed, Sabre was in desperate need of modernization. Early in his tenure as American's CFO Crandall traveled to Tulsa, Oklahoma, where Sabre was housed. The airline had purchased 1,000 CRT terminals to replace the keyboard terminals then in use, but American's marketing department had decided against using its budget money to fund their installation. Immediately upon Crandall's arrival in Tulsa, Max Hopper, who ran Sabre for American, took him to the basement storage room where those 1,000 terminals were gathering dust. The tech-savvy Crandall got the message—and the funding needed to refurbish those computers (which had been in storage so long they'd become outdated) and install them. That marked the start of an intense, Crandall-driven effort to update the airline's data processing and make automation and analysis of all airline operations a priority.

Crandall's time as CFO would be short. After Casey signed on he asked his three direct-reports—Crandall, Lloyd-Jones and Overbeck—to be part of the team screening candidates for the open position of senior vice president of marketing. It was a job that Crandall himself coveted. Although the shift was technically a lateral move, Crandall recognized that jumping over to become SVP of marketing would give him far more influence in shaping the airline's future in a period of dynamic change. The marketing chief would control route and network planning, pricing, data processing, Sabre, advertising and marketing, public relations, and customer service planning. And whoever held that job also would have a big voice on matters related to government relations and actual customer relations (even though flight attendants and certain ground employees technically reported up through the operations organization controlled by Lloyd-Jones). Technically the SVP of operations had a bigger job because about 60 percent of the company's employees answered to him. But in terms of influence on strategy, brand image, sales and, ultimately, profitability, the marketing chief's job was the more plum assignment.

So as Crandall and Casey began interviewing the half-dozen or so candidates for the marketing job, Crandall made a point of asking data-intensive questions he knew full well they could not answer. The strategy effectively convinced Casey that Crandall was the right man for that job, while Casey himself could handle the CFO duties. Crandall actually made such a good case for himself that full, rather than shared, responsibility for the airline's stations was shifted to his marketing realm from operations, where it had historically resided. "Al asked me to help interview guys, but I wanted the job myself," Crandall admitted:

I asked questions that the airline guys we were interviewing wouldn't have a clue about. Airline marketing is essentially a matter of analyzing data, not so much of one-on-one salesmanship or marketing. The [interviewees] didn't know anything about data processing, scheduling, the distribution of RPMs and ASMs, so I set out to demonstrate to Al that I knew more about the essentials than the candidates, and in the process I got the job. I ended up running marketing, including scheduling, and all the stations all over the system. It was a terrific job and it was absolutely a stepping stone to the CEO's office.[5]

By then, Crandall was known throughout the company as a gruff and unapologetic micromanager, quick to unleash streams of profanity at those who underperformed. "My style was very much hands-on, very much micro-manager," he said. "I don't delegate anything to anybody without checking up on whether it was getting done. People criticized me constantly for micro-managing. My response was always 'For me, that works.' Nobody else would do it the way I did it because nobody else gave a shit as much as I did. I wanted to know more than anybody else."[6]

For five or six years, Crandall was constantly on the road, repeatedly visiting American's five dozen station managers, personally scrutinizing each one's budgets in one-on-one meetings that became legendary for their excruciating detail. Managers squirmed under the gaze of the ultra-intense Crandall as he went over their budgets in search of waste. "I went to their offices and I said 'we're going to go over your budget line by line and if I ask you any question you can't answer, you're in trouble,'" Crandall said. "Then the word got around that you'd better know the goddamn answers." If a manager's budget included a line on expenses for rags, for example, Crandall demanded to know the supplier of these rags, their cost per pound and how that cost compared with the expense of rags purchased by other station managers. He maintains that only eight or ten of the 55 or so managers actually lost their jobs during these inquisitions, but those examples motivated others to build each year's budget from the ground up and closely manage their costs. "I didn't want them to be scared, but I wanted them to know every single dollar they spent and what they spent it on, and that they'd better not try bullshitting," Crandall said.[7]

The budget reviews were also Crandall's preferred method of learning the airline business in the kind of detail he believed was necessary. Crandall demanded deep immersion in detail from himself and from his top lieutenants. And he required all of the airline's senior officers to attend the annual president's conferences he hosted to explain the airline's business plan and solicit employee feedback from rank-and-file employees. He also frequently wandered through airports and encouraged workers to share their comments and questions with him. "My model was to always get to the airport an hour and a half early and go down to the ramp and wander around," he said. "Employees were very pleased then, and they still are."[8]

As Crandall micro-managed his way to the top, the airline industry was changing dramatically. Deregulation loomed in the mid–1970s; the debate over whether to reduce government control of the industry lasted four years and tested the commitment of airline executives to free-market principles. An unfortunate byproduct of deregulation for Crandall was the infamous 1982 conversation with Braniff's Putnam. In an interview, Crandall declined to discuss that famous phone call, a stance he has maintained for decades. He did, however, once grumble to a reporter that the tale of his phone call to Putnam undoubtedly will be included in his obituary. Amazingly, it did not derail his career. He was named American's president in 1982, and in 1985 he succeeded Casey as chairman and CEO.

The early 1980s also saw the dawn of yet another major airline innovation credited to Crandall and his team. American invented the world's first airline passenger loyalty rewards program, the AAdvantage Travel Awards Program. There had been other "clubs" for airlines' preferred passengers in preceding years, dating all the way back to the 1930s. But AAdvantage, which remained the largest frequent flyer program in the world until 2008's Delta-Northwest merger, represented an entirely new concept. It used Sabre's data tracking power to keep track of how many miles individual passengers flew on American, and offered "rewards" to those who racked up a certain number of miles on American flights—free flights, mostly, but also first class upgrades and other goodies. More than a million travelers enrolled in the program by the end of the first year. AAdvantage was immediately copied by nearly every other airline, eventually spreading to nearly all foreign airlines as well.

Crandall always distinguished between employees and the unions that represent them. "Most employees have no greater loyalty to the union then they do to the company," he said. But in negotiations, he said, "I wasn't dealing with employees. I was dealing with unions, and unions always want more. Anytime you don't give unions what they want, they claim you're not showing respect." In 1982, American was once again locked in tense labor negotiations with its unions. "There was continuing labor unrest at all the major carriers, and it was particularly profound at American," Crandall said. "Even during the years when CR was there—and he was revered by the pilots— there was a pilot strike every three years. The [American] pilots had broken away from ALPA and formed their own union, the Allied Pilots Association, the APA. The APA guys, of course, were always competing with ALPA, trying to be sure that Americans' pilots always had an industry-leading contract, thereby illustrating the wisdom of having formed APA."[9]

Faced with these obstacles, Crandall, with Casey's strong support, plotted an ambitious scheme that, if successful, would double the airline's fleet, pave the way for massive network expansion and reduce the carrier's average labor costs, which devoured about 35 percent of the company's annual revenue. "We said to ourselves: 'What do we do now?'" Crandall recalled. "The only thing I could think of to do was to find some way to get our costs down so that we could grow rapidly to compete with the new entrant, low-cost carriers." The proposal was to have a two-tiered wage system, tied to a major expansion of the fleet: a huge order of McDonnell Douglas MD-80 aircraft, which eventually totaled 250 planes. The planes, which seated 130 to 170 passengers, would allow the airline to expand its hubs at Dallas/Fort Worth and Chicago and to grow elsewhere as well. It was an appealing strategy for the unions, especially the Allied Pilots, whose leaders were eager to put furloughed pilots back to work. They also wanted to accelerate the time it took for a pilot to become a captain. American had been shrinking for nearly a decade by that time, so "it took 21 years for a first officer to become a captain," Crandall said. "A great many who were then first officers would never become captain. I said to the pilots, 'If we do this and double the size of the airline, all you guys flying in the right seat—we'll get that down to a couple of years.' We said 'We will start another airline, but we will not call it another airline. We'll do it differently than Frank Lorenzo, whose approach was to create a holding company and assign all the new flying to the low-cost airlines.' The unions called that double-breasting. We said that instead of that, we would create a lot of growth, but all within American Airlines. However, all the new employees would come to work on a different wage scale. That's exactly what corporate America is doing today," Crandall added. "It's precisely what Ford, GM and Caterpillar are doing. We did it in 1982."[10]

APA members approved the "B-scale" deal in 1983. The Transport Workers Union narrowly agreed to similar terms that also provided incumbent employees with lifetime job security. The leaders of the 6,000-member Association of Professional Flight Attendants initially were inclined to reject the approach, but reluctantly agreed when it became clear the rank-and-file were not strongly behind a threatened strike. Crandall promptly placed the McDonnell Douglas order, living up to his part of the deal, and the MD-80 became the workhorse of the American Airlines narrowbody fleet for the next three decades. "We got the pilots to agree, got the flight attendants and the TWU to agree, and we went from 250 airplanes in 1982 to something like 800 when I left," Crandall said. "And once we got into a growth mode, the company became very successful. We had good labor relations for ten or twelve years."[11]

International expansion meant acquisitions. In 1990, American purchased a Miami-based Latin American route system from Eastern for $349 million. Rights to serve every major South American nation except Brazil were included in the network, as were service rights to Costa Rica, Guatemala, and Panama in Central America. American also got rights held by Continental Airlines, Eastern's sister company under Lorenzo's Texas Air Corporation umbrella, to fly between Miami and Madrid and between Miami and London. "We were expanding internally, buying airplanes, and hiring people, and we needed places to fly the planes," Crandall said. "We wanted access to international markets. Eastern had neglected its Latin American assets. We were ambivalent about buying it, but Peter Dolara said he could fix Latin American. So we bought the assets from Eastern and Peter did fix Latin America."[12]

Dolara went on to serve for three decades as the highly regarded head of what became American's Miami hub and its Latin American and Caribbean division. Crandall remembers Lorenzo as "a guy who had a hard time pulling the trigger—he was always trying to improve the deal. I said, 'If you want to sell it, I will give you this much,' and we made the deal." Also in 1990, Crandall paid TWA $445 million for six slots—time-specific landing and takeoff rights—at London's Heathrow Airport. American used those slots to serve Baltimore, Boston, Los Angeles, New York, Philadelphia and St. Louis. Crandall negotiated that deal with TWA chairman Carl Icahn. "I always found Icahn to be a satisfactory negotiating partner," he said. "We did deals over the phone and afterwards, his lawyers would try to improve on the details. I said, 'Carl, that is not what we agreed to,' and he said to the lawyers, 'That's right.' I don't know that he was easy to deal with, but when I did business with Icahn, I always found him to be an honest negotiator."[13]

Although he made successful deals to expand into Latin American and Europe, Crandall never managed to secure sufficient Pacific routes for American. In 1985, United Airlines agreed to buy Pan Am's Pacific division, including 18 jets and landing rights in 13 cities, for $750 million. "I woke up one morning and read about it," Crandall said. "I always thought Pan Am got less than they could have gotten. Why the f—— would Pan Am sell to United without having an auction? You tell me. That isn't a natural way to sell anything." Another potential solution to American's lack of presence in the Pacific would have been for the government to require that carriers holding route authorities to China use those authorities to fly to China from the U.S., rather than to fly to Tokyo, Crandall said:

> I lobbied for this when I was there. I don't understand why if you have a route to China, you aren't required to fly it non-stop. The Chinese hated having all that traffic flowing over Tokyo, and if the government had required the airlines holding the routes to fly them non-stop, there would have been a lot more opportunities to serve China and there wouldn't have been a nascent Asian hub in Tokyo. Letting the carriers that had routes to China serve it via Tokyo simply made it impossible for other airlines, like American, to get routes to either Japan or China.

"The U.S. government just never seemed to focus on the vitality of the U.S. industry," Crandall said, echoing decades-old criticism of the senior bureaucrats and elected officials in Washington who control the nation's air transportation policy levers. "I have never understood, for example, why the U.S. government allows European carriers to codeshare in the U.S., which gives the Europeans much greater advantages than U.S. carriers can get from reciprocity, since the U.S.-beyond-gateway market is much larger than the European-beyond-gateway market. It's another example of the government not seeking to support the U.S. industry."[14]

Later in the 1990s, Crandall considered a merger with Northwest, which had been acquired by investors Alfred Checchi and Gary Wilson in a 1989 leveraged buyout. "They wanted too much money for it," Crandall said. "It didn't make any sense. It got to the point where they said what they wanted and we said, 'That's too much.'" American under Crandall generally grew organically as a result of its huge aircraft orders. An exception was American's 1986 purchase of AirCal for $225 million. While the Eastern Latin division and TWA Heathrow slot deals did not include aircraft, the AirCal deal came with a small fleet. "At the time it was very hard to get access to California cities [where] there was a lot of concern about noise," Crandall said. "That acquisition had to do with getting access to a number of cities we couldn't get into. It was just a collection of access rights." Crandall said he also "looked at USAir from time to time, but it didn't make economic sense. I don't do deals that don't make sense. You need to know the net present value of what you're acquiring, and it has to exceed the price they are asking for it. I would remind you that roughly 85 percent of all the mergers in the history of America have been failures."[15]

Crandall retired from American in 1998, saying labor conflict drove him away. "By the early 1990s the pilots couldn't stand to have one guy making more than another guy doing the same job, and they decided to force us to abandon the two-tier wage system. It was very contentious from 1993 to 1998, and I just got tired of it. I said, 'The hell with it, you guys won't let me do anything creative so I will retire.'" Looking back, Crandall said, "It would have been nice if the pilots had been more agreeable to my view of what was appropriate in the long term. American would be bigger and more competitive today if they hadn't decided to undo the two-tier wage system." While he will not criticize his successors, Crandall said he believes American should have filed for bankruptcy when its peers did. "The so called consensual deals American made with its unions were not good enough to remain competitive with the lower costs the bankrupt carriers got," he said. "You cannot have higher costs than the average. There is only one criterion, my friend: competitive costs. American didn't have competitive costs and couldn't get them because the unions simply would not agree to give American deals that would yield costs equal to what the bankrupt carriers got. So American lost a billion dollars a year for ten years."[16]

In 2013, at the age of 77, Crandall was happy with his legacy as a son of a bitch. "It's fine with me," he said. "Everybody would prefer to be Mr. Nice Guy rather than a son of a bitch. But I always did what I thought was best for American Airlines. I loved being CEO of American. I thought it was a marvelously interesting business." Told that it is ironic that today he is widely viewed as an industry saint, Crandall responded: "I don't think it's ironic. You often see virtue in the rear-view mirror."[17]

6

How Bob Crandall
Changed the Airline Industry

Was Bob Crandall the best airline manager in history? It's difficult to claim that definitively. There have been many good ones—and some bad ones, too. But no one would dispute that Crandall was, by a wide margin, the most influential airline manager ever. Crandall not only rebuilt American into the industry's biggest carrier during his nearly 25 years there, but also put his visionary, creative and managerial stamp on the entire U.S. and global airline industry. The list of American's major inventions, and innovations, plus its cutting-edge tactical and strategic moves, literally changed the way airlines do business. The list of highlights is long, and includes the following:

- Hub-and-spoke operations. Credit for the invention rightly goes to Delta under C.E. Woolman, who used the Atlanta-centered route rights, which the government granted Delta in the 1930s, to build the first real hub. It was, however, a "natural" hub because although nearly all flights began or ended in Atlanta, Delta only loosely scheduled its flights in and out of the hub. Any connection opportunities created for travelers were either accidental or were a secondary factor in building the flight schedule. In those days, Delta passengers could wait several hours at the Atlanta airport between flights. American, under Crandall and his two key route planners and strategists, Wes Kaldahl and Mel Olsen, was the first airline to maximize the potential from hub-and-spoke operations by purposely scheduling waves of flights to arrive at the hub around the same time and then depart roughly an hour later. American turned on its DFW hub for the first time on June 11, 1981. The hubbing "bank" came to be repeated 8 to 11 times a day, creating enormous passenger traffic flows through the hub. Then American led the industry in building multiple hubs at major airports around the nation, effectively creating a national—and even global—network of interconnected hub-and-spoke operations.
- Data-driven marketing and operations. The Sabre computerized reservations system was born out of a partnership with IBM in the late 1950s. But it wasn't until Crandall arrived in the mid–1970s that Sabre was developed into both a powerhouse information technology management tool and a world-leading ticket sales system available for use first by travel agents and, eventually, by consumers them-

selves. When United sought to build Apollo, a single public travel sales network serving all airlines, Crandall's team scrambled to take Sabre to the public market first and quickly established it as the market leader among all such systems over the next 20 years.

- Advance-purchase discount fares. Airlines had conducted small experiments with differentiated ticket prices for years, but because fares were regulated by the Civil Aeronautics Board, little incentive existed to step outside the lines. In the mid–1970s, Frank Lorenzo's Texas International was the first to succeed with what it called "Peanut Fares," deeply discounted tickets sold only to those willing to purchase well in advance of traveling, and only on flights for which there was slack demand (usually evening flights and those on weekends and slow midweek days). But with the arrival of deregulation, American began to push the advance purchase discount fare envelope much further, using Sabre's predictive capabilities (based on both real-time data and a deep well of historical travel data) to effectively manage seat inventories on a route-by-route, flight-by-flight and seat-by-seat basis. Deeply discounted tickets required four-week advance purchases, round trips and Saturday night stays, effectively blocking business travelers from snagging them.

  By filling many seats that otherwise would have gone empty, American generated lots of extra revenue while incurring little extra cost. Just as important, the strategy enabled American to maintain higher-frequency service on important business routes than it otherwise would have, which enabled American to attract an out-sized share of the so-called "premium" traveler market. As a result, throughout most of Crandall's tenure, American held a lead in revenue per available seat mile and revenue per passenger. And it maintained a bigger share of the industry's total revenue than its share of the industry's total capacity justified.

- Frequent flier programs. Many airlines had developed rudimentary customer loyalty programs over the decades in order to please their most frequent customers. But in 1981, American introduced AAdvantage, the industry's first (and still largest) frequent flier program. Such programs enable passengers to earn "miles," or points, that can be redeemed for "free" travel later on. AAdvantage was immediately copied by virtually all other U.S. (and eventually most foreign) airlines. In the three decades since, those programs have expanded and evolved so that now more than half of all mileage points are earned for non-flying activities such as using airline-branded credit cards, renting cars, staying in certain hotels, buying groceries at certain stores, or even taking out a mortgage through preferred lenders. As a result, frequent flier programs have become major sources of revenue for airlines because merchants pay airlines approximately two cents for each mileage point they give away.

- Yield management. The complex differentiated pricing system that grew out of American's advance purchase fares innovation naturally led to American's development of what it called "yield management," or "revenue management." By harnessing historical travel demand data and marrying it to real-time tracking of advanced ticket sales (made possible by the development of Sabre's database and analytical tools), American developed the ability to continually adjust the price of every seat on every flight almost continuously until the door was shut for takeoff. The idea was to sell every seat for the maximum price its occupant was willing to pay. The trick came in identifying how many seats on each flight could be sold at top dollar, how many could be sold at mid-range prices, and how many could be sold at the most steeply discounted price. All carriers now have yield management capabilities, but American remained light-years ahead of the pack well into the 1990s.

- Two-tier labor contracts. In 1983, American succeeded in negotiating the first-ever set of two-tier labor contracts with its unions. Crandall and his associates believed in 1982 that circumstances finally had given them the tool needed to win concessions from organized labor without taking a financially crippling strike. They promised rapid growth in exchange for dramatically lower compensation for every employee hired after the new contract was signed. After several months of tense negotiations and tough public rhetoric that included the threat of a strike, all three of American's big unions accepted B-scale contracts.

  In response, Crandall's management team launched a historic airplane-buying binge. The fleet grew to more than 800 planes by the late 1990s, employment at American and its sister companies nearly quadrupled in 15 years to a peak near 120,000, and tens of thousands of American employees saw their incomes escalate rapidly. It was not unusual for a pilot's pay to grow from around $60,000 to around $175,000 annually in a decade. But predictably, American's B-scale contracts (copied to varying degrees by companies inside and outside commercial aviation) also planted the seed for long-term labor-management tension. It took less than a decade for the number of employees hired on the second, lower pay scale to out-number their predecessors who had voted to approve the B-scale. And once they took over union leadership, it didn't take those B-scalers long to eradicate the two-tier wage system to which they owed their careers.

Not all of American's innovations in the Crandall era were huge successes. Several failed, and one failed on a colossal scale. In April 1992, American attempted to solve the industry's perennial problem: hyper-competitive, self-destructive pricing schemes featuring dizzying numbers of fares for every flight. American created a simple four-tier pricing plan it called the Value Plan. First-class tickets were priced at 50 percent below what they had been prior to Value Plan's launch. Standard coach fares became "AAnytime Fares," priced at least 38 percent lower than the pre–Value Plan standard coach fares. Then American offered two levels of discounted "Plan AAhead" fares requiring 7- and 21-day advance purchases. Each of those discounts was set at a percentage off the "AAnytime Fare." By doing that, American reduced the number of different fare offerings it sold via Sabre from more than 500,000 to just 70,000.

American expected dramatic reductions in the cost of administering its pricing system. Its executives were certain the far lower prices would entice many more people to fly, generating more revenue than before. Those executives also knew that when American and its competitors initially implemented the scheme, the conversion would lead to a severe, short-term run on every airline's cash reserves as travelers holding more expensive tickets rushed to convert them to lower-priced Value Plan tickets, getting big refunds for the difference in prices. American also anticipated that its rivals would try to undercut the new pricing initiative on a piecemeal, market-by-market basis. So Crandall publicly warned competitors that if any rival tried to undercut any single price or aspect of the Value Plan, American would respond by lowering all Value Plan prices in all markets in order to retain the percentage relationships between those four prices. American argued that maintaining those percentage relationships between the four pricing levels was the only way it and the rest of the industry could expect greater total revenues in the long run.

It was an argument based in math and sophisticated economics. Rival carriers reacted emotionally, believing either that the evil Darth Vader of the airline industry, Crandall, was trying to run them out of business or that their own cash balances couldn't survive the short-term bleeding. Northwest, followed first by Continental and later by others, tried to undercut Value Plan prices in niche markets. In response, American did exactly what Crandall had warned it would do, lowering all of its fares on all flights. American also matched and expanded on Northwest's limited deal allowing a child to fly free with a parent, offering a simple two-for-one deal with no limitations on the age or identity of the second traveler. What resulted in the summer of 1992 was the biggest fare sale in industry history. Consequently, every American alive, it seemed, took a flying vacation in the summer of 1992. Then Continental and Northwest filed suit against American in federal court in Galveston. American easily won the case—the jury took less than 90 minutes to decide, and that's counting an hour break for lunch. But American spent well over $20 million to defend itself in that case. Worse, although American prevailed in court, Value Plan ultimately failed because of the huge loss it incurred in trying to maintain the scheme's critical mathematical integrity once rival airlines reacted based on emotion and, in some cases, on poor analytical understanding of their own financial conditions. They simply refused to follow Crandall's lead in taking the industry in a radically different direction.

Of course, Crandall did not do all of those things by himself. The truth is, he took personal credit for only one of the big innovations—the development of Sabre into what became the world's leading travel sales system and, for a time, one of the world's most advanced commercial computer networks. "I think that's the one thing where we clearly saw—and where I clearly saw—that this was going to be very important to us and to our industry over the long haul," he said in a 1992 interview.[1]

Ultimately Crandall's greatest contribution, both to American and to the industry, wasn't any one innovation, or group of them. It was his identification and development of a small army of elite managers who went on to profoundly impact not only American, but all airlines. He had a few experienced hands on whom he relied heavily. They included Wes Kaldahl, American's chief planner and strategist during the critical growth days of the 1980s; Mel Olsen, the scheduling and pricing genius who taught American—and the industry—how to generate maximum revenue out of hub-and-spoke networks; Barbara Amster, who worked with Olsen and Kaldahl in developing the industry's pioneering yield management system, and the team of Max Hopper and Jim O'Neill, who played critical roles in making American not only the airline industry's leader in the use of information technology but one of the technology leaders in all of U.S. industry, at least in the 1980s and early 1990s.

But, for the most part, Crandall surrounded himself with young, brilliant and aggressive executives, many of whom went on to successful careers at other carriers. The list is long and impressive. One was Stephen Wolf, who had been at American seven years when Crandall arrived and who stayed for eight more as vice president of the airline's western division before departing to work in marketing at Pan Am and then to run four other airlines. Additionally, Tom Plaskett was the first senior American executive commonly viewed as Crandall's heir apparent. As head of marketing under

Five American CEOs gathered in one place: (from left) Don Carty, Bob Crandall, Doug Parker, Tom Horton, Gerald Arpey, summer 2013 (courtesy American Airlines).

Crandall in the early and mid-'80s, Plaskett oversaw many of American's early marketing innovations including advance purchase fares, the AAdvantage program and the development of the hub-and-spoke route system. He eventually left to become president of Continental Airlines under Frank Lorenzo, and then CEO of Pan Am until it shut down. Plaskett then became something of a turnaround specialist, nurturing both Greyhound, the bus company, and GameStop, a video game retailer, back to health after runs through bankruptcy. Other executives nurtured by Crandall were Frederic "Jake" Brace, later United's CFO; Randy Malin, later vice chairman and a board member at USAir; Doug Hacker, later a top executive at United; Jack Pope, later United president under Wolf; Ben Baldanza, later CEO of Spirit; David Cush, later CEO of Virgin America; Craig Kreeger, later CEO of Virgin Atlantic, and Jeffrey Katz, later CEO of SwissAir and then of Orbitz.

In addition to all those highly regarded graduates of the "Bob Crandall School of Airline Management," four young executives did, in fact, eventually succeed Crandall as American's CEO. Don Carty, who immediately followed Crandall, lasted only six years in the top job, but his fingerprints were on nearly every important decision at American from 1980 through 2003. Gerard Arpey joined American fresh out of grad school at the University of Texas and rose rapidly through the ranks, replacing Carty in 2003 and staying until November 2011, when he chose to retire without a severance package rather than take the company into a Chapter 11 bankruptcy. Tom Horton, Arpey's contemporary and close friend, succeeded him and led the airline during its two years in bankruptcy.

Ultimately the merger with US Airways, which Horton initially opposed, brought Doug Parker back to the airline where he too began his career in the finance department in 1986. On December 9, 2013, the day when the new American Airlines emerged from bankruptcy, Parker stood on a podium in Dallas and rang the opening bell for the NASDAQ stock exchange, where the new airline's shares were to be traded. Standing to his right was Horton, who remained as non-executive chairman of the company for a short transition. On Parker's left stood Bob Crandall. At 78, Crandall was a bit grayer, but otherwise didn't look much different than he did the day he retired in 1998. He was beaming, cheering and applauding the re-creation of his beloved American as the world's largest carrier once again.

The celebration made clear just how long a shadow Bob Crandall cast over the airline and travel industries. No fewer than 14 American-trained executives from the Crandall era have gone on to hold the title of president or CEO at other airlines or travel companies. Throw in all those who rose to the rank of at least vice president, and the number runs into the dozens. And when you add in the impact all those American-trained, Crandall-influenced executives have had on their own subordinates over the years, the numbers grow exponentially. Beyond that, executives throughout the airline industry who never set foot in the door of American's headquarters in Fort Worth are heirs—reluctantly in some cases and unwittingly in others—to Crandall-era airline management practices and concepts. Indeed, even ordinary travelers today continue to be influenced by Bob Crandall, even though he left the industry more than 15 years ago. Before Crandall broadly implemented Frank Lorenzo's vision, few had ever thought about buying their plane tickets well in advance to save lots of money. Now the entire world thinks that way. Before Crandall, no one kept track of how many miles they flew on one carrier. Today the practice is common, and some frequent fliers amass hundreds of millions of miles. And while our parents or grandparents thought of flying as a rare privilege, often one that merited dressing up in their finest clothes, today we grumble about "having to fly again" and we typically step aboard in our jeans and sneakers.

That, too, reflects the influence of Bob Crandall.

7

America West: The
Little Airline That Could

Deregulation unleashed a frenzy of entrepreneurship, with dozens of people eager to start their own airlines. Among them was Ed Beauvais, a young accountant, whose early career path ran through a series of small western airlines, including Frontier and Bonanza. The two merged in 1968 to form Air West, which Howard Hughes purchased in 1970, leading Beauvais to depart in order to start an aviation economics consulting firm with offices in San Francisco and Washington, D.C. In 1979, he opened a third office in Phoenix, a city he knew well after a dozen years of studying its route possibilities for the various carriers that employed him. Over time, the possibility of starting a Phoenix-based airline came to preoccupy him. Beauvais likens this period in the development of the U.S. airline industry to a similar period, at the start of the 20th century, when the U.S. auto industry was new and automakers seemed to grow on trees. "There were 100 airline startups during the ten-year period after 1978, just like there were dozens of startups in the auto industry at the turn of the century," Beauvais said. "It was wonderful. The airline industry was being revolutionized at the time, and we were the revolutionaries."[1] On the negative side, in the airline industry, as in the auto industry, the survival rate for the new businesses was minimal. In fact, America West Airlines was the only survivor of the period.

To create America West, Beauvais joined with two young Continental Airlines executives, Michael Roach and Mike Conway. In 1981, Roach was working for Los Angeles–based Continental as assistant to the president, Al Feldman. Feldman killed himself later that year, at a time when Frank Lorenzo was battling to take over Continental and seemed close to winning control. The extent of the resistance to Lorenzo seemed limitless: some Continental loyalists came to believe that Lorenzo planned to dismantle the airline. In Feldman's case, Lorenzo-phobia was compounded by the death of his wife the previous year. Additionally, Feldman was "a very closed guy [who] wouldn't let any of us get near him emotionally," Roach recalled. "I spent most of my waking hours with him for a year and a half, but I never really knew him."[2] Roach also recalled having lunch with Beauvais one afternoon at a restaurant in Los Angeles. "I said, 'Why are we doing this for other people when we could start our own airline?' and right away Ed pulled the first business plan for America West out of a briefcase.

He had identified Phoenix as an underserved market, and he convinced me. I was still in my 30s, filled with optimism, so it wasn't hard. I said, 'Let's do it.'"[3] Among the attractions: Beauvais had been working on the Phoenix airline concept for about a year and had already raised close to $1 million.

Conway, meanwhile, was an accountant, who in 1980 had resigned from Price Waterhouse, where he was the firm's lead airline specialist, to help with a planned merger between Continental and Western Airlines. "I was at Continental only a few months when Lorenzo made a hostile takeover move," Conway said. "I spent most of my time fighting that. Beauvais had the idea for a hub in Phoenix, and Beauvais and Roach approached me before the outcome at Continental was decided. My position was that I had to see it through at Continental, but if Lorenzo was successful, I was out of there."[4] Conway left the day Lorenzo took over, and he and Roach moved to Phoenix.

The trio set up shop in the office of a real estate firm that Beauvais owned, and set out to raise more money. They scraped up $500,000 from friends, family and their own pockets, taking out second and third mortgages on their homes and even tapping high-interest credit card borrowing. The next step was to raise more money from "wealthy Phoenicians who didn't care whether we succeeded but wanted to invest in a Phoenix airline," Roach said.[5] Once it had $2 million in seed capital, the group was able to fund a public stock offering. "It took over two years," Beauvais said. "It was a long time coming for us, but we were finally able to make the arrangements to have an IPO."[6] The offering in February 1983 raised nearly $19 million, bringing their total to just over $20 million. The mood was joyous, shared by a group of believers who came together and accomplished a dream of starting a business that was, at the time, on the frontier of technology. Morale, Beauvais noted, was further heightened because employees owned a meaningful stake in the airline.

At first, the three men complemented one another. "Beauvais' expertise was in route development and marketing, mainly route development, and he was very good at it," Conway said. "Roach was a very bright lawyer, who had worked for the CAB in the development of deregulation, and my expertise was in finance."[7] Eventually, however, as often happens, the joy and camaraderie dissipated along with the investment. In fact, the same thing had happened in the auto industry, when GM founder Billy Durant was ousted, later to return, and in many if not most other startup businesses. In the case of America West, it turned out that a shared dream underscored by an abhorrence of Frank Lorenzo was not enough to bind the young entrepreneurs. Roach left in 1984, and in the ensuring years Beauvais and Conway came to disagree on various aspects of the airline's strategy. "Obviously, Ed and I clashed or I wouldn't have left," Roach said. "As these things usually are, the clash was both personal and about the direction/culture of the company. Mike wanted my job and he got it. I went back to California, licking my wounds, and started in real estate. Later I joined Beauvais' former partner, a guy named Phil Roberts, in an aviation consulting business in the Bay Area."[8] After Roach left,

Mike Conway (left) and Ed Beauvais guided America West in its earliest days (courtesy American Airlines).

Conway, who had been CFO, became president and chief operating officer. After America West filed for bankruptcy protection in June 1991, Conway was elected CEO. The unraveling of the founding group would continue—but the airline managed to survive.

The early days were characterized by growth. America West followed a model defined by People Express, perhaps the best known startup airline of the time because it occupied Newark Airport, near the world's media center. People Express began flying in 1981, founded by Don Burr, who had left Lorenzo's Texas International Air. The two airlines, along with Southwest, spent the 1970s trying to find ways around various restrictive federal regulations. Beauvais had worked as a consultant for both Burr and Lorenzo. "They were very keen on the opportunities that deregulation presented," he said. "People Express and America West were the two startups from the time that had the most profound impact on aviation. Newark [Airport] was almost dead before People Express started, and we built the Phoenix hub in what was a sleepy city before that. It's what Thomas Jefferson said: Every generation ought to have its own revolution."[9] Bob McAdoo, the People Express CFO who was the third person hired at the airline, said: "America West was trying to do on the West Coast what we did at Newark. Like us, they tried to copy as much as they could of the Southwest model, and they copied our idea of cross-utilization of employees. From the day we started, we said everybody is cross-utilized: gate agents, reservations agents, flight attendants, baggage handling. We were worried that we would be unionized. What unions do if they unionize is to freeze you in the status quo. If you already cross-utilize people when the unions walk in the door, it doesn't hurt as much."[10]

America West copied the low-cost model, but sought to distinguish itself from People Express and Southwest by offering more amenities than either. "We were cast as the People Express of the West, but our concept bore little similarity to People Express," Conway said:

> People Express was bare bones with no frills, while we offered a fair amount of amenities like free drinks, assigned seating, and more seat pitch. We had no flight attendants per se: people were cross-trained to be flight attendants, reservationists and ticket agents, and to work the ramp. The employees were 65 percent female and 35 percent male. The concept behind it was that it allowed for a better-informed, better-educated customer service rep. If the terminal was crowded, the flight crew could be ready to board the passengers onto the aircraft. It was rather expensive, because the training was four times what a flight attendant gets at a major airline. But our employees were much more involved in the operation and much better-educated about the different disciplines, and [many] were able to move into management.[11]

For a decade, America West remained union-free, making it for a period the largest non-union airline in the world. "There were eight or nine different attempts by various unions to organize, but the workers elected not to," Conway said. "People say, 'Employees don't create unions; bad managements do.' Certainly, when the founders and initial management of America West was no longer there, the work environment changed."[12] In the 1990s, nearly every work group was organized.

On August 1, 1983, America West began service from Phoenix with flights to four cities: Kansas City, Wichita, Colorado Springs, and Los Angeles. The carrier started with 277 employees and three Boeing 737–200s. It rapidly added employees, destinations and aircraft; by early 1984 it had ten 737s. "It was a very tough experience to get everything organized, but once we started flying, it was a great experience," Beauvais said. "We had very aggressive expansion, adding 100 new employees a month for ten years. By 1990, we had 15,000 employees."[13] America West built Phoenix into a major hub, serving about 30 West Coast cities and connecting them with Midwest and East Coast destinations. It became the second largest post-deregulation airline, exceeded in size only by People Express. Competitors included West Coast carriers AirCal and PSA, which were acquired by American and USAir, respectively, and of course Southwest, which began Phoenix service in January 1982 and has remained the second largest Phoenix carrier. "We both created major operations in Phoenix, and it became one of the busiest airports in the world," Beauvais said.[14] The competition was intense: Conway recalled that America West commercials referred to Southwest as offering a cattle car experience. "We had a more personal touch," he said. "They were herding cattle."[15]

Despite the thrill of running snarky ads, competing with Southwest was a tough proposition. Southwest, which began flying in 1971, has long been an icon among airlines: its strategy has been the clearest, its approach the most disciplined and its profits the most consistent. "Our primary competitor was the most successful new airline," Conway said. "The presence of Southwest kept a lot of [other airlines] out of Phoenix," although the legacy carriers served Phoenix from their hubs and competed ferociously to protect their routes. "We started flying to DFW early on," Conway said. "It was a monopoly route for American. When we cut the fare by two thirds, we could still make money. But then they cut it to something even lower than their costs, and their frequent flier program was a huge advantage for them. We had a tough time getting passengers who originated in DFW to want to accumulate miles on us. That was a huge obstacle."[16] In general, America West would fly routes where incumbents significantly overcharged—where its fares were inevitably matched—or less desirable routes that lacked competition.

Besides route competition, problems for startup airlines included the lack of access to the congested, slot-controlled airports of the East or to regulated international routes. In many cases, "the fares the incumbents charged were several times what they charged in other areas, and the profits from those routes went to subsidize predatory pricing vs. startups," Conway said:

> The purpose of deregulation was to allow anyone to fly where they wanted to fly and charge what they wanted to charge, which was good in theory, but you had to have the real estate to do that. We didn't have any monopoly routes and it was very difficult to get into Chicago O'Hare, Washington National or the New York airports, and our main competitor Southwest had a legislated monopoly out of Love Field. The main advantages of the new entrants were efficiency and cost advantage, but it became largely a matter of whether you had enough staying power to survive.[17]

In an age of airline expansion, Beauvais was the archetypal expansionist, as he sought to mitigate the established carriers' strangleholds on congested airports and international routes. In 1988, America West, largely at the behest of Conway, bid for the Eastern Shuttle—but lost out to Donald Trump. It also made a pitch for the Pan Am Shuttle. When US Airways and Piedmont merged in 1989, Beauvais went to court

America West aircraft gather at airport gates at Phoenix International Airport (courtesy American Airlines).

to try to secure divested slots at Washington National. In 1991, Conway, who was by then CEO, opened a small hub in Columbus, Ohio. According to Conway, Columbus "was a key factor in the airline achieving record profits in 1993."[18] The Columbus hub was closed in 2003.

In the best example of what was widely thought to be overreaching, America West in November 1989 extended its Phoenix-Honolulu flight, aboard a Boeing 747, on to Nagoya, Japan. "We had a very successful B747 Phoenix-Honolulu flight to Nagoya, Japan," Beauvais recalled. "We had three flights a day, using 747s. They were making money and so we decided to extend it. We got a route authority [to Nagoya] and then we had to start the service or lose the authority."[19] It was a strategic priority for America West to operate in the Pacific. At first, it applied for an LAX-Australia route; the idea was to offer one of the industry's first code shares, because it had a ready partner in the Australian carrier Ansett Airlines, which owned about 21 percent of America West and which had a domestic Australia route network. But America West didn't get the route because, at the time it applied for the route authority, it lacked an aircraft with sufficient range to make the flight. "The next lucrative route that became available was LAX-Tokyo, so we got four 747s from KLM on a lease deal," Conway said. "But we didn't get Tokyo, we were awarded Nagoya instead, and we had to do something at that point."[20]

As the 1990s began, the aviation economy entered a difficult period. Fears surrounding the August 1990 invasion of Kuwait pushed oil prices from $17 a barrel in July to $36 a barrel in August and $40 in October. In 1991 Eastern Airlines folded after two years in bankruptcy, while Pan Am entered bankruptcy in January and folded in December. It was said that Eastern died of cancer while Pan Am died of a heart attack, because on the day it was supposed to emerge from bankruptcy Delta backed away from a plan to fund a new, Miami-based Pan Am that was to be focused on Latin America. Additionally, Continental filed for bankruptcy protection 1990, Midway filed in 1991, and TWA filed in January 1992. America West's filing occurred in June 1991. Two months later, Conway was named president and CEO, while Beauvais remained as chairman. Beauvais was forced to sell the Hawaii-Japan route authority, after just six months of operation, for $15 million.

The bankruptcy filing marked a turning point in the evolution of America West, because it led to the involvement of Bill Franke, a Phoenix business leader who developed an interest in airlines and, two decades later, remained a major airline investor. Franke, a Texas native and Stanford graduate, was brought in because he was experienced in restructuring, and the Phoenix community badly wanted its airline to survive. In 1987, Franke had overseen the acquisition of Phoenix-based Southwest Forest Products by rival Stone Container for $445 million plus the assumption of $300 million in debt and preferred stock. Subsequently he became chairman of Circle K Corp, which he restructured in bankruptcy. He was also chairman of the executive committee of Valley National Bank, the region's largest bank, helping to restructure it. In the area of fixing prominent businesses that are broken, "you start getting a reputation,"[21] Franke said. Early in 1992, Arizona governor Fife Symington called Franke to discuss America West. Recalled Franke: "He said, 'The creditors will file to convert from a Chapter 11 to a Chapter 7 and they will liquidate and we will lose thousands of jobs in Arizona. Would you be willing to talk to the management team with me about alternatives?' I said, 'Fife, I know nothing about the airline sector, but I will talk to them.' We talked to Conway and Beauvais. They were pretty cool to our having any involvement in the restructuring and they thought they had found a way past the creditors."[22] But three or four months later, at the insistence of Guinness Peat Aviation (GPA), an aircraft leasing company that was a major America West creditor, Conway and Beauvais called Franke and invited him for another visit. He came to stay.

The relationship between Franke on the one hand, and Beauvais and Conway on the other, quickly soured. Beauvais was the exuberant, growth-oriented, bet-the-ranch founder with a compelling sense of humor, while Franke was, and is, a no-nonsense, no-frivolity, buttoned-down manager. "We say hello when we see each other," Beauvais said in 2013, "but we hardly ever see each other."[23] Conway said the difference between them "was night and day—Beauvais was a charismatic individual who was easy for me to work with: He was a 'glass always half full' type,"[24] while Franke was not. For instance, while Franke said liquidation was a concern, Conway insists that no actual liquidation threat existed. "Liquidation is always a possibility if a plan of reorganization does not come to fruition, but it never got close to that," Conway said.[25] Nevertheless, he said, Franke "came on board as a result of GPA insisting that for them to put more money in, they wanted to have a showing of local support."

The arrangement created an awkward situation in which two groups were raising money, primarily from backers who were in conflict. Franke was allied with GPA, Beauvais and Conway with Ansett. Franke was allied with Republicans, Conway and Beauvais with Democrats. Conway and Franke disagree strongly on who raised how much, but both totals were apparently in the $7 million or $8 million range. In any case, it was the Franke backers who won out, as the creditors, led by GPA, asked Franke to manage implementation of a reorganization plan. "They said, 'We don't know whether the management team is up to that job,'" Franke said. "And I said, 'Okay, I will be chairman for six months.'"[26] As part of that agreement, GPA agreed to put in more money and Beauvais left as chairman in July 1992. "I got kicked out,"[27] Beauvais said. He lost not only his job but also his home, because a second mortgage was secured by stock in the bankrupt airline. He and his wife moved in with their son. "Losing America West was a heartbreaking experience, but I loved every minute I spent there,"[28] he said. Beauvais would return to the airline industry to start two more airlines, Western Pacific and Mountain Air Express. Although they too filed for bankruptcy after Beauvais retired, in those cases he managed to keep the money he made.

Conway, meanwhile, remained as CEO in charge of running the airline. He implemented a downsizing plan that led to break-even cash flow by the end of 1992 and a record first quarter in 1993. As the next step in emerging from bankruptcy, America West sought to link up with a financially strong partner. Early on, Franke backed a plan, called Operation Cowboy, to sell out to American Airlines. Conway said that neither he nor a board member from Ansett learned of the plan for a month or two. "To say I was pissed would be an understatement," he said. "American did not have a good track record with acquisitions: it would have been a disaster for America West."[29]

When that deal collapsed, Conway began to work with a group that included Continental Airlines and its major shareholder, Texas Pacific Group. A key player in putting that deal together was Jon Ornstein, then executive vice president of planning for Mesa Air Group, a Farmington, New Mexico, based regional airline that initially sought to acquire America West on its own.

Ornstein began his pursuit by meeting with Conway. "Conway said Mesa needed partners and 'we respect guys at Mesa, but this is probably more than you can handle,'" Ornstein recalled. "He suggested we talk to Continental."[30] Ornstein believed a deal was desirable because "America West was already doing well—they were already profitable after [cutting unprofitable flying]. So many airlines are just one schedule change from profitability. When you have overexpansion, you need to pull it back in."[31] Following Conway's advice, Ornstein met first with Continental executives, and then with TPG principal David Bonderman. "I explained why the deal made sense," Ornstein said. He worked to structure a partnership that included TPG, Continental, Mesa and eventually mutual fund company Fidelity Investments. Eventually, Franke came to back the deal, which enabled America West to emerge from a three-year stay in bankruptcy in August 1994 with Franke as chairman. Conway, in the end, backed a deal with financing provided by hedge fund manager Michael Steinhardt and Mutual Shares, a mutual fund company. "I thought Conway was a good guy, but the tent wasn't big enough for all of us to work together," Ornstein said. "Franke had already raised money, he had gained control, and he was doing a good job. As a result we sided up with Franke. I was told that Franke is very serious—they told me not to curse in front of him—but it turned out he had a good sense of humor and he and I got along."[32]

On December 31, 1993, Conway became the last of the three founders to leave America West. He went on to form Las Vegas–based National Airlines, and over the next few years, almost all of the top management at America West elected to join him there. The airline began flying in 1999 but shut down in 2002, a victim of rising fuel costs, a recession and finally the September 11, 2001, terrorist attacks. Franke remained at America West: "My six months there turned out to be nine years, broken up by two interim departures," he said.[33] Meanwhile, the exodus of executives created the openings for Franke to hire a bevy of new employees, including Doug Parker.

Franke hired Parker, then 33, from Northwest Airlines in 1995 as senior vice president and chief financial officer. "I was looking for a significant upgrade on the revenue management side of the airline," he said. "We hired about four people from Northwest, most of whom had started at American. Doug was one of those. He had been a very young vice president at Northwest and he joined us as CFO."[34] In 1998, Franke selected Parker as the airline's future CEO and set up a training program in which he would run through a series of roles, from CFO to chief commercial officer to revenue and network planning and then to chief operating officer, and have most of the airline's executives reporting to him. "We didn't anoint Doug," Franke said. "We felt he had the right qualities and had the ability and we wanted to expand his experience so he had the best opportunity to succeed. But had he failed along the path, he would not have gotten the job." What did Franke see in Parker? "My own view of Doug was that he projects himself as a very easygoing, go-along get-along guy, but in fact he has very strong analytical skills and the ability to absorb a significant number of facts, which might overwhelm others, and to sort through those facts to make a decision."[35]

Being a leader in the airline industry "takes a certain ability to take limited facts and make a decision," Franke said. "It's hard for traditional managers. But stuff happens so quickly in the airline sector. It's not like having 15 manufacturing plants, [consistently] making widgets. There are decisions around fuel and revenue and pricing and new markets, and they have to be made frequently, with limited information. You have to have good instincts and be able to survive while not always being right. A lot of executives want to be right all the time, but in the airline sector you try to be right 75 percent of the time."[36]

Franke takes pride in having selected Parker and the other young executives. "Whether it was good fortune, blind luck or skill, the bottom line is we put together a hell of a management team," he said. The transition was scheduled for August 31, 2001. That day, "we had a nice press conference and we had a $250 million line of credit," said Franke, who quickly left to vacation in Australia. Eleven days later, he was awakened by a phone call from one of his sons, who told him to turn on the television, where he could watch scenes of the terrorist attacks on the World Trade Center. With all commercial flying to the U.S. canceled, he was stuck in Australia for eight days. Franke had a few conversations with Parker, but said, "He was in charge, doing what he needed to do, managing the airline, and my understanding with him when I left was 'Doug, I am going to stay out of the way.'"[37] And that is what he did.

8

The House That Jerry Built

In many ways the story of Charlotte Douglas International Airport is the story of US Airways—an airline that, like the airport, not only survived deregulation but also prospered because of it, despite substantial odds against success. In deregulation, not only did many airlines fail, but also many airports were reduced to secondary status in a system that enabled just a handful of winners, all of them either international gateways or major hubs for network carriers or, as a consolation prize, became principal Southwest Airlines cities. The Charlotte airport was perhaps the biggest winner among airports, becoming a major hub—the second biggest for the world's biggest airline—even though it is neither located in a major city nor is a principal gateway to the U.S. In 2012, the Charlotte metropolitan area was ranked 23rd by the U.S. Census Bureau. Yet by 2013, US Airways offered nearly 700 daily Charlotte departures during the peak summer season, making the airport the world's fourth largest single-airline hub. Stephen Wolf once said that Charlotte has more air service than any city its size in the world. Charlotte became particularly valuable as the world was settling on a global commercial aviation system with three global alliances and three global U.S. airlines, but with only two hubs in the Southeast.

Charlotte Douglas grew for three reasons. First, it is located 80 miles from Winston-Salem, where native son Tom Davis started Piedmont Airlines in 1948. Soon after deregulation, Piedmont chose Charlotte over Greensboro as the site of its first hub. Second, Charlotte is not Atlanta, where Delta has long operated a hub and today operates the world's biggest single airline hub with approximately 1,000 daily departures. Rather, Charlotte emerged as the only alternative to Atlanta as a hub for the Southeast, which is home to 80 million people. The third reason for the airport's growth was the management provided by Jerry Orr, who became aviation director in 1989, and who had an intense commitment to keeping airport service levels high and airport costs to carriers low. In fact, in 2013, Charlotte Douglas was charging US Airways just $1.15 per enplaned passenger, lowest among major airports, at a time when many major airports had costs exceeding $10, with several close to $20. Orr was frequently quoted in the media, which holds him in particularly high regard because of his frankness, his accessibility and his oft-displayed gifts for humor and plain-spoken wisdom, making remarks such as this one: "When you produce the highest-quality product at the lowest possible cost, people will beat a path to your door."[1]

Tom Davis began Piedmont Airlines three miles from the house where he was born in 1918. In fact, he went to work at Smith Reynolds Airport nearly every day for six decades, starting in 1940, when he left the University of Arizona—where he had gone hoping the dry climate would ease his chronic asthma—to help reorganize a company that sold single-propeller airplanes to private pilots. "I haven't gotten very far," laughed Davis during an interview with the *Charlotte Observer* in 1997, by which time he had long since become a hometown hero. Davis recounted how his father took him to watch one of the early barnstorming pilots perform over a cow pasture south of town, and how Charles Lindbergh flew his plane, *The Spirit of St. Louis*, to Winston-Salem a few months after its historic 1927 transatlantic flight. Davis read Lindbergh's book, built a model of his plane and took flying lessons at the airport while he was in high school. Afterward, he recalled, "My interest in airplanes and aviation kept gnawing away at me."[2]

Among the early improvements Davis made at the Winston-Salem aircraft distributorship was to change its name from Camel City Flying Service—even then, the limitations were obvious, despite Winston-Salem's tobacco city heritage—to Piedmont Aviation, Inc. During World War II the company couldn't get any planes to sell, so it set up training schools for military pilots in Greensboro and Winston-Salem. The staff grew from 5 to 20. Then the war ended. "We scratched our heads and said what could we do to keep everybody on the payroll," Davis recalled. "Then we thought of scheduled service."[3] Like Allegheny, its eventual partner, Piedmont was among the dozen smaller airlines given permission by the Civil Aeronautics Board to offer regional service. In 1947, the CAB approved Piedmont's application to fly between North Carolina and the Ohio River Valley. The first departure occurred on February 20, 1948, when a DC-3, with a capacity of 21 passengers, left Wilmington, North Carolina, bound for Cincinnati, making 6 stops on the 5-hour, 15-minute flight.

Because it started as an effort to ensure its workers' continued employment, and because of its small-town origin, Piedmont had a paternalistic culture that never disappeared. The carrier was so homey that Davis' home number was listed in the phone book. "He got many calls at one or two in the morning—for instance, if we messed up and lost somebody's luggage," recalled Bill McGee, a former Piedmont executive vice president. "Sometimes, he'd call me right afterwards and say, 'Get this matter straightened out.'"[4] In the early days, Davis searched the country for airplanes, buying some from George Batchelor, a Miami aviation entrepreneur with a gift for finding used military aircraft. "In those days, I used to go to Honolulu and fly the planes back myself," Batchelor recalled.[5] Piedmont grew gradually into one of the most successful regional carriers. "We had a leg up because we had experience and we had people," Davis said. "We had the background and knowledge of a lot of instructors, mechanics, bookkeepers and pilots. Most of the other applicants were paper companies. They put in applications but had nothing to back them up."[6]

Of course, the small-town, small-company approach also had a downside. Gordon Bethune, who left Piedmont for Boeing and later ran Continental Airlines, once recalled that on his first day at work at Piedmont in 1984, he found a rotary dial phone on his desk. "Where is this from, World War II?" Bethune asked his secretary, Sue Lineberry, beginning a discussion of the airline's policies regarding telephones. When Lineberry brought him a form to log each of his long-distance phone calls, Bethune said he wouldn't do it—and Lineberry threw her own form into the wastebasket. "I'm not doing it either," she said.[7] Another time, when the head of maintenance wanted to hire a foreman, Bethune insisted that a written job description be posted. Then he demanded that a requirement of five years of Piedmont experience be excluded. "What's this s——— in here for?" Bethune asked. "It ain't how long you worked at Piedmont that makes us successful."[8] Gradually, Bethune learned to love the place. In 1966, Piedmont had begun flying to New York's LaGuardia Airport and in 1967 the company entered the jet age, placing an order for Boeing 727s and 737s. In 1969, Piedmont reported a profit, the first in a string that continued for two decades until it was absorbed into USAir. In 1978, Piedmont was listed on the New York Stock Exchange. It gradually added

Piedmont founder Tom Davis (left) and longtime executive Bill McGee, two Winston-Salem kids who started a hometown airline, with a Piedmont DC-3 (courtesy American Airlines).

flights to major cities, including Boston, Dallas, Denver, Phoenix, Los Angeles and San Francisco. Adding flights was easy, Davis said. All you had to do was to send "the feds a penny postcard saying you're going to fly to here or there, and they send you one back saying okay."[9]

In 1979, Piedmont began to connect a handful of flights in Charlotte. At the time, Eastern Airlines was already operating a small hub at Charlotte, with service to more than a dozen cities. Piedmont began working with Orr, a North Carolina State graduate who had left a family surveying company to become an airport engineer in 1975. Orr oversaw planning, financing and construction of a terminal, a runway and a maintenance base for Piedmont. "We had a tremendous relationship with Jerry Orr," said George Mason, who oversaw construction of the Piedmont base and later became a Continental Airlines senior vice president. "He had the vision to see what increased transportation would do for Charlotte, and he facilitated the construction."[10] Mason said Orr's cooperative attitude helped persuade Piedmont to put its hub in Charlotte instead of Greensboro. In fact, Piedmont planned to move its headquarters from Winston-Salem to Charlotte, Mason and Orr said. The 1980s were a period of rapid expansion for Piedmont, especially after the airport opened a new terminal in 1982. In 1985, Piedmont purchased Utica, New York–based Empire Airlines for $42 million,

Piedmont's first 737–300, tail number N301P, out for a spin (courtesy American Airlines).

providing access to Northeast markets. Piedmont opened small hubs in Baltimore, Dayton and Syracuse. By 1987, Piedmont operated 177 aircraft and was considered a star of deregulation: in June of that year, it inaugurated Charlotte-London service with its newly acquired Boeing 767 aircraft. Despite the expansion, Piedmont enjoyed a sterling reputation in the airline industry, where it was known for its smooth operation, customer focus, family atmosphere and consistent profitability.

But the end of Piedmont's run as a successful independent airline was coming. In 1981, Norfolk and Western Railroad bought 20 percent of the carrier and agreed to let it remain independent for five years. At that point, the agreement gave the railroad the option to either bid for more or sell its shares. In 1986, the railroad, by then called Norfolk Southern, offered to buy the rest of Piedmont for $1.5 billion, or $65 a share. But USAir offered $1.6 billion and the railroad refused to top it. Davis retired as chairman in 1983, although he remained on the Piedmont board.

"It never occurred to me that anybody would outbid Norfolk and Western," he said. "But their board of directors decided, on the advice of their bankers [that] they should not go beyond $1.5 billion. We were disappointed, but we were glad to see the shareholders treated nicely, and we knew USAir was a reputable company. Hindsight is pretty good, but I don't want to second-guess anybody."[11]

USAir was not the only airline interested in Piedmont. In a 2013 interview with *TheStreet,* Orr disclosed that before the railroad put Piedmont on sale, American Airlines had expressed interest in a purchase, which might have made Charlotte an American hub two decades earlier. Before the USAir/Piedmont merger, Orr said, American inquired about buying Piedmont. "Everything goes round and round," he said. "You just have to stand in one place and be patient—The same deal will come back. Some people think deals never come back—That's wrong."[12] Additionally, Sandy Rederer, then senior vice president of strategic planning for TWA, recalled that TWA owner and chairman Carl Icahn talked with Piedmont CEO Bill Howard about a purchase. "Bill Howard tried hard to find an alternative to USAir," Rederer said. "We had talked to him before the USAir bid and I tried to talk Carl into it. But Carl wanted a deal for Piedmont to buy TWA. We produced assessments of the value of TWA and projections of the synergy between TWA and Piedmont. I also worked on various other merger ideas, including TWA-USAir and TWA-Northwest."[13] After retiring from Piedmont, Howard worked for several years as TWA CEO.

One of the most emotional days in the history of Charlotte Douglas occurred on February 20, 1988, when a portion of Piedmont's first flight 40 years earlier was recreated with a restored DC-3 flying from Wilmington to Charlotte. Tom Davis was aboard. Many ex-employees lined up to greet Davis, to hug him or to have pictures taken with him. Amazingly, Davis recalled the names of people he had not seen for decades. "You will never find loyalty to a company like you did at Piedmont," said Colleen Fields, a US Airways ticket agent who went to work for Piedmont in 1981. "There was a feeling there no one place else could capture. I have seen grown men with tears in their eyes, just talking about it."[14] Fields also recalled a pilot nicknamed "Stick It in the Mud Bud" who once taxied off the runway in Roanoke. Many credited Davis' employee-oriented approach for the airline's success. "We worked for a man who made us feel proud," said Nigel Adams, US Airways Charlotte station director, who started at Piedmont in 1981.[15]

Davis noted that he had gone into the cockpit and piloted the plane for about 10 minutes on Friday. "I didn't get lost," he joked.[16] Among the crowd that gathered on the ramp Friday was 78-year-old J.B. Simpson of Greenville, South Carolina, the purser on the 1948 flight. After the plane arrived in Cincinnati, Simpson recalled, it couldn't return for eight days because the weather was bad and Piedmont's temporary certificate didn't allow limited-visibility flying. Simpson was pleased when the weather cleared. "We were ready to come home and get that other shirt," he said.[17] Piedmont executives spoke warmly of Charlotte. Said Bill McGee, a passenger on the inaugural flight who eventually became Piedmont chairman, "The Charlotte hub was the crown jewel of the Piedmont operation."[18]

Bill Wise joined Piedmont in 1986 as a mechanic. To do that, he had to leave his home in Orlando, Florida, where he was working two jobs—one as a part-time fleet service worker and customer service agent for Piedmont, the other as a full-time mechanic for Page Avjet, which provided third-party line maintenance service to airlines such as People Express, Florida Express and Braniff. Wise started with Piedmont in Rochester, New York, moved after six months to Baltimore, and then in 1989 moved to Charlotte, where he was to remain. In 1991 Wise became active in the International Association of Machinists, which represented Piedmont mechanics. "I got active because of something my dad taught me," Wise said. "He was a government worker, and he was not in a union, but when Piedmont offered me a job as a mechanic, I also had a chance to go to Delta (where mechanics were not unionized), so I called my dad and asked him what to do. He said: 'Don't be afraid of unions. Unions are good. They did good things for the United States. But the one thing you have to do to make it work is to participate; don't just be a member.'"[19]

Wise started in the union as a shop steward and trustee and worked his way up. In 2000, he was elected president of IAM Local 1725 in Charlotte, which represented thousands of mechanics; by 2013, he had been elected five times and was in his 13th year as president. Wise had little regard for any of the five CEOs who ran US Airways following the Piedmont merger. In fact, he said, the only CEO he ever saw in the hangar was Tom Davis. "Piedmont was a first-class airline with good working conditions," he said. "It was like a family airline. Tom Davis knew who everybody was. He always came into maintenance, which is what happens when you get CEOs from aviation. They're all bean counters now, they know you as an employee number only, but at Piedmont they knew you as an individual. Tom Davis would walk up to you, shake your hand, and call you by name."[20] Wise recalled that he once met Davis in Rochester. The next time the two met was in Baltimore, and Davis remembered his name.

Wise was a bit surprised by the changes that occurred following the merger with

USAir. "I'm sure, from a business standpoint, it was good," he said. "It was certainly good financially for the Piedmont mechanics because our wages increased. But it was a culture change. The contracts were different, the conditions were different. At Piedmont, we were all very young mechanics. And we didn't do pushbacks or [aircraft] receipt. We would sit in the break room until we were needed. With USAir, the contract had mechanics doing receipt and dispatch. The mechanics would handle mechanical and they would also marshal the plane in, chalk it, do a walkaround, hook the tow bar up and do the logbook."[21] Switching to the USAir contract meant higher costs, not only because wages were higher but also because mechanics were paid more than the fleet service workers who worked the gates at Piedmont. In Baltimore, Wise said, Piedmont had 28 mechanics who worked the three shifts at the hub, which had about 300 departures a day. Because of the mechanics' dispatch responsibilities, however, USAir needed about twice as many mechanics.

For years, the USAir/Piedmont merger was considered to be an example of a merger gone badly, primarily because the more corporate, less flexible USAir corporate culture won out. The need for more mechanics was just one example. George Mason

Jerry Orr discusses the creation of a new Charlotte airport authority with reporters on July 18, 2013 (Jeff Siner, courtesy *Charlotte Observer*).

recalled that of Piedmont's top 40 officers, only about 4 went to USAir. "It wasn't a convivial merger," he said,[22] noting that USAir was unwilling to yield on any point. For instance, even though Piedmont was building a new maintenance base in Charlotte, USAir wouldn't move any work from Pittsburgh—nor would it shut the old base in Winston-Salem. It wasn't until almost a decade after the merger that Stephen Wolf, hired as USAir chairman in 1996, shut down the Winston-Salem base and moved to consolidate maintenance and other functions. Another frequently cited example of bad policy was that while Piedmont gave passengers a full can of soda, the USAir policy of offering only a cup was what survived. That angered passengers.

"In the end, USAir got rid of the people who had talent," said Bethune. "They ran us off. And as soon as they did that, they lost their shirt."[23] The cultural conflict also reflected the North/South conflict that long divided the entire country. One prominent Pittsburgher was Teddy Xidas, the longtime leader of the Pittsburgh chapter of the Association of Flight Attendants. In 2004, Xidas ran for national president of the US Airways AFA chapter. Her opponent, Steve Hearn, the eventual winner, was the Charlotte local leader. During the campaign Xidas was asked to characterize the differences between the two cities. "We come from labor, steel mills, blue-collar workers," Xidas said in a 2004 interview with the *Charlotte Observer*. "The culture is different than in Charlotte. They are like little daffodils. They wear their hair in a bow and say 'I just hate that for you.' Charlotte is very delicate—gentle, soft souls," she said. "Pittsburgh is rough and tough. We're rough around the edges. We like to rumble."[24]

Orr, meanwhile, was a prominent advocate for Piedmont and Charlotte. "We were on a good track with Piedmont here," Orr said in a 2007 interview. "They were making money and growing rapidly, and we planned ahead and grew with them." Things changed when USAir bought Piedmont. "USAir ran hot and cold," Orr said. "They thought the sun rose and set in Pittsburgh."[25] To an extent, Charlotte remained an outpost of Piedmont gentility. "Sometimes I overhear people talking, people who have never flown through Charlotte before, and they say, 'This is such an easy, pleasant airport to travel through,'" said Terri Pope, US Airways station director, in a 2007 interview. "That's our draw here. We are a big airport but we have a small-town feel, and we pride ourselves on that."[26] Before displacements following the industry's 2001 slowdown, former Piedmont employees accounted for perhaps 75 percent of Charlotte's customer service and fleet service workers.

Orr became airport director in 1989, the year the merger was completed and the two carriers could blend their operations. At first, Orr benchmarked airport performance against that of Pittsburgh International, then USAir's largest hub. In the late 1980s, Pittsburgh underwent a $900 million expansion that produced a beautiful airport but also created a more costly place to operate. Orr just tried to keep costs down. "We understood deregulation," he said.[27] Eventually, US Airways cut Pittsburgh flying by 90 percent while growing in Charlotte. When the competition with Pittsburgh ended, Orr adopted new benchmark: Atlanta. "In any competition, you have to win one battle and then move on to the next," he said.[28] To ensure Charlotte's standing, Orr had to maintain its position as the principal alternative to Atlanta. He built a fourth runway and expanded terminals, creating a spacious international terminal, and still kept costs low. "If we can have a cost half of what the competition has, and we can produce a good product, we can win," he said.[29] Executives from US Airways, as well as those from competing airlines, routinely praised Orr for creating an environment in which airlines could prosper. In 2013, Doug Parker said Orr "has done a phenomenal job of building an airport for this community."[30] In a 2010 interview, JetBlue CEO Dave Barger called Orr "an institution" and "an industry gem."[31] Stephen Wolf once described Orr as one of the country's two best airport directors. Asked the other one's identity, Wolf said there was no one, but he wanted various others to believe it was them.

It wasn't just a strong airport

Terri Pope, US Airways vice president for airport customer service/Charlotte hub, a station manager with people skills (courtesy American Airlines).

manager that made the Charlotte hub a success for US Airways. Starting in 2000, the airline also benefited from having a gifted, instinctive executive in place as station manager, charged with overseeing operational performance at its biggest hub. Like Seth Schofield, Terri Pope never attended college. Yet she rose to become one of the more prominent women in the airline industry, at least partially because of her innate ability to get the most out of the people who worked for her. By 2013, Pope oversaw 5 department heads, 30 shift managers and 1,500 people in Charlotte who staffed the airline's ticket counters, passenger services, baggage handling, ground airplane movements and other airport operations.

Pope began her airline career soon after graduating from Davies County (Kentucky) High School, joining commuter carrier Air Kentucky in 1976 as station director. In 1983 she moved to USAir as a club representative in its Boston airport club. Like many airline employees, she moved frequently during her early career, working as station manager at Palm Beach International and Washington National airports before taking over at Charlotte. Pope's job involved a constant obsession with the performance numbers that are the guts of the airline industry. Throughout her work day, she would glance at a video screen showing the latest numbers on US Airways airport delays, the reasons for delays, the length of time between arrivals and departures, departure times relative to scheduled departure times and other performance measures.

Another pursuit was the carrier's weekly quality review meeting: an hour-long conference call and slide show of nearly 200 charts, one by one, each showing various aspects of the airline's performance for the past week. The measurements included food and beverage complaints, the amount of time reservations clerks spoke to each customer on the phone, the number of inoperable bathrooms per day and each key station's "PAWOBs," or passengers arriving without baggage. Among Pope's favorite topics is "turn time," which refers to the amount of time an aircraft spends at the gate, because that is what she controls at Charlotte. During an airplane's turn time, often around an hour for a narrow-body aircraft, passengers disembark and board the aircraft while workers clean it, fuel it, stock it with provisions and load and unload baggage. Pope calls turn time "the only pure measure of performance." In Pope's small office, the window offered an uninspiring view of the roof of the US Airways club, with the roof of an airport concourse and a few airplane tails beyond. The few personal possessions included photos of her husband and son and models and photos of airplanes, tributes to the lure of the airline industry. "I've never done anything else," Pope said during a 2001 interview. "We've had so many people leave the airline to do something else and then come back. Other jobs are not the same."[32]

On December 9, 2013, the day shares in the new American Airlines were listed on the NASDAQ stock market, Pope told reporters at an airport media event that mergers were nothing new for her or her airline. She listed the four that occurred during her career, starting with Piedmont. For that one, she had been brought from Boston to Charlotte to coordinate changes in airport operations including policies involving ticketing and gate and curbside procedures. The transition took two years, after which she had left temporarily to be station manager in West Palm Beach. The mergers with PSA and America West had followed. "I've had experience in merging airlines,"[33] Pope told reporters, as she envisioned months of work before the American merger was complete.

Unlike Pope, Jerry Orr could not look forward to being involved in the merger that would even more firmly establish Charlotte Douglas as one of the country's most important airports. In July 2013 the city fired the 72-year-old Orr, who became collateral damage in a political battle between a Tea Party–dominated North Carolina state legislature and a heavily Democratic Charlotte City Council. The battle exemplified how pettiness and spitefulness are often components of human behavior, and how being Democrat or Republican makes no difference in that regard. The first step occurred when the legislature seized on a perceived need to wrest control of the airport from the city, which had run it successfully since 1936. The legislators sought to create an airport authority, with its members selected primarily from people outside Charlotte. The city, not surprisingly, objected. Orr had little or nothing to do with the Republican power grab, although he later conceded, "I went to work at the airport in April 1975 and on the second day I figured out that it desperately needed to be run by an airport authority. I have believed that consistently, and that's what I always said if anybody asked."[34] It was not what city politicians wanted to hear. Additionally, throughout his career, Orr had been able to fend off politicians' efforts to get their hands on the hundreds of millions of dollars that annually flowed through the airport. For them, the chance to oust him proved too tempting to resist. Wrangling over the airport authority continued in the courts, but Orr officially retired from the city in December, saying he wanted to do what was best for the airport.

On US Airways' October 2013 quarterly earnings call, *Charlotte Observer* reporter Ely Portillo asked about the airline's latest take on Orr, three months after he had been removed. At first, Robert Isom, chief operating officer, took the politically correct course, saying relations "with the city and airport have never been better." But then Doug Parker spoke up, saying, "Jerry has been a phenomenal airport director." He added: "Jerry Orr has done an amazing job, and we'd like to see him back in there." Earlier in the call, which came soon after US Airways announced that it would operate 10 daily flights to Europe during the summer, Scott Kirby had said, "It's a remarkable story of growth in Charlotte. It shows you the power of a hub to be able to connect customers and offer customers service to far more destinations, in the microcosm of the Southeast." Parker referred to the hub capabilities that Kirby spoke of, and said: "All that is due to Jerry."[35]

9

How Stephen Wolf
Almost Fixed US Airways

During a 35-year aviation career, Stephen Wolf presided over four carriers as they adapted to deregulation. He followed a remarkably similar pattern at all of them. He would paint airplanes, and sometimes buy new ones: reduce costs, typically through carrot-and-stick negotiations with labor; reconfigure route systems, often adding international service; and grow revenues. When Wolf brought his method to USAir in January 1996, one of the first things he changed was the airline's name. The switch from USAir to US Airways was mocked by some, who viewed it as a meaningless deck-chairs rearrangement, as name changes often are. But in fact it had enormous implications. For one thing, Wolf wanted to unite the disparate workforces from the two primary predecessor airlines, Piedmont and USAir. A decade after their 1987 merger, many Piedmont employees still resented everything about their acquirer. Additionally, Wolf thought that "USAir" sounded like the name of a regional airline while "US Airways" was classier, bringing the élan of an international carrier like British Airways. Wolf was obsessed by the concept of class. He had high standards not only for his airlines but also for himself.

Wolf strove for exactitude, always pushing himself and those around him to do more, to work harder and to carefully consider the way things would appear to others. At times, the concern for appearance conflicted with his sense of elitism: When Wolf was running US Airways, he stayed much of the time in the upscale Four Seasons Hotel in Crystal City, despite employee complaints that the financially troubled carrier was spending far too much on lodging for its imperial CEO.

Wolf's most distinguishing characteristic was his height: He stood six foot six and towered over people. He wore a mustache and red suspenders, which had the effect of making him look taller and more imposing. A workaholic, he often started at 7 a.m. and stayed at the office until late in the evening. He was consumed with minute details of the airline business, such as the length of the ticket counter lines, the color of the carpet in the airplanes and even the color of the paper used for timetables. With people, Wolf was sometimes aloof and remote. On the elevator in US Airways' Crystal City headquarters, when he rode up or down with other airline employees, Wolf would rarely chat, preferring to stare straight ahead. Additionally, during his six years at the carrier, Wolf rarely gave media interviews, at a time when many other airline CEOs regularly did so. Yet on the occasions when he did talk with reporters, he could be warm and engaging and he would reveal intimate details about his work and his life.

Perhaps the oddest, most revealing instance in Wolf's career came at the company's May 1999 annual meeting, which took place in a hotel in downtown Charlotte. At the time, the airline's unions were incensed over compensation levels for Wolf and US Airways president Rakesh Gangwal, a protégé whom Wolf was grooming to one day run the airline. Wolf's 1998 base pay was $580,000, while Gangwal's was $566,538: Future stock awards and incentives boosted their reported 1998 compensation to about $35 million each, although it should be said that the total included stock and incentive gains that were not necessarily ever going to be realized. Wolf, in fact, never sold any US Airways stock. Rather, his holdings were wiped out in the carrier's 2002 bankruptcy. In 1999, however, the outlook was bright. Wolf was fixing the airline, with share price gains expected to follow. But contract negotiations were dragging, as they often do in the airline industry. Outside the annual meeting, about 150 workers protested, with high executive compensation as a focus. The workers included flight attendants as well as airport agents and reservations agents, members of the Communications Workers of America, which had about 10,000 agents at the airline. They had not had cost of living increases since 1992.

In the meeting, Wolf described the slow pace of negotiations with the agents in his usual detached style. "In 1990, when the company was at death's door, the company changed agent compensation in a draconian fashion," freezing pensions and reducing the number of holidays,[1] he said. Then, when he joined the company in 1996, the group was in the midst of a union organizing drive, followed by contract negotiations. During both events, labor law prohibited pay increases. Among the employees who stood to question Wolf was Danny Carter, a Charlotte passenger service supervisor. Carter offered a narrative about the difficulties he faced living on a fixed salary eroded by eight years of inflation. While his pay had been frozen, Carter said, there was no freeze on the cost of braces, auto insurance for his two teenage daughters or formula and diapers for his 2-year-old. As Carter spoke, revealing the innermost details of his life, he began to cry. "I worked overtime, and I paid a terrible price," he said. "I seldom spend time with my family. I've grown apart from my wife and I don't really know my teenage daughters. I want to fall in love with my wife again. I want to see my daughters graduate from high school and college [and] I believe with the help of the CWA this will happen."[2]

Wolf was moved and he responded in kind, offering a rare glimpse into his own life. "You deserve to be compensated at a fair level for a number of years," he said, adding: "My wife and I don't have any children. At 57 years of age, I wish we did, because I'd love to be spending time with them today." Later that day, Wolf announced that he and Gangwal would give up their long-term incentives, which made them eligible for bonuses equal to 220 percent of their base pay over the next three years. Wolf said he had made his decision the day before the meeting, noting, "Rakesh and I had a long conversation."[3] It is possible to imagine that Gangwal, who had a young family, was not as enthusiastic about giving up his incentive pay, but of course he went along with his mentor.

Although Wolf by 1999 was living as an aristocrat, his origins were humble. He led a difficult childhood. He was born August 7, 1941, in Oakland, California, into a lower-middle-class family. When he was 15, his father walked out. "There was nothing much to leave," Wolf said, during a 1997 interview. "He left, but there was no animus."[4] His father's departure meant that it was left to Wolf, then a student at Oakland High, to support his two sisters and mother. His first job was to wrap gifts and sweep floors at a jewelry store in downtown Oakland. He then worked on the loading dock at United Parcel Service while attending San Francisco State University. After graduating, he took a job in an American Airlines management training program. It was a 12-month program, but Wolf made supervisor after 12 weeks. In 10 years, he rose to the number two spot on the airline's cargo side before moving to the far bigger passenger side. There, his ascent up the management ladder hit a snag because he saw five people ahead of him on the corporate ladder. One was the airline's president, Bob Crandall. "I couldn't have been happier, but I wanted more responsibility,"[5] Wolf said. He left in 1981 for Pan American World Airways, where he was made a senior vice president. At Pan Am, "Wolf was a hard-nosed budget guy," said Al Topping, an assistant to the chairman who occupied a nearby office. "Once he was at a meeting and somebody brought in some coffee in Pan Am Clipper Club paper cups. Wolf got mad. He said 'These are for the customer; we should use plain paper cups.'"[6]

The next stop was Frank Lorenzo's Continental Airlines. Late in 1982 Lorenzo, chairman of holding company Texas International, offered Wolf the Continental presidency. When Wolf arrived, Continental was in a state of chaos: it was in the midst of moving its headquarters from Los Angeles to Houston at a time when it was running out of money and could barely pay its bills. Some Continental executives would say later that Wolf concerned himself primarily with minute details, such as color schemes for the new carpet in the airport club at Denver and the flight attendants' new ties and blouses, and that he made little contribution to addressing the airline's more pressing problem: survival. Wolf left after nine months, perhaps because of his approach to his job and perhaps because he would not fully embrace Lorenzo's strategies, which included the first bankruptcy of a major U.S. airline, which Continental filed in 1983. "I thought bankruptcy was the ultimate symbol of failure in business and I wouldn't go along with it," Wolf said. "You can flip a coin [as to] whether I was leaving or I got fired."[7] In any case, Wolf's departure enhanced his reputation because he came to be viewed as an executive who would not go along with Lorenzo's strategy, at a time when Lorenzo-phobia was rampant.

Five months later, Wolf found a job as president of Republic Airlines in Minneapolis. The good news was he once again became an airline president; the bad news was that Republic was close to bankruptcy after overexpanding through a series of mergers. Republic served more cities than any other U.S. carrier but lacked a dominant presence in any of them. Wolf secured wage concessions from Republic pilots by threatening to file for bankruptcy protection. He also repainted the airplanes, consolidated resources in the airline's strongest cities and made Republic profitable. Then, in 1985, he sold out to another Minneapolis-based airline, Northwest. The sale was first discussed in a clandestine meeting between Wolf and Northwest chairman Steven Rothmeier at the Cherokee Sirloin Room, a neighborhood steak place in St. Paul. "Republic was at a point where they had cut costs and maxed out their growth opportunities, and they could barely finance any additional fleet," Rothmeier recalled. "We were an international airline, looking to acquire domestically, and Republic was right here in the Twin Cities."[8] In the $884 million deal, made in January 1986, Wolf collected $2 million in options profits and $1 million in severance. More importantly, perhaps, he had for the first time acted to implement his model: He reduced costs, painted the airplanes and focused on the hubs. Then he sold the airline, enabling profits for investors. Over the next 15 years, the same model would work at two more airlines and almost work at US Airways.

Again Wolf was out of a job, but that didn't last long. By this time he was a hot property, and Los Angeles–based Flying Tiger Line, then the world's largest all-cargo airline, was adapting poorly to deregulation. This was largely because new legislation enabled shippers such as Federal Express and UPS to buy their own airplanes rather than to lease cargo space from Flying Tiger. As Wolf was awaiting governmental approval of the Republic acquisition, he received two phone calls encouraging him to join Flying Tiger. One was from officials of the Air Line Pilots Association in Washington. The other was from financier Saul Steinberg, who controlled the airline, which was close to bankruptcy. Both parties thought Wolf's management could enable Flying Tiger to survive. Again, Wolf seized the opportunity to impose both his operating model—labor cost cuts, paint jobs, enhanced route system with expanded international flying—and his compensation model, which involved securing a sufficient quantity of stock options that would enable him to collect millions of dollars if he succeeded.

But there was one very dramatic change. On his first day on the job, Wolf went to lunch with the man who became his most important lieutenant and whom he would later describe as his best friend. Larry Nagin, Flying Tiger's chief counsel, was a Los Angeles native who joined the airline in 1980 after six years as an attorney for the city of Los Angeles, including a stint as senior assistant city attorney representing the Los Angeles Department of Airports. As a child, Nagin's principal interests included attending Pacific Coast League baseball games of the Los Angeles Angels—years later, he was pleased that he once spoke to Bobby Bragan before a game—and spending time poring over airline schedules, collecting airline memorabilia and watching airplanes take off from Los Angeles International Airport. Nagin always felt fortunate to have transformed a childhood love of airplanes into a lasting and singular career in aviation.

Years after that 1986 meeting with Wolf, Nagin recalled that the two men bonded instantly over their decision to take a long lunch at an expensive restaurant. They also shared a sense of humor. But in other ways, Wolf and Nagin were opposites. While Wolf was aloof and formal, Nagin was warm and engaging, a big bear of a man who relished personal contact with people and who mentored dozens. While Wolf shied away from reporters, Nagin enjoyed working with them, always seeking to shape their perceptions and stories. He also enjoyed politics, and years later delighted in developing a relationship with the conservative North Carolina senator Jesse Helms, whose political views he did not remotely share, because the two men agreed that US Airways should have a Charlotte-London route. Over time, as Nagin and Wolf worked together at three airlines, Nagin, a man of profound intelligence, would develop political strategies that sometimes worked, as when they won a Chicago-Tokyo route for United, and sometimes did not, as when they attempted to spin off US Airways operations at Washington's National Airport to black entrepreneur Robert Johnson in order to secure regulatory approval for a United–US Airways merger. One person Nagin mentored was Rahsaan Johnson (unrelated to Robert Johnson), who went on to a career as a spokesman for various airlines after joining US Airways in 1999. Nagin once interrupted

Steven Wolf (left foreground) meets employees including dispatcher Don Wright (right foreground) in US Airways Charlotte hangar, September 17, 1997. Larry Nagin is at right background (Gayle Shomer, courtesy *Charlotte Observer*).

a staff meeting to thank Johnson, who a week earlier had made a small mistake in describing an airport's layout, and then had corrected it. "Beneath Larry's big, gruff exterior was a guy who wanted to see people do well," Johnson said.[9]

Nagin was immensely loyal to Wolf: David Castelveter said regularly that "Larry would step in front of a bus to protect Steve." After Nagin died in 2009 at the age of 67, Jerry Grinstein, who met Nagin, then a law student at the University of California, in the 1960s, described him as Wolf's *consigliere*. "Stephen is a very creative, innovative guy, very demanding and very precise, and he needed someone who was going to be his right hand, his adviser," Grinstein said. "When you are someone who is trying to make changes, you've got to have somebody alongside you making sure that you are being careful, that what you are doing is OK."[10]

In one of the most famous stories from Wolf's career, leaders of the Flying Tiger chapter of the Air Line Pilots Association showed up for their first meeting with Wolf wearing red suspenders. The relationship quickly became contentious because Wolf wanted the 650 pilots to immediately accept a three-year, 15 percent pay cut. Eventually the pilots capitulated, the carrier became an attractive acquisition candidate, and FedEx agreed to pay $895 million to buy it, a transaction that enabled FedEx to dominate the overnight package carrier business into Asia, perhaps permanently. Nagin would later describe the Flying Tigers years as the most joyous chapter of his long partnership with Wolf, because once costs were reduced, improvements were easily made and quickly translated into a financial turnaround. Once again, an options deal was going to make Wolf rich—but this time, he did not even stay to cash in his options. In 1986, before the transaction closed, United Airlines called. Former astronaut Neil Armstrong, then chairman of the United board, wanted Wolf so badly that he arranged to award him options on 250,000 shares of United stock as compensation for giving up his Flying Tiger options. Wolf joined United in 1987; Nagin followed in 1989. Together, they would transform United, just as they had transformed Tiger.

United is known today for its vast international route system, yet when Wolf and Nagin arrived the carrier did not offer a single flight to Europe. In fact, United in 1987 was an ugly cauldron of labor conflict combined with a misguided plan to create an integrated global travel empire that included the airline, hotel chains, and Hertz rental cars, all under the mantle of the Allegis Holding Company. In May 1985, pilots had staged a 29-day strike over a proposed B-scale pay rate for new hires. On the plus side, in 1985 United made perhaps the best asset purchase in airline history, buying Pan Am's Pacific division, including a hub at Tokyo's Narita Airport, as well as U.S.-China routes. To make matters more confusing, United's employees were seeking to buy the airline. The pilots in particular feared that if Wolf succeeded in fixing it, the purchase would be more costly, so they decided to generally oppose his efforts. At one point, they refused to fly two new Boeing 747–400 jets because their contract did not specifically include rates for the aircraft type. "Those boys up there were goal-oriented," said David Morrow, a former US Airways pilot who later became a national ALPA leader.

"They decided that the best way to deal with Wolf was to smack him right in the face and keep on hitting. Wolf laughed about it later. He told us, 'Those pilots didn't give me a chance to earn their disdain; they bestowed it upon me.'"[11]

By most measures, Wolf made vast improvements at United. He quickly sold off the hotels and rental car company. He added routes in Europe as well as Latin America, so that the total number of international destinations expanded from 11 when he arrived to 33 when he left. Nagin engineered a successful political battle to win the rights to fly between Chicago and Tokyo in an intense political battle with American. The pair also ordered hundreds of new airplanes, including the first 777 jets that Boeing produced. Following a trend of the time, Wolf also created an airline-within-in-an-airline, a low-cost version of United that flew in California. It failed, but United retained an intra–California route system that still supports its hubs at San Francisco and Los Angeles

Though he initially opposed employee ownership, Wolf eventually backed it and joined pilots to negotiate concessions worth $4.9 billion in exchange for 55 percent employee ownership. When the deal was finally set, pilots no longer wanted Wolf to stay, so he left with $37 million in salary and gains from stock options and grants. Later he declared, "When I left, United was the best-positioned airline in the world by a wide margin. Under different conditions, I would very much have liked to stay and run the company."[12] Instead, he went to work for investment banker Lazard Frères and Company, advising Air France, while Nagin went into private practice and Rakesh Gangwal became United's executive vice president. Years later, during a 2010 press conference, Wendy Morse, the newly elected chairman of the United ALPA chapter, praised Wolf. She noted that United had had seven CEOs during the past 25 years and that "only one left the company better than he found it."[13] That one, she acknowledged, was Wolf.

Wolf was at Lazard when US Airways, then the world's sixth-largest airline, came calling. He turned down the first few approaches but eventually yielded. "I had quite consciously decided it was indeed time to smell a rose," he said. "[But] then, I focused on the challenge."[14] Wolf was only 55, and here was the chance to repeat what he had done three times, working with the same team and collecting a big payoff—tastefully, of course, with options that would appreciate only if he succeeded. On joining US Airways in January 1996, Wolf received options for 1.3 million shares of stock, vested by 2000, as well as 325,000 shares of stock, vested by 1999.

By 1996, US Airways had become an also-ran airline, a regional carrier confined largely to the eastern half of the country. It survived by charging high fares on relatively short routes. But low-cost competitors such as Southwest, ValuJet and Delta's low-cost Delta Express were starting to pick off choice routes, knowing they could fly them more cheaply than USAir could. In the six years before Wolf signed on in January 1996, USAir had lost $2.9 billion and had failed in repeated efforts to negotiate lower-cost contracts. In general, USAir had not yet figured out how to operate under deregulation, while Wolf was a master of that transition. In his early days at the carrier, Wolf discussed potential mergers with nearly every airline. Northwest, Wolf said later, would have been the most desirable partner, given its access to Asia and its strength in the Midwest, where US Airways was weak. However, in 1997 Wolf said merger efforts had been "put to bed."[15] What he meant was that he had to fix the airline if he were going to be able to sell it.

The inefficiencies in USAir's pre-deregulation organizational structure were striking. When Wolf arrived, the carrier housed management functions in three cities: Pittsburgh; Crystal City, Virginia, and Winston-Salem; Wolf consolidated management in Crystal City. Three maintenance bases were located within 100 miles of one another, in Charlotte, Greensboro and Winston-Salem. Despite union protests, Wolf closed the latter two bases. Closing Winston-Salem was particularly emotional since Piedmont had been founded there. Even today, US Airways still employs about 700 people at its Winston-Salem reservations center. Wolf also closed a reservations office in Utica, New York, which had been the site of Mohawk's headquarters. Another problem was that hubs in Baltimore, Charlotte, Pittsburgh, Philadelphia and Washington were all within a few hundred miles of one another. Over time, beginning after Wolf left, the Baltimore and Pittsburgh hubs would cease to exist. Wolf only began to address the problem of route redundancies, which included 21 daily connecting flights between Hartford, Connecticut, and Greensboro. As Gangwal described the situation: "You can basically say that we are our own largest competitor."[16] Another change was in management: within two and a half years of Wolf's arrival, only 10 of the top 32 officers remained, and hundreds of lower level managers had also departed.

USAir's labor contracts were filled with costly work rules, because every time the airline had completed a merger, the most generous components of the two previous contracts were retained. One day in April 1997, at a meeting with employees in Charlotte, a reservations agent asked Wolf what he was going to do about "swaps," which enabled trades of shifts with other workers. At one time, the swaps policy allowed the carrier's 4,000 reservations agents to trade up to 50 percent of their shifts, but the number had been cut back to 20 swaps per quarter, irritating the clerks, many of whom drew night shifts for years. Wolf expressed compassion, followed by exasperation. "I don't know of a company in the world that has unlimited swaps," he said. "I don't think most companies know what swaps are. I almost don't know what to do about it…. It may be the goofiest thing anybody ever heard of. Some of our policies are beyond goofy—the fact that they went on for 1,000 years doesn't make them right."[17] Among the problems, he said, was the necessity to consistently replace a worker at one salary level with a worker at another level. He went on to say that the unlimited swaps policy was a holdover from Allegheny Airlines. "The principal culture in this company is the Allegheny culture," he said. "Allegheny flew monopoly routes in the East for 2,000 years at monopoly price. It was wonderful and profitable every day of its life and as a result of that, we are very generous with our employees."[18]

For all of its problems, USAir had a major strategic asset: On the East Coast, home to the highest concentration of airline travelers in the world, it dominated. In 1996, it carried 41 percent of East Coast departures, while number two Delta had 21 percent. At its largest hub, in Charlotte, the airline offered 344 daily departures, most of them connecting passengers between the Northeast and the Southeast. National Airport, which USAir dominated, was essentially closed to new competition because the supply of gates and runway times was so restricted. National has long been a profit center. Wolf focused on adding transatlantic service from Philadelphia, building it into a major European hub. But while USAir dominated the market for intra–East Coast flights, it trailed competitors in the markets between the East Coast and other regions. On transatlantic flights, US Airways had just 3 percent of the market, even though 69 percent of all U.S. passengers to Europe departed from east of the Mississippi.

Of course, Wolf linked his plan to fix the airline with the need for employees, particularly pilots, to make concessions in their generous contracts. The biggest incentive Wolf offered was an order for up to 400 narrow-body Airbus aircraft. The order eventually made US Airways the biggest Airbus operator in the world, a distinction it retained after the 2005 merger with America West, which had 94 Airbus aircraft in its own fleet. Wolf had placed the order in November 1996, but tied confirmation, scheduled for a year later, to approval of a new pilot contract. "The way Stephen Wolf would get pilot concessions at United and US Airways was that he would go out and buy a bunch of new airplanes for them, tied to a contract," said veteran airline analyst Bob McAdoo. "It was a bribe. He would say 'We will put you in nice new airplanes if you sign the contract.'"[19]

Wolf argued that at every airline he ran, pilots benefitted. By 1996, Republic pilots were flying jumbo jets to Japan for Northwest; Flying Tiger pilots had senior jobs at FedEx, and United had expanded so fast that its pilots were making captain in six years instead of the 19½ years it took when he arrived. The Airbus deal would mean that Wolf had bought nearly 1,000 airplanes, more than any civilian in history. Unfortunately, the principal concession Wolf was seeking at US Airways was the ability to start a low-cost division, to be called MetroJet. In retrospect, although low-cost divisions were popular at the time and were being tried at Delta and United, Wolf would have been far better off seeking some other concession, such as the right to fly more regional jets. Little-remembered MetroJet began flying in 1998 and shut down in 2001.

Despite the efforts to build US Airways as an independent airline, it hardly came as a surprise when, on May 25, 2000, United announced a proposed $11.6 billion acquisition. The two airlines said they expected Justice Department approval, partially because they provided three sweeteners: a two-year freeze on airline fares, except for fuel cost and cost-of-living adjustments; a guarantee not to lay off any of US Airways' 42,275 employees; and an arrangement to spin off most US Airways assets at Reagan National Airport to Robert Johnson. The merger would have combined the largest U.S.

United CEO Jim Goodwin (left) and US Airways CEO Stephen Wolf (right) announce in May 2000 that their airlines would merge (courtesy American Airlines).

airline with the sixth-largest, creating a mega-carrier with more than $26 billion in revenues, more than 140,000 employees and more than 1,000 aircraft. US Airways' East Coast routes would fit nicely into an airline that was domestically strong everywhere but the East Coast. United was to pay $60 per share for US Airways stock.[20] That meant Wolf would leave US Airways with $86 million, including $11.6 million in incentive and termination pay. The remaining $74 million represented the value of the stock he had accumulated at the airline. As it turned out, when the merger failed and US Airways filed for bankruptcy, Wolf had not sold a single share. His $74 million turned into nothing.

Fourteen months after the merger was proposed, the Justice Department rejected it on July 27, 2001, saying it would reduce competition, raise fares and harm airline passengers. United had to pay US Airways a $50 million breakup fee. Why did the deal fail? Many explanations were offered, but by far the most compelling one is that United lost interest. The deal's collapse followed a sharp decline in the economy, which meant that the airline industry was expected to lose as much as $2 billion in 2001, its biggest loss since 1993. United had committed to pay $60 a share for US Airways stock, but the shares closed on July 27 at $17.26 each. In fact, United had tried to pull out of the deal in June. Nagin said later that United ceased to lobby or negotiate with regulators on behalf of the deal. Additionally, airlines at the time were among the least popular U.S. industries. In 2000, United pilots, in the midst of contract negotiations, staged a slowdown that created what was known as "the summer of hell." One out of every four U.S. flights that summer was delayed because of the United slowdown, bad weather and scheduling overloads at the nation's most congested airports. Why would the Justice Department have approved a difficult $12 billion deal, in an industry that was making everybody angry, when the buyer had totally lost interest?

10

Plan B as in Bankruptcy

The September 11, 2001, terrorist attacks came just two months after the US Airways/United deal fell through. The attacks exacerbated the problems of an already weak airline economy, bringing a sudden sharp decline in traffic that led to huge numbers of losses and layoffs. The domestic industry's revenues fell to $107 billion in 2002, down from $130 billion in 2000, while domestic airline employment fell to 450,000, down from 520,000 in 2002. US Airways was particularly hard-hit because 80 percent of its departures were on the East Coast, where travel fell precipitously, and because Washington's Reagan National Airport, where US Airways was the dominant carrier, was closed for three weeks. Stephen Wolf had anticipated capping his career with an adroit transaction creating the biggest, best-balanced airline in the world. Instead, he found himself, at 60, managing through a disaster. He had spent years grooming his protégé Rakesh Gangwal to take over for him, naming Gangwal to be US Airways CEO in 1998. But in November 2001, Gangwal resigned suddenly, just as Wolf had planned to retire. The airline said Gangwal preferred to go to work in the venture capital business. It was also speculated that Gangwal feared his compensation package would diminish should the carrier file for bankruptcy. His departure forced Wolf back into a day-to-day role. Wolf ran the airline until March 2002, when the airline's board named David Siegel, a former Continental Airlines executive who was running Avis Rent a Car, to be president and CEO.

Siegel had spent seven years at Continental from 1993 to 1999, a period during which outgoing executive Gordon Bethune took over the airline and, building on the base that Frank Lorenzo had established, turned it into an industry leader. Siegel felt that he too was ready to run an airline, but he arrived at US Airways at a particularly bad time. Travel demand was down, costs at the legacy airlines were high and low-cost airlines such as AirTran, JetBlue and Southwest were expanding rapidly. US Airways at the time had the highest operating cost of any major airline—12.46 cents per mile, compared with 10.14 cents for Delta and 7.54 cents for Southwest—and it spent about two-thirds of its revenues, the highest of any airline, to pay labor costs.[1]

"The honeymoon ended for David Siegel two weeks after he took office," the *Charlotte Observer* reported on March 26, 2002.[2] According to the newspaper, "Siegel was blasted by labor leaders hours after he posted a telephone message for employees,

US Airways CEO David Siegel, seeking employee concessions, speaks in Charlotte Douglas International Airport, May 8, 2002 (Patrick Schneider, courtesy *Charlotte Observer*).

saying the airline's 'parity plus one' compensation plan doesn't make sense."[3] Parity plus one had been a linchpin of the high-cost union contracts Wolf signed in order to facilitate a merger with United, but the situation had changed dramatically. One month after Siegel arrived, US Airways reported a $269 million first-quarter loss, marking its seventh consecutive losing quarter. Two months after he arrived, US Airways stock plunged to an all-time low, closing under $3 a share as talk of bankruptcy protection spooked investors. Soon thereafter, on May 17, Siegel unveiled a reorganization plan that included about $950 million annually in labor concessions. It was designed to meet the terms required to secure a government-backed loan from the Air Transportation Stabilization Board, which was charged with helping airlines stay in business following the Sept. 11 attacks. Five months after Siegel arrived, on August 14, 2002, US Airways filed for bankruptcy protection, becoming the first major airline to file following the attacks.

The day before the filing, Bill Wise, president of the IAM lodge that represents US Airways mechanics in Charlotte, spoke with Siegel in one of a series of phone conversations between the two men that month. Wise suggested that the airline could save money by moving maintenance to Charlotte and by changing some of its processes. "They were talking about building a huge mega-hangar in Pittsburgh and moving all the work there," Wise said. He continued,

> I said Jerry Orr has done a tremendous job here and wants to have more maintenance here. Also, I told Siegel I knew how the airline could save money. I was working in the flap shop at the time, working on outboard flap assemblies for the 737. I would rebuild them. Each assembly had eight bearings that cost about $1,200 apiece. In the past, we would remove them and send them to Winston to the machine shop, which could rebuild them, making a ship set of 16 bearings for around $2,000. But they had switched the policy, so that when we rebuilt the flap assemblies we were instructed to discard all the bearings. We would pull a trash can over, remove the bearings from the assembly, throw all eight of them in the trash can and pull eight new ones. That cost $9,600 a wing or $19,200 for a set of two.[4]

"Siegel told me the airline didn't have two nickels to rub together—I remember him saying that," Wise said. "He also said he would come to Charlotte and walk through the Charlotte hangar with me and explore how he could save money. But he never came. The next day, he filed for bankruptcy."[5] After two bankruptcies, Wise said, the airline doesn't repair its flaps anymore. Nor does it work on its own batteries, coffee makers, escape slides, flight controls or brakes. Instead, all of that work is contracted to outside vendors.

In bankruptcy, the carrier continued to lose money, reporting a $794 million fourth-quarter loss, the largest in the industry, and a $1.65 billion loss for the year, as it sought concessions from its unions in a tough airline environment. In March, Siegel got a new, unexpected management partner as US Airways accepted a bid from the state of Alabama's $25 billion retirement system to invest in the airline. At first, the system's three pension funds provided bankruptcy financing of $500 million, which was repaid. The airline emerged in March 2003 after cutting annual costs by $1.9 billion, including $1 billion in employee costs. At that point, Retirement System of Alabama put up $240 million in return for a 37.5 percent ownership stake, eight board seats and the chairmanship for its own outspoken chairman, David Bronner. Bronner had made a name for himself by using Alabama pension assets to make unusual investments, including a Manhattan office tower as well as the Robert Trent Jones Golf Trail, a collection of upscale public courses that helped lure tourists to Alabama. Bronner said he wasn't planning to interfere with the airline's management, but he made it clear that he thought more flights to Alabama and more employees in Alabama would be a good idea. He fought off charges that an airline investment was too risky, saying: "You have to understand how big the retirement system is. If the Dow drops 100, I've lost $100 million. A 1 percent interest-rate rise means $1 billion to me, up or down. You have to put it in perspective." He added: "I'm a big boy. I make my bets and take my losses."[6]

It quickly became apparent that, despite Bronner's financial savvy, US Airways had not secured all the cuts it needed. One indication came during a Delta Air Lines earnings call on January 14, 2004, when respected CEO Jerry Grinstein told analysts that US Airways had failed to finish the job. "The current situation at US Airways is a cautionary tale that we will all heed well," Grinstein said. "We will not cripple our company for the long term in order to obtain a short-term deal."[7] At the time, Delta, which had lost $790 million in 2003, was seeking cost cuts from its own pilots. Grinstein called US Airways' plight a "reminder that the business plan we pursue must be fully capable of leading us all the way to our goal of sustained profitability." Grinstein also said that Delta had expressed interest in some assets at US Airways, which had retained investment banker Morgan Stanley to explore their value. "It's no secret that almost every airline has had discussions with US Airways," he said.[8]

Siegel was not in an enviable position. Months after emerging from bankruptcy, there he was, trying to get more cost cuts. On March 25, 2004, he turned to an emerging technology—a webcast—to make his point. But if the technology was new, the message was the same. In a half-hour program, Siegel told the carrier's 28,278 employees that Southwest was "trying to kill us and take our franchise away."[9] Southwest had announced it would begin flying to Philadelphia, then US Airways' most profitable hub, in May. Southwest planned to start in Philadelphia with four gates, and then expand to eight. "They go to eight and it's over," Siegel said. With eight gates in St. Louis, Southwest was a principal contributor to the failure of hub carrier TWA, Siegel pointed out. "I refuse to follow that same path," Siegel said. "I'm prepared to lead this fight against Southwest." He said he needed more cuts, more furloughs and a 25 percent cost reduction, and he vowed to take an unspecified cut in his own salary. "We've tried small fixes," he said. "We know those don't work. Everybody's going to participate in this, no exceptions."[10] In the IAM union hall in Charlotte, a half-dozen members stared cheerlessly at the screen showing Siegel's webcast. They occasionally joked or cursed. Afterward, some employees said they might prefer to see the airline close. "I'd rather all of us walk out together with our heads held high," said Fred Coors, 50, a 30-year fleet service worker. "I don't want them to dismantle the airline one person at a time."[11]

The Web presentation probably sealed Siegel's fate at US Airways. Many employees thought it was overkill. Unions were reluctant to go back to employees for more cuts, and most had a poor impression of Siegel. Jack Stephan, who later became president of the US Airways ALPA chapter, recalled that Siegel did not bond with the pilots. "He was not a guy whom I would call an 'everyman' type of guy," Stephan said. "He added a layer of formality to the process that didn't have to be there. He didn't have the approachability that [Doug] Parker had."[12] David Castelveter remembers Siegel differently, as an executive who tried assiduously to be liked by employees but was hopelessly encumbered by the carrier's troubled financial picture. Early in Siegel's tenure at the airline, Castelveter was called to Siegel's office along with a photographer. It was Halloween and Siegel was dressed as Austin Powers, a popular, goofy-looking, action-comedy film series character with bad teeth. Siegel entered the senior staff meeting in the costume. Then he went from office to office, handing out candy, and to nearby

IAM Local 1725 president Bill Wise speaks during employee day of solidarity at Charlotte Douglas International Airport, May 8, 2002 (David T. Foster, III, courtesy *Charlotte Observer*).

National Airport to greet passengers and crew members and give them candy. "It was a big change," Castelveter said. "We had gone from Colodny, who was very educated and proper, to Seth, who was grassroots, to Wolf, who was button-down conservative, to handing out candy in a costume."[13]

Siegel also sought out new ways to recognize employees, including awarding Jeep Cherokees to some, as Continental had done. Sadly, his efforts to be liked were often stymied. "One day he went to an employee meeting and people sitting in the front row showed up with tomatoes to throw at him," Castelveter said. "I can't remember if they threw them or wanted to throw them, but it soured him a bit."[14] In December 2003, the pilots called for Siegel to resign. Meanwhile, pilots were bonding with Bronner and his longtime advisor Bruce Lakefield, a former Lehman Brothers executive and submarine commander. In April 2004, Bronner asked Siegel to resign, and Lakefield took over as CEO. "I am really happy that Dave Siegel is gone," said Bill Wise. "I think right now anyone would be more palatable to the labor groups."[15] Mike Flores, who at the time was president of the Charlotte local of the Association of Flight Attendants, said, "I'm not sure Siegel left because he was a bad guy or because he was thrust into a situation by David Bronner where he had to become the bad guy."[16]

In a 2006 interview, Siegel told *TheStreet* that he knew his situation would be damaged by seeking concessions on top of the concessions he had already gained. "I knew when I went to the second round that it would be tough for me to survive politically," he said. In the first bankruptcy, he recalled, "I said we hope this works, the world has to get better. But I always feared we weren't getting enough. When the world didn't get better, I said now we have to step up to reality."[17] The timing compared very unfavorably to Bethune's or to Doug Parker's, Siegel said. "Like Doug, Gordon came in when all the cost cuts had been made," he said. "Somebody had taken the hits for that, and now [Parker] can be the builder, the positive guy. If I had the choice, I'd rather do that than what I had to do." Siegel was well compensated for his time on the job. His departure resulted in a $4.7 million severance payment and a payout of more than $773,000 in defined contribution benefits. Siegel says he worked 80 to 100 hours a week and earned the money. "Don't cry for me," he said. "I know the employees went through a lot. But had I kept my old job, and never gone to US Airways, I would have made a lot more money and nobody would have complained about it."[18] Immediately after leaving the carrier, Siegel was named president and CEO of Gate Gourmet, which provides catering for airlines, where he worked for five years. In 2012, he was named president and CEO of Frontier Airlines.

US Airways filed for bankruptcy protection for the second time on Sunday afternoon, September 12, 2004. That morning, the headline in the *Charlotte Observer* proclaimed, "Airline Expected to File Today." Several sources had told the newspaper that "a last-ditch effort to reach new cost-saving labor agreements collapsed on Saturday."[19] The carrier had made proposals to its pilots and flight attendants on Friday—its plan called for an additional $800 million in annual labor concessions—but no talks occurred on Saturday. This was very clearly not an encouraging sign. Late Saturday, Castelveter, then US Airways' principal spokesman, said no decision on bankruptcy had been made. He said the board of directors would make the final call, but he would not say when the board would meet. The newspaper story hinted strongly at the likely outcome: "The airline has warned for months of the possibility of bankruptcy—under which it could still fly—and it has been consulting the past few days with hired bankruptcy advisers." The story continued: "One of the main incentives for going to bankruptcy court would be for US Airways management to get access to a new hammer to require concessions from labor unions."[20]

Meanwhile, flight attendant leader Flores labeled the proposal for his group "absurd." The proposal cut benefits, eliminated a pension plan and reduced pay. "I think they know that when they go into bankruptcy, they will get some or all of that,"[21] Flores said. Negotiations with the other major unions were even further behind those with the pilots and flight attendants. The airline's shares had closed Friday at $1.46, down 29 cents. After emerging from the first bankruptcy, shares had begun trading on the NASDAQ under the short-loved symbol UAIR. They had opened at $8.40 on October 21, 2003, and peaked at $15.25 in intraday trading on October 27. But the air quickly began to leak out of the balloon.

One of the problems that confronted every US Airways CEO was the sad state of the operation at Philadelphia International Airport, where a combination of lack of funds, airport administration issues and airport configuration issues had resulted in a long history of problems for the airline. In the words of one former USAir executive, who asked not to be named: "The only solution to Philadelphia was to nuke it." The airport authority generally responded to political concerns, rather than aviation concerns. Airport administrators generally seemed unwilling to upgrade aging terminals and other facilities, and they were prone to move slowly when upgrades were required. Airport operations were severely impacted by congestion in New York area airspace, leading to frequent air traffic control delays. A giant 210-foot-high crane, built in a shipyard near the airport in the late 1990s, impeded operations, as did a complex path for aircraft to move from the gate to the runway. When Southwest began flying to Philadelphia in May 2004, it seemed clear that airport administrators favored Southwest over the longtime incumbent hub carrier. They put Southwest construction on a fast track and gave Southwest gates at the outer corner of the terminal so that its aircraft could get out faster than US Airways aircraft could.

Whenever someone decides that things cannot possibly get worse, they tend to be wrong. During the Christmas 2004 holiday travel season, US Airways hit bottom at Philadelphia. A new baggage handling system, required by the Transportation Security Administration, broke down, and the airport faced a delay in getting the parts to fix it. That made it impossible to efficiently deliver passenger baggage to and from the airplanes. The problem was compounded due to understaffing, its impact magnified by high numbers of sick calls related to the carrier's effort to negotiate a new contract in bankruptcy and by flight cancellations resulting from bad weather around the country. Piles of baggage were everywhere. Yet the meltdown had a positive outcome because many US Airways employees and executives made their way to Philadelphia to pitch in to help sort out the mess. Their collective effort to restore the operation reinvigorated the company, inspiring employees who had been through so much. They came to believe that perhaps they could get through one more crisis.

When Lakefield succeeded Siegel as CEO, he had a single overriding mission: to save jobs. "I didn't really come into this for anything but that reason, and that mission was accomplished," Lakefield recalled in 2006. "Whenever I ride an airplane, and I ride fairly often, more people thank me than I could ever imagine."[22] The vast majority of US Airways' remaining 24,000 employees were retained in the merger, with the biggest exception being employees at the Crystal City headquarters, which was closed when the headquarters moved to Tempe. Lakefield willingly stepped aside as CEO, but he became vice chairman of the board. At US Airways' annual meeting in 2006, Doug Parker paid tribute to Lakefield, describing how he helped to establish the new company, and added: "Bruce, to his credit, said, 'I care about that [financial] stuff, but what I really care about is saving jobs.' Now 35,000 people work for the largest profitable airline in the U.S."[23]

Lakefield's path was not an easy one; he faced some dark days before the merger became reality. Early in 2005, US Airways came close to shutting down after it fell out of compliance with loan covenants from its banks, the ATSB and General Electric Commercial Aviation Services. A few other airlines, including JetBlue and Virgin America, expressed interested in buying takeoff and landing slots at Washington National and access to other key East Coast airports, but selling pieces of the airline's heart to competitors was not a particularly attractive option. Working with advisers, Lakefield came up with a plan to seek investments from regional airlines, which would benefit from ownership as well as by securing contracts to fly for US Airways. Additionally, Lakefield restarted talks with Parker, who had expressed interest in a merger. In February, Lakefield reached deals with two investors: Richard Bartlett, chairman of Air Wisconsin, and Ed Shapiro, a partner at Boston hedge fund PAR Capital Management. Lakefield had also courted Jon Ornstein, then CEO of Mesa. "Bruce Lakefield looked me dead in the eye and said, 'You should do this deal,' and he was right," Ornstein recalled. "Bartlett and Shapiro were very smart about it. They both made beaucoup bucks [and] Air Wisconsin also got a long-term contract to place aircraft at US Airways. We were offered a deal for $150 million, but we just couldn't do it. It was more than we could afford and it seemed too risky. Everybody had passed. A lot of people made fun of the deal. It was called Project Barbell but people were calling it Project Dumbbell. What I didn't understand at the time was that no one was going in until they raised $1 billion. Not doing that deal was maybe the biggest mistake in my career."[24]

Lakefield retained the support of the pilots thanks largely to the leadership of Bill Pollock, president of the US Airways ALPA chapter. Pilots provided more than $2 billion in pay and benefit concessions to save US Airways, the major part of the combined $3.4 billion reduction in annual costs that occurred during the two bankruptcies. Pollock's willingness to support the airline in bankruptcy was essential to ensuring its survival, but the former navy pilot weathered a storm of opposition from within his union during his four years on the job. "It was the full spectrum of human emotion and character," Pollock said. "It ranged from, on the one hand, the idealist cause of working hard to see the company return to profitability, to, on the other hand, every man for himself."[25] Among the groups, he said, were several hundred older pilots whose pensions were protected by the federal government's Pension Benefit Guaranty Corporation because they were older than 53. "Some of them would just as soon have seen the company liquidate as work under draconian pay cuts," he said. "They were not bashful in pursuing that outcome. It made leadership particularly challenging." Another group, several hundred junior pilots, had been at the bottom of the seniority scale for years, even though most had spent more than a decade on the job. "Their lifestyle was miserable," Pollock said. "They had almost no control over their flying schedule, they were facing more pay cuts and more shrinkage, and most of them didn't have much interest in whether the airline succeeded or failed." Other pilots, as a personal matter, "would argue, 'I'd rather die on my feet than live on my knees,'" Pollock said. "A large number of pilots had reached this point, and had become skeptical whether we were working to preserve anything that was really worth preserving."[26]

Mike Flores said Lakefield

was a smart man who was very sympathetic to labor and to the plight of airline employees in bankruptcy, but he knew he had to get his pound of flesh because otherwise the airline was going to fail. Siegel's attitude was "This is the way it has to be: If you don't want to be here and work for this money, then leave—you picked the wrong career." The thing about Bruce was he always listened to us. He helped Parker tremendously in putting together US Airways with America West. One day he said to me and my wife: "This is the craziest business, why can't we just raise ticket prices and get out of this mess?" even though, from a financial standpoint, he knew he couldn't do it and he knew why.[27]

Lakefield's leadership brought the airline through a period where it might easily have shut down, David Castelveter said. "He was a very level-headed, likable guy, with no aviation background at all, but with financial savvy and enormous integrity. Bronner told him to dress it up and sell it, but he tried to figure out what was the best solution for an ailing organization."[28] In May 2005, Castelveter sat in a conference room in Tempe with Lakefield as the America West board decided whether to sell. "I said I wasn't sure it was right," Castelveter recalled.

I said "Employees will think that you sold out an airline that has weathered every storm—a lot of mergers, five crashes, Sept. 11, a failed merger with United," and I said that "Every time people counted US Airways out, we survived. Every time somebody said there would be five airlines and not us, we survived." He said we didn't have the financial wherewithal to survive. He said if it didn't happen we would go to Chapter 7. Right after that, Doug came in and shook his hand and said that the board had approved the merger.[29]

11

America West Looks East

To understand Doug Parker, the best place to start is at America West, which provided the vehicle for his rise to the top of the airline industry. America West always struggled. It began as a small, Phoenix-based carrier fighting bigger, more established rivals. It operated under bankruptcy protection from 1991 to 1994. A decade later it barely avoided a second bankruptcy filing only because Parker, in his first months as CEO, coaxed loan guarantees from the Air Transportation Stabilization Board.

In keeping with America West's upstart image, Parker has always been an informal, approachable, youngish-looking executive, known within the airline as Dougie or even Doogie, a reference to TV's youthful-looking, teenage doctor Doogie Howser, MD. Perhaps recalling the airline's 747-to-Japan flight, which operated long before he arrived, Parker has an incautious streak. He ran with the bulls at Pamplona. He likes to play blackjack in Las Vegas. He has a record of four driving incidents involving alcohol: three came when he was in his 20s and one when he was 45. He made a quixotic run at merging with Delta in 2006, barely a year after the merger between America West and US Airways was approved and long before much of the integration between the two carriers had been completed. In 2013, Parker and his team seemed to dismiss the possibility that the Justice Department might object to the merger between US Airways and American, even though it was intended to create the largest airline in the world. At the same time, Parker has always been committed to rational airline behavior, including cost control.

Until the American merger succeeded, Parker seemed to be crashing a party dominated by older, more straightlaced executives running bigger, more established, more highly regarded airlines. In the Delta merger effort, he appeared as the young Tempe upstart who challenged Jerry Grinstein, a widely respected, silver-haired industry eminence with Yale undergrad and Harvard Law degrees, knowledgeable in the ways of Congress, where he had worked as an aide; broadly experienced as a former railroad and airline CEO, philanthropic and popular among employees. Parker departed inelegantly from his battle with Grinstein, even managing to be arrested for drunk driving the night it ended. Afterward, the "good Parker" emerged and dealt with the experience honorably. He did not squirm or deny guilt in the legal case, nor did he seek to pretend that the merger attempt was without flaws. And ironically, this colossal mistake of pursuing Delta worked to Parker's benefit, defining the framework he successfully used five years later to gain the upper hand in his assault on American Airlines.

The successful takeover of US Airways did nothing to diminish the airline industry's proclivity to take potshots at Parker and his merry band of outsiders. A drawn-out, failed effort to merge with United followed the Delta debacle. United CEO Glenn Tilton professed to be negotiating a merger with Parker, but ultimately oversaw a merger with Continental. In May 2010, in announcing that merger, Continental CEO Jeff Smisek said he had contacted Tilton after reading in the newspaper that US Airways was talking to United about a merger. "I didn't want him to marry the ugly girl," Smisek said then. "I wanted him to marry the pretty one."[1] Three years later, American CEO Tom Horton issued a barrage of derisive insults when he was in the early stages of attempting to stave off a merger. "This will be their fourth try at this: twice for United, once for Delta while they were restructuring, now American," Horton said, during a meeting with the *Dallas Morning News* editorial board. "I would argue that this will be every bit as successful as their prior tries." Describing US Airways, Horton said: "This is a small company, very strategically limited, I would argue—not any international flying, hubs of less strategic importance."[2]

It was all true, but Horton chose at the time to ignore the America West team's very effective management of the assets it had. Rather, he declared: "I'm not sure what's in the water out there in Phoenix. Maybe it's the cactus. I don't know what it is."[3] Two and a half months later, American released a letter to employees from Horton, who wrote, "It's easy to understand US Airways' sense of urgency to find a way to address the challenges it has faced for a long time."[4] Of course, almost exactly a year after Horton asked, "What's in the water?" he was drinking it, as American and US Airways announced their merger agreement. "I look forward to working closely with Doug Parker, whom I have known as a friend for more than 25 years, and with the leadership teams of both companies to assure a smooth integration and the creation of a new industry leader,"[5] Horton said then. His fealty was rewarded with a one-year job as chairman of the combined companies and an exit package of stock, cash and benefits valued at $17 million.

Parker was born October 31, 1951, the son of a meat cutter who worked his way up to become a Kroger executive. He attended Michigan's Albion College, where he majored in computer science, played tight end on the football team and graduated in 1984. Parker said he was drawn to the school for sports, which had consumed him at Farmington High School. But in economics and computer programming classes at college, he saw how his math skills could be put to use in a successful career. Parker went on to earn an MBA at Vanderbilt, graduating in 1986. At the time, American, which was setting up a Nashville hub, recruited from Vanderbilt's MBA program, and the carrier hired Parker as a financial analyst in Dallas. There, he worked with other young analysts who would become executives at various airlines. One of them, David Cush, introduced him to his wife Gwen, then an American flight attendant. On the honeymoon in 1990, Parker went bungee jumping, one more sign that he likes to take chances in life. In 1991, he left American for an executive finance job at Northwest, where Bill Franke found him.

Parker wasn't Franke's only hire. In fact, Franke brought together all but one of the six top officers in the America West management team that would take over first US Airways and then American. In 1995, besides hiring Parker, Franke hired Robert Isom and Steve Johnson. Isom came from GMAC, where he had been chief restructuring officer. Before that he had worked at Northwest in a variety of jobs, including overseeing ground operations and airport customer service. Johnson, meanwhile, was general counsel at leasing company GPA, an America West creditor. Franke hired him to be vice president of legal affairs at America West, and Johnson held various positions at aviation companies Franke controlled before becoming executive vice president at US Airways.

In 1996, Franke hired two more future AWA leaders. Derek Kerr came from Northwest, where he worked with Parker in financial planning and analysis; he joined America West as vice president of financial planning and analysis and rose to become chief financial officer. Scott Kirby, an Air Force Academy graduate, was working in an AMR reservations technology division affiliated with Sabre. Kirby joined America West as senior director of scheduling and rose to become Parker's number two executive and heir apparent. The youngish-looking Kirby has a quick mind and a gift for revenue management. Veteran airline analyst Bob McAdoo once said he was awaiting the completion of the American merger and the day when "Scott Kirby gets his hands on the American operation at LAX, because he will make it profitable."[6] If there is a link between the group's members besides airline experience, it is Michigan educations: Parker went to Albion; Isom has an MBA from the University of Michigan, and Kerr has a BS and MBA from the University of Michigan. Bev Goulet, the only top officer retained from old American Airlines, holds a BA and a JD from the University of Michigan.

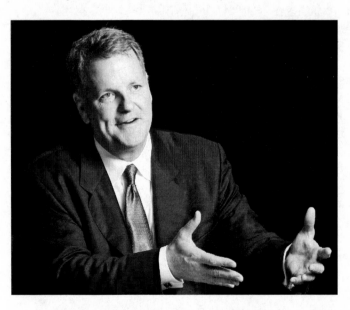

US Airways CEO Doug Parker advocates for American merger in meeting with *Charlotte Observer* editors on July 7, 2012 (Deidra Laird, courtesy *Charlotte Observer*).

Another 1996 hire was

Jeff McClelland, a former navy pilot and Stanford MBA who had worked at both American and Northwest. Within 10 years, McClelland was overseeing operations and other functions as executive vice president and chief administrative officer. He lost his life to cancer in 2006. When McClelland died, Parker, who had known him for 18 years, issued a prepared statement that went well beyond the norm for such an event, saying:

> Words can't describe the sadness we feel from losing not only an extremely talented executive but a close confidante and a great friend. Jeff's contributions, which are too numerous to list, went well beyond any job title. He brought insight, depth and vision to our airline and he did so with an unparalleled work ethic and the utmost integrity. He was the embodiment of leadership by example, setting a standard that drove those of us who worked with him to be better executives and better people."[7]

Scott Kirby has been Doug Parker's right-hand man at America West, US Airways and American (courtesy US Airways).

The Phoenix flight training center was renamed in McClelland's honor. In 2007, Isom, who had left America West, returned to replace McClelland. The sixth member of the leadership team was Elise Eberwein, a former TWA flight attendant who ended up running not only corporate communications but also human resources. Eberwein joined America West in 2003 from Frontier Airlines, where she had worked in a variety of jobs including corporate communications. By 2013, one striking characteristic of Parker's leadership team was that not a single person from US Airways was a member, even though US Airways was twice the size of America West at the time of the merger.

When the first airplane crashed into the World Trade Center on September 11, 2001, Parker, then 40, was at home in Paradise Valley, Arizona, getting ready to go to work. He had been CEO for 11 days. In the weeks that followed, he underwent a baptism by fire, presiding over a nearly broke airline that was carrying barely any passengers in a badly damaged airline economy. That morning, the phone calls came in, first from Parker's sister-in-law, who mentioned a crash, and then from the airline's operations control center, which said the Federal Aviation Administration had grounded all commercial flights. As he quickly drove the half-dozen miles to work, Parker said, "My first concern was making sure all our people were safe."[8] That turned out to be so. Another concern was not so easily resolved. America West, the ninth-largest airline, was about to run out of money. It had been negotiating with GE Capital and Airbus for a financing package; term sheets had been signed, but not definitive documents. The events of September 11 dramatically reduced air travel, which constituted a "material change in events," leading GE Capital and Airbus to pull out of the financing deal.

After a three-day shutdown, flights resumed but travel did not. "We were flying 10 percent loads," Parker said. "I would go to the airport and walk into the crew rooms. Our employees were there. They put on their uniforms and went to work. They weren't afraid." Unfortunately, the public was. From a Phoenix conference room, Parker joined in conference calls with top executives from other airlines and government officials, who discussed how to save the industry. The strangest part, Parker said, was that no airplanes flew by the windows, which looked out on the flight path for Phoenix Sky Harbor Airport. "It was a weird three days," he said. "You didn't see any airplanes all day." Within a few days, Parker was in Washington attending a series of meetings with other airline executives. They gathered at the Air Transport Association, at the White House and at a session of the House Aviation Subcommittee. The carriers all had different issues: American and United needed federal insurance after each lost two aircraft to terrorists. Every airline needed federal loan guarantees. And America West, which cut back its schedule by 15 percent, needed cash immediately. "We were the most in need,"[9] Parker said.

On September 22, Congress approved a $15 billion bailout for the airline industry. However, in October the newly formed ATSB turned down America West's loan request. "It was a bad day," said Parker, who thought to himself: "I'm 39. I've been CEO for a month. Now I'm going to liquidate. It is not going to look good on the resume."[10] On the flight home to Phoenix, a depressed Parker went to the rear galley and spoke with a flight attendant, a single mom, who asked how it had gone. "I couldn't lie to her," he said. "I told her: 'They don't want to do it. We're trying to get it done. Hopefully we'll be able to get through bankruptcy.' She just looked at me. She said: 'You can't do this. I've been doing this job for 15 years. This is what I do. I have my child care set up around it. I can't do anything else.'

"I realized this isn't about me," Parker said. "Management's job is to serve the people who do what she is doing." Parker said he "literally lived in Washington from September to December,"[11] fighting for a share. In October, America West got a $60 million federal grant, as funds were allocated to carriers according to their capacity. Then in December, America West received a $380 million loan guarantee, becoming the first carrier to get an ATSB loan guarantee. The funding enabled America West to reach a new aircraft financing deal with Airbus and GE Capital. It was in business to stay. Under Parker, America West positioned itself as a low-fare carrier and took the lead in eliminating Saturday-night stay and round-trip ticket purchase requirements. In February 2003, the carrier announced it would close the Columbus hub, where it had just 49 daily departures to 15 destinations, retaining only 4 daily flights to Las Vegas and Phoenix. In the second quarter of 2003, despite a weak economy and rising fuel prices, the carrier surprised analysts by earning $13 million excluding items, its first profit since the third quarter of 2000. It began to seem that Parker and his team had perhaps developed a formula to turn around an ailing airline.

The merger chase began with a run at Indianapolis-based American Trans Air in 2004. America West, at the time, had $2.4 billion in revenue and about $400 million in cash. "This was the first indication that Parker was going for market size, trying to break into the Chicago market," said aviation consultant Bob Mann.[12] The effort also made it clear to Parker that bankruptcy court was a good place to initiate a merger, given the obvious ability to negotiate lower costs and to jettison duplicative assets such as airplanes and airport facilities.

In 2004, ATA was the country's tenth-largest airline, with a route system based at its hub at Chicago's Midway Airport. It got into trouble because it was taking delivery of new airplanes, financed with high-cost leases, at a time of rapid increases in oil prices, which rose about 36 percent during the year to an average cost near $38 a barrel. Moreover, ATA was making a difficult transition from being a charter carrier to providing scheduled service. Like America West and US Airways, it secured an ATSB loan. But dissimilarly, its problems could not be solved, and it filed for bankruptcy protection on October 26, 2004. America West had pursued a deal before the filing, and it kept trying afterward, offering $90 million to acquire major portions of ATA including the prized Midway gates. But it was forced to drop out. It couldn't reach lease agreements with ATA's aircraft lessors, who felt they could get more value for their 34 Boeing 737–800s by leasing them to Asian operators. Furthermore, it was bidding against far bigger Southwest for the gates. Southwest took over the gates gradually after making a code-share deal with ATA, which emerged from bankruptcy and then filed again and shut down in 2008. In public statements following America West's failure to secure ATA, Parker made it clear he would be back in the consolidation game. America West had "chosen to pass on this particular transaction," he said then. But he added, "We feel confident there will be future growth and acquisition opportunities," and he promised to play "a role in the continued consolidation of the industry."[13]

The merger with US Airways was announced on May 19, 2005. During a media conference in Tempe that day, the most memorable moment came when *Arizona Republic* reporter Dawn Gilbertson asked Parker whether America West had "the bandwidth"[14] to take over the bigger carrier. He said that it did, but the question lingered for several years. Initially, Parker was greeted as a hero at US Airways. Within a few days of the merger announcement, he visited Crystal City to speak to employees in a hotel near the airline's headquarters. David Castelveter, Amy Kudwa and Christina Ulosevich of the airline's corporate communications team had gone "back into the files to find all of the logos of all of our predecessors, to capture our proud history,"[15] Castelveter recalled, and they put together a video recounting US Airways' historic past, mentioning all of the predecessor airlines. Parker seemed transformed by what he saw. While other airlines, following mergers, have sought to eradicate any vestige of predecessor companies, Parker embraced it. Soon, US Airways announced that it would paint four Airbus jets in the colors of four predecessor airlines: Allegheny, America West, Mohawk and Piedmont. The paint jobs became occasions for celebrations. In August 2006, Parker spoke at an employee event at the US Airways Charlotte hangar. Behind him was the airplane painted in Piedmont colors. It was a quintessential Parker moment. "People said stop talking about this [because] we're going to start a new culture," Parker said. "But what I realize is you can't kill that [old] culture. It's still here, it's vibrant, and frankly it's one of the best assets of US Airways. What you should do is embrace it."[16]

The new management team excelled at fix-it projects. To fix the lagging operations and on-time performance, Parker rehired Isom. Within a year, US Airways had become one of the best network carriers operationally, and it stayed near the top during each of the next four years. Yet another major improvement addressed the historically difficult operation at Philadelphia International Airport. The 2004 airport meltdown, while dramatic, was just one of many problems. In 2007, for example, US Airways fired more than a dozen baggage handlers in connection with an alleged scheme to manipulate the records of the hours they worked. That year, the airline had hired hundreds of new baggage handlers at starting pay of less than $10 an hour, while many veteran baggage handlers departed. Under Isom, the Philadelphia problems diminished dramatically.

By many measures, the merger was a stunning success. Soon after the management team from a small, regional, Western airline took over a long-established eastern carrier with a presence in both Europe and the Caribbean, both unit revenue and the share price improved dramatically. The merger closed on September 27, 2005. Shares resumed trading under a new symbol, LCC, opening at $20.40. By November 2006, the price would reach a peak of $63.27. Subsequently, the combination of the recession and rising fuel prices meant that by July 2008, the price fell to $1.45. But then an industrywide recovery began, as consolidation surged and newfound commitments to capacity discipline and ancillary revenue gained broad acceptance. Nearly two years after the post-bankruptcy low, shares reached double digit prices in June 2010. In October 2013, with the DOJ lawsuit opposing the merger pending, shares reached $23.16, their highest level since November 2007.

It was not simply management skills that fueled US Airways' renaissance. Throughout the eight years the America West team ran the airline before the American merger, it benefited from a unique advantage: artificially low labor costs, particularly pilot costs, reflecting the impact of the division in the pilot group. The controversial 2007 seniority ruling by arbitrator George Nicolau so divided the two pilot groups that they could not effectively overcome management reluctance to negotiate a new contract. The benefit included not only savings of nearly $400 million annually, but also the ability to allocate more time for flights, given the lower crew costs. More block time meant US Airways could consistently report superior on-time performance. The airline industry came to view US Airways as not only profitable, but also operationally superior. As an example, the airline's flight plans would typically allow a little over two hours for a flight from Charlotte to New York. On some days, given the congestion at New York airports, two hours were needed. But on many other days, the flight would take between one hour and one hour and 15 minutes. Low pilot costs meant that allocating extra time made sense.

US Airways "used the Nicolau award as an opportunity,"[17] said Bill McKee, the two-time chairman of the Charlotte pilot group, first when it was part of the Air Line Pilots Association and again after the creation of the U.S Airline Pilots Association. The outgoing McKee joined Piedmont in 1985 as a flight engineer on a Boeing 727 and eventually becoming an A320 captain. He could be proudly obstinate: Call McKee on his cell phone and, in the interlude before he answers, you hear the song "Won't Back Down" by Tom Petty. The Nicolau award, he said, led to "an orchestrated plan to keep the bankruptcy contracts in place for an extended period of time. Management constantly used the seniority issue, one section of the contract, to say they cannot negotiate the rest of the contract. It was bunk. We were absolutely getting stonewalled."[18]

During the decade following the first bankruptcy, US Airways pilots did not get a raise. Rather, they remained stuck at annual salaries between $75,000 and $90,000 for first officers, depending on aircraft type and the number of hours flown, and between $125,000 and $135,000 for captains. It was not a lot of money, particularly the first officer pay, for pilots with two decades of experience. Most US Airways pilots had joined the airline in the 1980s, anticipating they would continue to be paid the same as pilots at the major airlines throughout their careers. Instead, pilots at other carriers were being paid tens of thousands of dollars more annually, while US Airways pilots earned what pilots at smaller, low-cost airlines such as Spirit made, or less. "We were well below industry standard in almost every respect," McKee said. "Some commuter pilots at express carriers made more money."[19] The America West pilots were also at the bottom of the industry scale, although they were paid more than the east pilots and also had small increases in their contract.

Although union leaders at American worked tirelessly to assure a merger, McKee said American employees may someday cease to view Parker as a friend to labor. "The image has worked very well for him; he's been able to keep labor in his pocket, and Wall Street likes that," McKee said.

And why change it, as long as it works? If you're a lion or a tiger, and you find a good watering hole, you're going to keep going back there as long as it's full of water. Parker kept coming in with that good old boy, "aw shucks, I'm just really trying [demeanor]," but it got stale. He doesn't look at labor any differently than he looks at the tail numbers on the airplanes. We're just a part number. It's all business. The American Airlines guys thought they had it bad before, but they will find that they have the same animal, just with different mannerisms. I think they will get their eyes opened up and it will come as a shock, just like walking into a room and catching your wife in bed with another guy.[20]

Newly merged US Airways first reported financial results for the first quarter of 2006. The number that stood out was a 27.7 percent increase in revenue per available seat mile, the amount of revenue generated by each mile of flying, for the former US Airways. (RASM on former America West routes improved by 16.2 percent.) Overall, excluding special items, the company earned $5 million compared with a loss of $16 million in the same quarter a year earlier. Per-share earnings were 5 cents, a big surprise to analysts who had expected a loss of 16 cents. Much of the RASM increase reflected capacity reductions, as the combined airline took planes out of service following the merger. The first-quarter earnings call provided a key moment in the history of the post-merger US Airways, because it was then that, for the first time, the airline industry heard Parker and Kirby lay out the principles that would define them and much of the rest of the airline industry over the ensuing years. "Some people don't seem to recognize the value you can create if you can get out of airplanes and get out of some of your worst-performing markets," Parker said. "We were able to do that through the US Airways bankruptcy. Some of the other [airlines] are adding capacity, and they're not seeing anything like [this]."[21] Kirby, then executive vice president, added that when the former US Airways was in bankruptcy, "customers were defecting, there was lots of bad press—and US Airways got into the mode of deeply discounting because they felt like they had to. We don't feel like we have to do that anymore." Fares, Kirby said, had risen about 20 percent. "We're selling a lot fewer of the absurdly priced low-end fares," he said. "Whereas a year ago it was common to have $158 [transcontinental] fares in the market, today those fares are more like $300."[22]

Merger enthusiasm was in full bloom. That day, US Airways shares rose 9.2 percent to $51.63. JP Morgan analyst Jamie Baker reported that US Airways' margins improved more than any other carrier's, and he reaffirmed his price target of $100 a share by mid-2007. That is an example of a case where even a highly respected analyst, who is often the first to call attention to airlines' failed strategies, got caught up in the exuberance. But while Baker's irrational exuberance led to overly ambitious earnings expectations, Parker's led straight to Atlanta.

12

The Delta Debacle

On November 15, 2006, just 14 months after its own merger closed, US Airways unveiled an unsolicited $8 billion effort to merge with Delta, which at the time was reorganizing in bankruptcy court. (The bid was subsequently increased to about $10 billion.) Delta would not emerge from bankruptcy protection until April 30, 2007. But even at the time of US Airways' hostile attempt, its executives could see they were on the cusp of an opportunity to remake Delta as a leading global carrier, able to take advantage of the strategic resources it had underutilized for years. For instance, prior to Grinstein's arrival, managements had used Atlanta, the world's biggest hub, largely to connect passengers between New York and Florida. In 1996, the Atlanta hub had just 14 international departures. But 10 years later, following the bankruptcy reorganization, it had 67, with more planned. Another bankruptcy fact: Between June 2005 and June 2006, Delta added more than 50 international routes. So Delta was not a carrier looking for a merger partner, especially a merger partner that had few resources that could meaningfully benefit the Delta route system. Rather, Delta was just waiting to bust out of bankruptcy and show the world what it could do. The Northwest merger, which Grinstein did not support, would come later, although reports surfaced during the US Airways effort that Delta had in fact, already talked with Northwest.

US Airways by now viewed itself as a master of the bankruptcy process. It argued that a Delta merger would generate $1.65 billion in annual savings and benefits, and that more than half of the savings would be lost if Delta were to leave bankruptcy as a standalone carrier because the right to reject leases under bankruptcy law would be left on the table. In total, US Airways offered $4 billion in cash and $4 billion in US Airways stock to Delta's unsecured creditors. "Our timing is driven by the fact that Delta is in bankruptcy, [which presents] a unique opportunity to realize values," Parker said on a conference call with analysts and reporters. "There are not many industries more fragmented then the one we participate in," he said, reciting from his mantra. "In an industry this fragmented, we think there are opportunities for mergers."[1] He said that he had written Grinstein a letter in September, but that Grinstein had refused to meet with him.

That ought not to have been surprising. Grinstein had no interest in Parker's plan, and once the effort was unveiled he rejected Parker outright. Delta's goal "has always been to emerge from bankruptcy in the first half of 2007 as a strong, standalone carrier," Grinstein said, in a public response. The bankruptcy court had granted Delta "the exclusive right to create the plan of reorganization until Feb. 15, 2007 [and] we will continue to move aggressively towards that goal," he said.[2] Parker argued, "This alternative, we believe, is much more compelling than a standalone plan," and added, "The creditors will see that, and the management and employees as well will come to see that, once we get a chance to sit down and work with them."[3] Once again, Parker contemplated working with airline labor unions, as he had in the ATA attempt and as he would in the American attempt. He said the Delta deal would include a $90 million annual cost increase to "take labor costs to the highest common denominator in all groups."[4] In an interview with *TheStreet,* US Airways president Scott Kirby said he anticipated that all of the unions on the property at US Airways would also represent workers at Delta, which had traditionally been non-union except for its pilots.[5]

From a route standpoint, the merger made sense in the context that the combined carriers would save money by reducing capacity at duplicative hubs. Delta's Atlanta hub and US Airways' Charlotte hub are the two principal Southeast hubs, but Atlanta is far larger with far more local traffic, virtually assuring that Charlotte operations would have been diminished in a merger. "It's not inconceivable that we would have to give up gates in Charlotte," Kirby disclosed in an interview with *TheStreet.* "Giving up gates is something we might do, but I don't think divesting ourselves of the hub is conceivable."[6] He declined to specify how many gates might be shed. Looking at Charlotte's future following a merger, Kirby said he didn't anticipate that another carrier would want to establish a Charlotte hub, and he said Charlotte would likely become even more focused on serving smaller markets with regional jets, while even more connecting traffic would pass through Atlanta. The concept worried Charlotte leaders, including airport director Jerry Orr, but speaking out publicly against the airport's primary tenant did not appear to be the wisest course.

Fortunately for Delta and for Charlotte, the proposal to merge US Airways with Delta never gained traction. The denouement probably came at a January 2007 hearing of the Senate Commerce Committee subcommittee on aviation issues, where Grinstein and Parker both appeared. While Congress has no role in determining whether airline mergers will be approved by the Transportation Department and the Justice Department, hearings before Congress have historically provided an accurate indication of the country's mood regarding a merger. At this hearing, the mood was decidedly sour and consolidation appeared to have few fans. The hearing room was packed with uniformed Delta pilots, who strongly opposed a takeover. It has always been known in the airline industry that legislative hearings can be easily swayed by the appearance of large numbers of uniformed pilots, resembling nothing so much as a group of uniformed U.S. servicemen, which many of them have been, so that going against their wishes somehow appears to represent an assault on American values. "Take a look behind me at all of the people from Delta who have come here today to let you know by their presence how strongly they feel about this," said Grinstein, in his opening remarks.[7]

Delta pilots, led by Lee Moak, president of the Delta chapter of the Air Line Pilots Association, had in fact started a "Keep Delta My Delta" campaign. The airline backed 16 "Keep Delta My Delta" rallies around the country, not only in big cities such as Atlanta and Washington but perhaps more importantly in places such as Baton Rouge, Louisiana; Butte, Montana; Columbia, South Carolina, and Jackson, Mississippi, where they drew the attention of members of Congress. Moreover, the hostile effort to merge with the Atlanta-based airline came to be viewed as an attack on the South, instantly binding most representatives from the former Confederacy.

When Doug Parker mounted a misguided 2006 effort to merge with Delta, Delta employees fought back, and Parker learned the value of employee support (collection Ted Reed).

This became clear when Republican Mississippi senator Trent Lott told Parker: "I must say you are an aggressive suitor. But the lady from the South—Atlanta—doesn't seem to want to be forced into this shotgun wedding."[8]

Not only did Parker lose the South, a Republican bulwark, but also he managed to lose the labor movement, a Democratic bulwark. On the Democratic side, a telling moment came when Missouri senator Claire McCaskill related how many middle-aged flight attendants, most of them her constituents, lost their livelihoods because of the merger between TWA and American. "I have a great deal of angst over what has happened to the former TWA employees," McCaskill said.[9] She would later sponsor legislation, the 2008 McCaskill-Bond Act, intended to protect employees involved in seniority integrations. Parker responded by saying that the situations were not parallel and that his merger would not lead to the layoffs of any frontline employees. But then Grinstein said that when American executives said they would provide for TWA employees, "I am sure [they] meant every word. I am sure they were as committed to it as Mr. Parker is. But it's a volatile industry."[10] Also, Robert Roach, general vice president of the International Association of Machinists union, said aspects of the 2005 merger between America West Airlines and the former US Airways, including integrating labor groups, had yet to be completed. "Do they have the ability to merge an airline? That question is still open," Roach said.[11]

At the hearing, no one in attendance outside of Parker and Andrew Steinberg, assistant secretary for the Transportation Department, voiced support for industry consolidation. Perhaps the only other backers were the investment bankers who put the deal together and stood to profit from it. In an interview with *TheStreet,* Lee Moak summarized the Washington view. "Wall Street types say it is simply a financial transaction and it is the American way," Moak said. "But in the Senate, what comes out of there is 'Are we going to let Wall Street set public policy on airlines?'"[12] In other words, US Airways had been totally outmaneuvered, losing both Democrats and Republicans, and exposed as an amateur in the world of Washington politics.

As part of US Airways' campaign, its attorneys proclaimed that the Justice Department would permit a merger that would put the Charlotte and Atlanta hubs—the only two hubs serving a region of about 80 million people—in the hands of a single carrier. Six years later, that assertion was controverted in a media conference call on August 13, 2013, when Bill Baer, the assistant attorney general who heads the Justice Department's antitrust division, discussed his opposition to the planned merger with American. Asked to name previous airline mergers the DOJ had opposed, Baer mentioned the 2006 bid for Delta, saying, "We were looking seriously at the hostile bid for Delta when that got abandoned, [so] it's not the first time."[13] Later, on the November 12, 2013, media conference call when he discussed the settlement of the DOJ's case opposing the American–US Airways merger, Baer was asked whether DOJ would have opposed the Delta merger, given that it was "anti-competitive." He responded: "It's well known that is one reason why it was abandoned. We did not see it differently from the way you just characterized it."[14]

A backdrop to US Airways' hostile bid for Delta was that Northwest was also in bankruptcy. Delta and Northwest had filed for bankruptcy protection within minutes of one another on October 15, 2005. Their simultaneous filings had encouraged speculation that they planned to merge before their court cases ended. That speculation continued throughout the concurrent bankruptcy processes, but on January 31, 2007, a week after the Senate subcommittee hearing, Northwest announced it would emerge as a standalone carrier and Delta's creditors committee announced it would support Delta's independent reorganization plan, rather than US Airways' bid. The Delta committee said it "intends to work collaboratively with Delta towards confirmation and consummation of its plans."[15] Immediately, US Airways withdrew its offer. "We are disappointed that the committee, which has been chosen to act on behalf of all Delta creditors, is ignoring its fiduciary obligation to those creditors," Parker declared in a disparaging prepared statement.[16] Additionally, after the merger fell through, according to the *Arizona Republic,* Parker sent Delta CEO Jerry Grinstein an email in which he "made some quip like, 'At least now we don't have to go to Washington [for another hearing].'"[17] On a conference call the day before the creditors' decision, Parker had seemed at best resigned, at worst weary. "We're not going to keep chasing this thing," he said,[18] noting that he would be content to return to running US Airways if the deal failed.

What followed was easily the most troubling episode in Parker's public career, not only because of what happened but also because of the way the situation was managed by his corporate communications staff. At 11:30 p.m. on January 31, the day Delta's creditors announced their decision, Parker, then 45, was arrested on a charge of drunk driving after being stopped for speeding following leaving a golf tournament he had attended in Scottsdale, Arizona. The incident was not publicly known until February 9, 2007, when it was reported in the *East Valley Tribune,* a Phoenix-area newspaper. It was quickly picked up by the Associated Press, and it became the talk of the airline industry. Then came a startling public relations gaffe. In a press release, US Airways quoted Parker as saying that he had taken a blood test and that he believed it is "very likely those tests will come back under the legal limit." Within an hour came the announcement of the results, showing Parker to have been above the legal limit.

In the press release, the airline quoted from a letter Parker had written to employees, in which he said:

> Approximately one week ago tonight, I did something that I need to tell you about. After spending the evening with several friends at a local golf tournament in Phoenix, I agreed to drive a couple of these friends home. Unfortunately, I was in too much of a hurry and was pulled over for speeding. When asked if I had had anything to drink, I answered truthfully that while I believed I was okay to drive, I had consumed some alcohol during the course of the evening. I was taken to a location where blood is drawn so my alcohol content could be tested for the legal limits. I am now awaiting those results. While I believe it is very likely those tests will come back under the legal limit, our local press has learned about the incident and will be writing a story about it shortly. First and foremost, you need to know how embarrassed and sorry I am about this. I have let down all of you and also my family, and that is something I will have to live with irrespective of the outcome.[19]

Soon, US Airways put out a second press release to acknowledge its mistake. And that evening US Airways issued a third press release, prompted by newspaper inquiries, in which Parker confessed to three additional alcohol-related incidents (including two when he was driving) while in his 20s. At best, Parker's advisers failed to get ahead of the news cycle and also issued a public statement in which the airline speculated wrongly on the results of a sobriety test. The incident provided a textbook example of how not to manage corporate communications.

When the Delta bid collapsed, Parker's merger interest turned to United, the world's biggest airline, which had come close to merging with US Airways in 2000. Like Parker, United CEO Glenn Tilton, who joined United in 2002 after a long career at Texaco—where he served as CEO during a merger with Chevron—was consumed with the concept of consolidation. In fact, Tilton let United sit in bankruptcy for three years while he chased a merger. But Tilton's dream did not involve US Airways; rather, he avidly pursued Continental. However, Continental, which at the time was widely considered to be the best U.S. airline, was reluctant. In April 2008, Continental announced that it had dropped out of merger talks with United and was committed to remaining independent. This seemed to create an opening for US Airways. Despite the preference for Continental, "there were senior people at United who believed a linkup with US Airways made more sense than many people thought," said Jonathan Ornstein. "There was a lot of talk at the time that US Airways was a glorified regional, but it provided a lot of support on the East Coast, a lot of passengers who were all connect possibilities. The US Airways folks really believed the deal made sense and pursued it aggressively."[20] Ornstein recalled that in the mid–1990s, when Continental was still struggling and he was a Continental executive, he "went on a secret mission" to discuss a potential merger with United executives. "We approached United with the idea of their acquiring Continental," he said. "Continental stock was near its low. The pitch was simple: Just look at the map; it all fits."[21] But United could not be tempted.

Again in 2008, United would not make a deal. In May, United and US Airways announced they were halting their discussions. "After much work and many conversations with other airlines, we have come to the conclusion that consolidation involving US Airways will not occur at this time," Parker wrote in a letter to employees. "This is not to say that something won't occur in the future—as you know, I strongly believe that consolidation is required in our industry and that US Airways would benefit from participating. Rather it is simply unlikely that anything will happen in 2008 as our industry continues to struggle with how to function in a world with $130 [per barrel] oil prices."[22] Meanwhile, Tilton wrote to his employees, "After a considered review by our board of directors, United has determined that it will not be pursuing a merger at this time due to issues that could significantly dilute benefits from a transaction. We are evaluating other options, and will do what is right for United."[23]

But the two consolidation-loving CEOs could not stay away from each other. They resumed talks, either late in 2009 or early in 2010, and negotiated for months before the effort collapsed in April 2010. That was about a week before the merger between United and Continental was announced. In their second round of talks, Parker and Tilton reached agreement on many key issues, sources told *TheStreet*,[24] although they had not yet determined who would be CEO of the merged airline. One issue particularly troubled United executives: The US Airways pilot contract included a provision requiring that in the event of a change of control, US Airways pilot salaries would return to pre–2000 levels, which were very high. Such contract provisions were not uncommon, and were generally viewed as bargaining items, rather than absolute requirements that a specified condition had to be met. In fact, Parker's position was always that US Airways pilots, working under a 2004 bankruptcy contract, would benefit so much from contract improvements in a merger that they would be foolish to block one.

Nevertheless, it was clear that negotiations with the pilots would be difficult. And United executives were put off by the alternative, which had been utilized in the case of the America West–US Airways merger, in which bankrupt US Airways had to be the acquirer. Similarly, a United deal would have to be structured in such a way that US Airways acquired United. United executives felt it would be difficult for US Airways to assemble the financial resources needed to amply provide for shareholders in a far larger company that seemed to require three times US Airways' market capitalization. Nevertheless, the talks progressed. Eventually, the two sides agreed the company would be named United, be headquartered in Chicago and have two-thirds of the board from United. United's preference for a Continental merger was, obviously, not news to US Airways executives, but it did not deter them. They believed they had no choice but to pursue a deal that would so clearly benefit their company, and they believed they could convince Tilton of their wisdom.

Parker was of course concerned about the problems involved in structuring the deal as a US Airways acquisition. On March 17, at the conclusion of a meeting with pilots at US Airways' Charlotte training center, he unexpectedly raised the topic, saying that change-of-control snapback trigger was a barrier to any merger the carrier might pursue. Four to five dozen pilots attended the meeting, and many said afterward that they found it odd that Parker would raise the topic on his own, unprompted. "We've had talks with airlines in the past," Parker said, at the meeting. "This [provision] always comes up. [It] is a large issue in consolidation talks. There will not be a merger if that's where the pay rates go. Anybody we would merge with can't let the pay rates go to those levels." He added: "You can't have both. You can't have a merger with that provision. [It] will either result in a merger never being done or it will be a merger that doesn't trigger that provision."[25] Later, Parker met with USAPA leaders to discuss the potential merger, and they agreed to work with the airline to facilitate it.

In many ways, a deal between United and US Airways looked good in 2000 and still looked good 10 years later. United had neither a Southeast hub nor a strong New York presence, while US Airways had Charlotte and a lot of slots at LaGuardia. At Washington Dulles and Philadelphia, each carrier had a serviceable East Coast hub; it would have been left to Scott Kirby to rationalize their respective roles. In the West, it is likely that Phoenix flying would have been reduced given United's strength at Los Angeles, San Francisco and Denver. But in the end, these were issues that never had to be raised, because Continental had far more to offer United. Its hub at Newark was the best in the New York area, the world's busiest travel market, and according to Kirby, the most profitable U.S. hub.[26] (US Airways' hub at Washington National was the second most profitable, United's Houston hub was third and Charlotte was fourth, Kirby noted.) Eventually, some on the US Airways side came to believe that United's resistance to the proposed structure for the deal was an indication that the talks were a façade, intended to entice Continental to step in. That belief intensified as US Airways executives read media reports about ongoing discussions with Continental. In any case, Continental and United announced their merger agreement on May 3, 2010.

It was clearly a blow, but US Airways didn't miss a beat. Speaking to pilots in Charlotte on May 27, Kirby said a merger between US Airways and one of the Big Three airlines remained "a pretty high probability for the endgame" of major airline consolidation. "Further down the road, there's a high probability that US Airways will wind up merging with either United, Delta or American," Kirby said.[27] He noted that if regulators approved the planned merger between United and Continental, the combined carrier would have a 22 percent share of the domestic market—the same percentage that Delta had, while American had an 18 percent share. "None of those are anywhere close to dominant market shares," said Kirby. "We'll be about 8 percent. We could merge with any one of those [three]. At most, you take Delta or United up to 30 percent. That still leaves a very competitive, vibrant industry and one of the industries that's most competitive today."[28] At the same meeting, Kirby ticked off the reasons why US Airways would not merge with a smaller carrier or low-cost carrier, saying JetBlue's costs were lower; AirTran could not get bigger and still compete with Delta only in select markets; Alaska's costs were too high; and Southwest pilots wanted to staple new pilots at Frontier to the bottom of the seniority lists, a concept that would be a nonstarter in a US Airways merger. In any case, Kirby reiterated, US Airways had no immediate need to do a deal. The economy was improving, the airline had recently projected 18 percent to 19 percent gains in second-quarter revenue per available seat mile, and US Airways shares were up 80 percent year-to-date. "Things look brighter than they have in a very long time," Kirby said.[29]

13

The War Between
East and West

While the merger between US Airways and America West was in many ways a vast success, it will forever be tarnished by the ugliness of the failed integration of the two pilot groups. The process stalled following a controversial 2007 seniority ruling by George Nicolau, a respected, longtime arbitrator. Seven years later, the resolution remained in doubt, although the merger between US Airways and American appeared to provide a methodology to end the conflict through the application of the McCaskill-Bond Act, labor legislation that Congress approved in 2008 in response to the troubled integration of TWA workers into the American workforce. At its most contentious point, the Nicolau seniority ruling placed a 56-year-old pilot with 17 years at US Airways, never laid off, behind a 35-year-old America West pilot with a few months on the job. In hundreds of similar cases, US Airways pilots with 15 or more years at the carrier went behind America West pilots with just a few years.

The ruling became the subject of thousands of hours of cockpit conversations, in which pre-merger, Crystal City–based US Airways was invariably referred to as "the east," while America West was "the west." It drove a wedge into efforts to merge the cultures of two airlines, always a difficult job, although it did not diminish a successful management effort, which began in 2007, to improve operational performance. For many, a telling sign was that the ruling was so firmly embraced by the west pilots, who constantly reminded that it resulted from both sides' agreement to participate in binding arbitration, at the same time as it was so firmly rejected by nearly all of the east pilots. "In a successful seniority integration, everybody is pissed off," observed Mike Flores. "That's what happened at PSA and Piedmont. But in the America West merger, you have one side that is ecstatic and one side that is pissed off. That's how you know the arbitrator screwed up."[1]

For its part, the airline's management generally sought to stay as far away from the ruling as possible, consistently maintaining that it would let the courts decide. But in fact, the ruling vastly benefitted the airline, which consistently maintained that it could not negotiate a contract until the seniority matter was resolved. The two pilot groups, east and west, worked under different contracts with one important commonality: they included wages and benefits that were substantially less than the industry standard. Lower costs helped enable US Airways to consistently be an industry leader in its financial performance, and that helped Doug Parker and his team to make the case to the investment community and to the American creditors that they could successfully manage a merged airline. In announcing the merger on February 14, 2013, the airline said the new contracts accompanying the merger would increase its annual payroll by about $400 million, with most of that going to the pilots.

In retrospect, it is easy to suggest that Parker and his team should have done something different, in advance of the merger, to assure that pilot integration would proceed smoothly. But who could have foreseen that the ALPA merger process would fail so dramatically? In every subsequent merger, airlines took pains to assure that what happened in the US Airways seniority integration would not happen to them. Delta and United built processes in which contracts were signed in advance of the completion of seniority integration, and arbitration was, in fact, binding. Southwest, when considering whether to merge with Frontier in 2009, said it would not go ahead unless its pilots approved the seniority integration plan. When the Frontier pilots would not agree to go to the bottom of the Southwest seniority list, the merger was abandoned. For his part, Parker relied on the history showing that ALPA merger policy had functioned reasonably well in nearly every past merger that involved two airlines with ALPA contracts. The procedure involved negotiations and, if that failed, binding arbitration with an arbitrator approved by both parties. The selection occurred in the same manner as jury selection, where the two parties begin with a list of names and take turns removing them, so that the last person remaining on the list becomes the one who will preside over the case.

The principal problem was that ALPA merger policy did not include longevity as a factor in determining seniority. Longevity had been removed following the failed 2000 attempt to merge United and US Airways because United pilots—the largest single ALPA constituency—were concerned that they would have lost ground if the more senior US Airways pilots had been able to impose a "date of hire" seniority list. Also, in retrospect, the east pilots may have been doomed the moment Nicolau was selected, even though many had considered him acceptable because they approved the seniority formula he devised following the 1996 merger of US Airways with the Trump Shuttle. The shuttle had been operated by Eastern Airlines before Donald Trump bought it. In the merger with US Airways, Nicolau devised a seniority formula that gave shuttle pilots little credit for their long careers at Eastern. Rather, the Eastern pilots were slotted into the US Airways list based on their relative seniority on their own airline's list rather than their date of hire. The Trump Shuttle ruling showed that Nicolau was "a slot guy," US Airways pilot leader Bill McKee said. "Once he was picked, there was going to be slotting."[2]

Initially following the America West–US Airways merger, the east and west pilot leaders sought to find common ground. "This was the first merger for the America West guys, while we had gone through this before," said Jack Stephan, who became chairman of the US Airways ALPA chapter in March 2006 and led the group during and after the arbitration process.

> They respected the fact we had a lot of experience doing mergers. However, they approached the process very tentatively, cautiously, fearful that we might use our experience to our advantage. We went to great lengths to try to put them at ease. The merger committees met in Phoenix and in Pittsburgh, and when we met in Pittsburgh we would occasionally take them to Pirates games. We wanted them to feel comfortable and let the process play out, to trust the process. But we weren't getting any significant counterproposals from them. For them, there may have been a fear of being the guy who blinked first. On our side, we felt we were on solid ground—date of hire with some flexibility as we had in all our past mergers—but we wanted to give negotiations every chance to succeed.[3]

Jack Stephan was the last president of the US Airways chapter of the Air Line Pilots Association (courtesy Jack Stephan).

In his ruling Nicolau, who was 80 in 2007, took the top 512 east pilots, who were or could have been flying widebody jets on international routes, and left them at the top of the list. Then he took all of the active pilots at the two airlines and slotted them according to relative seniority and aircraft type at their own airlines. This is the portion of the ruling that engendered the greatest controversy. As for the 1,700 east pilots who were laid off at the time of the merger, Nicolau put them at the bottom of the list. That conforms to precedent, but for this group, the suggestion that date of hire—or at the least, years of active flying for the airline—should be the guiding principle in a merged list had a particularly strong appeal.

The hearing took place in Washington, D.C., over 18 days from December 2006 to February 2007. It considered testimony from 20 witnesses and 14 volumes of exhibitions, and resulted in a 3,102-page transcript. The 3-man arbitration board, consisting of Nicolau and two neutral pilots from other airlines, dealt with vast differences in seniority at the two carriers. At the time of the merger, US Airways had 5,098 pilots on its seniority list, of whom 1,691 were on furlough. The most senior furloughed pilot had been hired in 1988. America West, however, had started flying in 1983. At the time of the merger, it had 1,894 pilots on its seniority list, and not a single one was on furlough. The least senior pilot at America West was hired on April 4, 2005, a month before the merger, close to 5 years after the hiring date of the least senior pilot on US Airways' furlough list.

"As in many other mergers, the airlines differ in size, with US Airways substantially larger than America West," Nicolau wrote in his ruling. "The former, a product of previous mergers over the course of a number of years, is also much older, which consequently reflects a wide disparity in pilot dates of hire as between the two airlines. Additionally, US Airways has a substantial international presence in which planes not in America West's fleet are flown. However, in most categories, America West's pay scales are higher. Beyond this, at the time of the merger announcement, US Airways had a significant number of pilots on furlough while America West had none. Moreover, the financial future of US Airways was not comparable to or as bright as that of America West. These factors, as could be predicted, led to great differences in the parties' concepts of a fair and equitable merger."[4]

In the many thousands of discussions that have followed the ruling, some have said that Nicolau did not consider the carrier's relative financial situations, but that is not the case. "There were differences in the financial condition of the two carriers," Nicolau wrote. "For a short time, America West had been in bankruptcy but [it] emerged in 1994 as a low-cost carrier operating out of hubs in Phoenix and Las Vegas. US Airways had also declared bankruptcy, not once but twice. And it was still in bankruptcy at the time of the merger and was unprepared to present a reorganization plan for its emergence. Despite these differences, it is clear from the evidence that the more financially able needed the other and that both have benefited financially from the acquisition."[5] Later, after summarizing the positions of the two pilot groups, Nicolau reiterated: "It cannot be disputed that that there were differences in the financial condition of both carriers and that US Airways was the weaker. This necessarily means that career expectations differed and that US Airways pilots had more to gain from the merger than their new colleagues."[6] This point continues to be widely disputed, especially because Scott Kirby subsequently indicated to both groups that "Project Zanzibar," a potential bankruptcy filing by America West, was being analyzed in the event the merger did not take place and America West was left as a stand-alone carrier.

In explaining his rationale, Nicolau wrote, "Giving sole consideration to date of hire and length of service would put the senior America West pilot some 900 to 1,100 numbers down the combined list. US Airways' proposed restrictions, both as to aircraft and length, would unduly deprive too many senior America West pilots of upgrade opportunities for too long a time, and would also put a number of active America West pilots below long-furloughed US Airways pilots who, until the merger, had little prospect of an early return."[7] Acknowledging the imbalance the ruling would create, he continued, "We also understand that our choices will place pilots with disparate lengths of service next to each other. That, however, is a result of the balancing of the equities inherent in ALPA merger policy, a balance [resolved by] neither a top to bottom active pilot ratio as advanced by America West or a top to bottom length of service integration as proposed by US Airways."[8] In December 2007, ALPA officially presented the Nicolau merger list to the airline—which formally accepted it, although it lacked the ability to impose it.

Jack Stephan turned out to be the last chairman in the history of the ALPA chapter at US Airways. Unlike many pilots, Stephan had a liberal arts education, rather than one that led directly to flying. In 1975, he graduated from Notre Dame after earning a degree in American studies, with a concentration in American literature, a major he selected after reading a roommate's books. He focused on Jazz Age authors such as Fitzgerald and Hemingway, and was also a member of the football team for four years, including the national championship year of 1973, although he was a walk-on who rarely played. After college, Stephan taught American literature and coached football at a high school, taking flying lessons in his spare time, not knowing where that would lead. But in 1977, at 25, he enlisted in the navy in order to be trained as a pilot. He spent the next seven years stationed in the Indian Ocean and the Mediterranean, before leaving to join USAir in 1984.

It was a good year to join the airline, before the rapid pilot hiring that began in 1985 and lasted for two years, and Stephan made captain in less than five years. After 25 years as a pilot, he began to experience problems with his vision. He went on medical leave in 2010 and began a second career as a mediator, involved in a variety of district and circuit court cases, including divorces and child custody. This should, perhaps, provide an indication that Stephan is someone who in general would like to see a deal made, recognizing that most deals involve some level of compromise by multiple parties. Soon after joining the airline, Stephan became involved in union activities, and he rose to become communications chairman during Bill Pollock's term and a half as president. He took over as chairman when Pollock was prevented from seeking a second term by the chapter's divided leadership group, called the master executive council (MEC). Conflict over Pollock's future reflected a historic division within the MEC between hard-line factions on the East Coast, particularly in Philadelphia, and a more moderate group in Charlotte, composed primarily of former Piedmont pilots. Like Pollock, Stephan represented the union's moderate wing. In choosing the union's post-merger leadership, Pollock's allies lacked the votes to determine the body's parliamentary guidelines but had enough votes to elect his successor.

As Nicolau conducted arbitration in late 2006 and early 2007, both the US Airways pilot MEC and the America West pilot MEC were represented by merger committees, which functioned semi-autonomously. In conducting negotiations over the seniority ruling, "The merger committee enjoyed a longer tether than most other committees at ALPA," Stephan said. Although ALPA's national organization nominally presided over the seniority integration process, the policy was that an independent arbitrator in charge of a binding arbitration had considerable latitude to formulate a ruling, with little likelihood that ALPA would interfere afterwards. At the time of the Nicolau deliberation, ALPA's merger policy "was vague at best," Stephan said.[9] Even though longevity was no longer a criterion, early in the negotiations ALPA asked each side to submit certified membership lists that included every pilot's birthday and date of hire, so that the other side could consider the information in formulating its proposal. For any ALPA represented airline, the cost of assembling this information could approach $100,000, which paid for certified mailings as well as remuneration for pilots on leave to preside over a time-consuming process that included thousands of phone calls and verifications.

The compilation of the date-of-hire membership list fed the US Airways pilots' desire to believe that Nicolau would favor date-of-hire seniority, which had prevailed in both of the recent mergers with Piedmont and PSA. "The Trump shuttle was the first one for us that was not DOH," Stephan said. "It was slotting with restrictions." Why then did the US Airways pilots approve the selection of Nicolau? "If we had our choice, we would not have selected him," Stephan said. "The west pilots knew that, and they excluded arbitrators who were sympathetic to our case, just as we excluded arbitrators who were sympathetic to their case. But Nicolau was the last guy standing in the selection process."[10] As Nicolau deliberated, he encouraged leaders of the two ALPA chapters to move away from their initial demands, but that did not occur. "Like that of US Airways, America West's position was not substantially modified during the proceedings," Nicolau wrote in his ruling.[11] In later years, various non-pilot sources involved in labor negotiations declared in private conversations that Nicolau was particularly frustrated by the east leaders' unwillingness to move off their position. But some east leaders said they had no idea what Nicolau was contemplating and no real opportunity to propose a compromise.

Perhaps the most contentious portion of the US Airways pilots' position was the desire for date of hire even for the 1,691 pilots who were furloughed at the time of the merger. Historically, furloughed pilots went to the bottom of seniority lists in mergers. Stephan said that while DOH was sought, he was receptive to considering only those pilots' length of service, which would mean crediting them only for time they had actually worked, which would have excluded, in some cases, years of being on furlough. "Both sides felt they had a good case," Stephan said. "We felt we had a very strong case for DOH, with restrictions and conditions. We knew that the furloughed pilots were going to be an issue, and we felt there was room to move, but we weren't going to go in there on day one and throw them under the bus." In any case, Stephan said, while the issue of the furloughed pilots became "a red herring" in the postmortem discussions of why the east had lost so badly in the arbitration, "it wasn't the thing that kept the sides apart. There were a lot of stumbling blocks."[12]

In retrospect, Stephan says he should have studied the Trump Shuttle ruling much more closely than he did. "While I in no way agree with the current ruling, a closer look at the shuttle award would have provided much more clarity to what Nicolau was thinking, not just in the slotting but in his rationale as to why he slotted the way he did, why he shuffled the cards the way he did. If you look at the Trump Shuttle decision, his respect for international flying jumps right out, and you could easily see that DOH was not at the top of his radar screen." At the time of the Trump Shuttle decision, Stephan was the ALPA captain representative in Baltimore, and the first officer representative had been disadvantaged by the ruling, losing "a lot of numbers" on the seniority list, largely because Nicolau had considered aircraft types, the 727 at the shuttle and the 737 at US Airways, to be equal and flight engineers equal to first officers. Similarly, in the America West ruling, "Nicolau said you are not equal internationally, but below that yes, you are equal," Stephan said.[13]

As the arbitration hearing proceeded, Stephan said,

It was made clear to both sides that Nicolau was not going to accept either proposal. What we were proposing, and what America West was proposing, those things weren't going to work. We should have seen that coming, if we had looked more closely at Trump. At that point our counsel came back to us and said that both sides were being given an opportunity to adjust their seniority approach. Our counsel said that even with the conditions and restrictions we had on DOH, we were not gaining Nicolau's ear. In merger negotiations, you don't want to disenfranchise the arbitrator. You want him to be reading off of your sheet of music. But on our side, we had different ideas of what to do; our MEC was conflicted on how to respond. The question was did we want to provide the merger committee with the ability to call an audible, to come off strict DOH and offer something less than

US Airways Airbus A319, tail number N768US, taxies at Charlotte Douglas International Airport on June 25, 2013 (Jeff Siner, courtesy *Charlotte Observer*).

that, in the hope that Nicolau would say, "These guys are working with me and I will be more sympathetic to their case." I am a big fan of having options, because in any negotiations the more options you have the more likely you are to succeed, but the MEC was uncomfortable with providing our merger committee with the authority to move off our original position. I had heard from enough of our pilots that they were not expecting to get a straight DOH list through arbitration, but that there would be some respect for DOH and that they expected us to do our best in protecting their current seniority and career expectations. But nobody on the MEC wanted to be the guy who backed off DOH. Nobody wanted to show a sign of potential weakness before the arbitrator. Nobody wanted to blink first.

I have often thought about what could have been if I personally had done something different. I still believe there should have been more effort to negotiate this thing. Our counsel seemed to want to do it, and our merger committee [of three] was composed of capable individuals who, if given the opportunity and authority, could have worked out a deal without compromising our list or giving away the store. I trusted them. There were attempts by the MEC to get rid of these guys, but they were capable. If I am disappointed in my role, it is because I should have made sure that they knew they had more autonomy, even though they were reluctant to get on the head of that spear without the full support of the MEC. It would have taken my making a statement to the MEC, that "Here's what I am going to tell these guys." I was comfortable with not doing that then, because I thought the worst we would get would not be that bad. But when I saw the list, I saw how badly we got hurt. At that point, anyone in leadership says, "What could I have done to prevent this? What was my role in this travesty?" Little did I know that Nicolau would come up with a rogue decision. I think he realized that this was the first time the America West pilots had gone to this dance, that they were David in this David-and-Goliath scenario, and so he was looking at us to be the kinder, gentler leader in this process, to realize that we were not going to get it all and to say "Let's talk about that." So I believe that we needed more negotiating flexibility and shouldn't have been or appeared to be so dogmatic.[14]

US Airways CEO Doug Parker advocates for American merger in Charlotte (John D. Simmons, courtesy _Charlotte Observer_).

The ruling appeared to violate ALPA policy that prohibited a windfall for one pilot group over another, but, Stephan said, "ALPA was paralyzed." Its president, John Prater, had just taken office in 2007, after a narrow 51 percent election win, and the union feared a lawsuit by the America West pilots if it tried to overturn a decision reached, under its procedures, by a respected arbitrator in binding arbitration. Prater made several attempts to get the parties to meet and discuss remedies, but those attempts were unsuccessful. For their part, east pilots found the ruling unpalatable. They began a move to withdraw from ALPA, which had represented them since 1950, in order to create a new union, the U.S. Airline Pilots Association. In November, 2007, USAPA filed with the National Mediation Board for a representation election.

Meanwhile, the moderate leaders from both sides were making one more effort at compromise, gathering in February 2008 for a conference at the Aspen Institute Wye River Conference Center near Wye River, Maryland, the same site where Israel and the Palestinian Authority reached a historic agreement, brokered by President Clinton, in 1998. "That's where we went when we found that we weren't getting anywhere with ALPA national's efforts to remedy the situation," Stephan said:

> We had a "Come to Jesus" meeting. With the impending representational vote looming to decertify ALPA, we knew this was our last chance to strike a deal with the America West pilots, to make our case for mitigating the damages that the Nicolau Award would create for all of our pilots. The attrition that would be created by eventual east pilot retirements formed the foundation of our proposal. We were willing to provide some of that attrition, especially on our widebody international flying up front to the AWA pilots in exchange for providing our first officers the ability to capture narrowbody attrition later on. In other words, when an A330 captain retired, that vacancy might go to the west initially in exchange for protecting captain vacancies for our first officers on our narrowbody aircraft. This arrangement was not available to them under the Nicolau Award and we thought this was a big enough move on our part to get their attention.[15]

The west delegation was led by MEC chairman John McIlvenna, whom Stephan described as a "very reasonable" leader. "We got their attention; we got real close," Stephan said:

> I always believed that we could have come to a deal that would have been satisfactory. But the decertification process was spooking the west guys, and they were afraid to agree to anything. They were afraid that it was a trick, that should USAPA prevail in the election, it would take everything away from them. Besides, they felt that we wanted them to give up things they had already won. And while we reminded them that they had a lottery ticket they couldn't cash in, I had doubts whether our proposal would pass our membership, let alone our MEC. Anyway, as soon as the election happened, and USAPA won, that was the end of it. But I was extremely proud of what we attempted in Wye River and proud of the US Airways pilots who took part in that effort.[16]

In a message to pilots on February 8, 2008, following the failure of the Wye talks, Stephan wrote: "After nine days of talks between the US Airways and America West Steering Committees, the America West contingent has chosen to stand down talks. At this time they are not prepared to address seniority implementation issues, specifically, mitigating the damages caused by the Nicolau Award."[17] Stephan wrote about the dissension within the US Airways MEC, which was exacerbated by the campaign to replace ALPA with USAPA. "The odds of any plan we develop succeeding are greatly diminished by members of this MEC continuing to cower behind their fear of failure and seeking to sabotage any process we elect to pursue," he wrote. "There was no cram down, no end-run deal, no deal-chasing and no backroom conspiracies. We said we were going to look under every stone to find solutions and we meant it." He defended the MEC members who had sought a compromise, saying "they did their best trying to reach a solution to the Nicolau award [but] at this time the America West pilots are unwilling to address our seniority concerns."[18]

The USAPA election results were announced on April 17, 2008. USAPA won with 2,723 votes or about 55 percent of those who voted. The vast majority of 1,800 pilots from the former America West voted for ALPA, meaning that only about 500 of the pilots from the former US Airways failed to support the new union. In Charlotte, which was to become the site of the new union's headquarters, about two dozen USAPA backers gathered at an airport-area hotel to await results. They were pleased when the phone call came from USAPA leaders at the National Mediation Board offices in Washington, but beyond a few cheers and some brief hugs and handshakes, little celebration occurred. Leaders assured that USAPA would seek a peaceful accord with the west pilots. "We will welcome them into the process, so that we can represent all pilots," said Mark King, a Philadelphia-based captain who became USAPA secretary-treasurer. "I wouldn't be here if it wasn't that way. We can't succeed as a union if we are fighting each other."[19] King said the Nicolau ruling no longer had any standing since it was issued under the auspices of ALPA, which has been replaced. But an ALPA spokesman told *TheStreet*, "While [USAPA's] glee in the moment is understandable, it is a sad day for all airline pilots." USAPA was bound to face litigation, the ALPA spokesman said, noting: "The new representational agent will inherit all the agreements we had, including the seniority list, and if they fail to implement it, they are likely to be sued for a lack of fair representation by the west pilots."[20]

And that is what came to pass as USAPA, from the day it took over, faced continuing court challenges from the America West pilots. Each of the three east pilots who served as USAPA president sought to reach an accommodation with the America West group, but the efforts were always stymied. The west pilots believed that they had agreed to go to binding arbitration, had won there and did not need to make any concessions. The principal court case, alleging that UPSA had not fulfilled its duty of fair representation, was brought by six America West pilots. They won in a 2009 jury trial in U.S. District Court in Phoenix. But USAPA appealed, and in 2010 the Ninth Circuit Court of Appeals in San Francisco overruled the district court decision. The appeals court said the seniority issue was not "ripe" because no one had yet been damaged by it.

In a broader context, of course, every pilot from America West and US Airways had been damaged to the extent that the ruling delayed their ability to secure a better contract. At the same time, when the merger with American was finally announced, nearly six years after the announcement of the Nicolau ruling, many pilots benefitted from the delay, at least to the extent that it contributed towards US Airways coming to occupy a position from which it could force the merger to occur.

14

A Tough Act to Follow

Don Carty faced a tough decision in the summer of 1979. Seven years removed from Harvard Business School, he'd landed a job in the big leagues of the business world at American Airlines' headquarters in New York City in 1977. It was the kind of position where he thought he could make an outsized impact and, in so doing, punch his ticket for a ride to the top of the corporate world. Carty was to be put in charge of straightening out an enormous managerial and accounting mess at Americana Hotels, American's odd assortment of high-end, mid-market and tourist-class hotels, so that CEO Al Casey could figure out whether Americana was worth keeping. Two-thirds of the way into that process, Casey announced that AMR's headquarters would be moving to Fort Worth, Texas. Carty, Toronto-born and Montreal-raised, had never been to Texas. "I wasn't at all sure I wanted to live there," he said. "But the opportunity with the airline was so exciting I couldn't pass it up, so I went even though I was not at all certain I would like living down there."[1]

In Fort Worth, Carty quickly climbed the executive ladder. Less than a year after moving, he was promoted to vice president and became Bob Crandall's personal emissary, watching over the more than 200 projects—big and small—aimed at reducing American's operating costs, generating new revenue and driving bigger profits. He had no direct authority to make any of that happen. But everyone understood that he spoke for Crandall.[2] The assignment put him at the center of the hundreds of discussions—or intense raging debates—that Crandall loved to preside over as he and his team of young guns, plus a few graybeards, debated the future of American and the airline industry. For the 34-year-old Carty, the early 1980s at American were a very heady time. One critical-thinking exercise involved American's aging fleet of Boeing 707s. They had become unaffordable gas guzzlers compared with the Boeing 727 and other, newer aircraft. They also represented 21 percent of American's capacity. In November 1980, Casey shocked the industry by announcing that American would park all 67 of its 707s within a year. "It was a very hard decision to make," Carty said. "We kept studying the possibility of grounding them and concluding that if we proceeded, the company was going to shrink dramatically and we couldn't find enough overhead costs to get rid of to offset the revenue we were going to lose. What finally convinced us was our determination to get rid of an entire fleet of inefficient planes and to make enough fundamental change in the company that we could force sufficient cost reduction."[3]

Eliminating the 707s meant American could no longer serve dozens of small eastern and Ohio Valley cities it had served for decades. However, it launched new service to cities in the South, Southwest and Central United States that it had never before served, tying all of them to its new DFW hub. Like the decision to ground the 707s, Casey's decision to move American to Fort Worth had valuable results that no one could have predicted. "We changed the whole culture of the company to a culture more willing to embrace change," Carty said. "We got to see the country differently, from a new perspective."[4] The third major change during the period involved acquiring the MD-80s and implementing the B-scale compensation levels in 1982 and 1983.

Carty left American in 1985 to be president of CP Air in his native Canada. There, he helped form Canadian Airlines through the merger of CP, NordAir and Pacific Western Airlines. In 1987, he returned to American as senior vice president for airline planning; in 1989 he added supervision of American's financial operations to his planning duties and his title was bumped up to executive vice president. That made him one of American's two number-two executives. Bob Baker, Crandall's long-time managerial Mr. Fix-it, was promoted on the same day to executive vice president of operations—a position from which he basically ran the airline's day-to-day operations without much input from Crandall or anyone else. Outsiders mostly figured it was an even race between Baker and Carty to replace Crandall upon his eventual retirement, while those close to Crandall and the board always assumed that the top job was Carty's to lose.

For all the glorious successes of the '80s under Crandall, one nagging issue would not go away. American's labor costs may have been dramatically altered in management's favor by the B-scale contracts signed in 1983, but labor issues simmered. The 1987 round of labor contract talks was contentious. Given its growth and success over the previous four years, American could not avoid granting significant pay and benefits increases. It succeeded in getting approval from its pilots to farm out more short routes to smaller planes flown by regional airline pilots who weren't members of the Allied Pilots Association, but the fight over the "scope clause" nearly triggered a strike. Ground workers and flight attendants got better deals in 1987, but negotiations were contentious. By 1992, when all of American's contracts were up for renewal, management had lost control of the labor cost debate. In late July 1991, only days before Saddam Hussein's Iraqi tanks rolled into Kuwait to trigger what became the first Persian Gulf War, Delta agreed to give its pilots—its only large unionized work group—big raises and benefits gains, setting a higher bar for the entire industry.

American took a hard line in flight attendant talks that began in 1992, based on the presumption that flight attendants were easier and less costly to replace than highly trained pilots and mechanics. Flight attendants were not pleased. They struck the airline on Thursday, November 18, 1993, one week before Thanksgiving. That morning, most of American's early-morning flights took off but few carried passengers, because federal regulations require that flight attendants staff aircraft that carry passengers. Although the vast majority of flight attendants honored the picket lines, a small number eventually crossed. (It was never clear how many, but estimates are around 20 percent or less.) On Monday, November 21, President Clinton brokered a settlement. That meant airplanes were in place to carry passengers on the Wednesday before Thanksgiving, the year's heaviest travel day. The relief was short lived. On Thanksgiving Day in 1993, a major ice storm struck Dallas and American shut down its biggest hub.

Meanwhile, Crandall had grown increasingly frustrated by the company's inability to move quickly and innovate as rapidly as it had a decade earlier. His frustration led to the announcement in February 1993 of what came to be known as the Transition Plan. The growth plan had been all about bringing in new planes, new employees, new routes and new marketing innovations, as American took advantage of its ability to reduce its average cost per seat mile while it improved its profit margins. But by 1993, the carrier's ability to grow its way to improved profitability had been eroded by union contract gains and competitive pressure from rival airlines. The transition plan was really a very slow shrinkage plan, though company officials steadfastly refused to publicly acknowledge it. They portrayed the transition plan as a status quo approach accompanied by modest efforts to grow internationally. In fact, Carty always referred to it as putting the car into "neutral." But there was no hiding the fact that American had slammed on the brakes and put the car into very slow reverse. It was in this environment that in 1995 Crandall announced Carty's promotion to president of the airline, formally beginning the succession process. Carty, however, still had to earn the top job. And his first big task was to build a better relationship with labor.

Unions had generally taken a negative view of Crandall for more than a decade, in large part because of his bluntness in talking about American's cost problems and his tough-as-nails persona. Carty, like many others on both sides of the management-labor divide, hoped to change the tone. That thinking proved to be naive. American's 1996 pilot contract talks were unusually slow and ineffective, partially because of turmoil between warring factions of pilots. Management sought to rein in what it saw as out-of-control cost growth, while some B-scale pilots demanded to be to be compensated for their years on the B-scale. The longer the contract talks dragged on, the more heated the internal war within the pilots' union got. By the fall of 1996, the most anti-management faction of pilots had gained control of the union's board. And they made it clear they wanted a showdown.

That showdown came late on Valentine's Day, 1997. For a week management negotiators, led personally by Carty, and union leaders engaged in high-profile, federally mediated negotiations in Washington, D.C. Swarms of reporters and cameramen representing virtually every major media outlet in the country, and many minor ones, surrounded Carty and his union counterparts every time they were spotted in the lobby of the hotel where the talks took place. On Valentine's morning, Carty even made a point of displaying his toothbrush, declaring that he was ready to work through the night to avoid a strike. At midnight, union leaders stepped into the lobby and announced that their strike was under way. The strike was brief. At 12:07 a.m., the White House announced that President Bill Clinton had intervened, employing seldom-used powers granted him by the Railway Labor Act, and ordered the pilots back to work. It took another four months and four more dramatic rounds of mediated negotiations, but a deal was reached, and ratified. Management generally got what it wanted, but Carty personally came out of the 1997 pilots' contract ordeal relatively intact. He had gotten a deal without having to absorb a real strike.

In 1997, American and the rest of the U.S. airline industry were riding high on the strength of booming national and global economies. AMR earned a then-record $985 million that year, and topped that in 1998 with a $1.3 billion profit. The transition plan was still in place, but demand for travel and the pricing environment were so strong that American had added a bit of domestic flying and a considerable amount of international flying to its schedule. Still, Crandall made no effort to conceal his continuing frustration, or his disgust with American's labor unions and how they were blocking American from achieving the greatness he thought it could reach. His mood was buoyed by American's financial performance, but Crandall knew that American was riding the crest of one of the occasional waves that can push airlines to big cyclical highs. He also knew that such waves don't last. So, given his, frustration, Carty's readiness and the airline's good financial performance, Crandall decided that 1998 would be a great time to retire. The baton was passed graciously.

The only change Carty instituted was to relax the company's dress code. But Carty did have an agenda. He thought "it was time for us to do things to gain [American's marketing] leadership position back," he said. "There was a long period there under Bob, probably 15 years or more, where American was the unquestioned leader in every category…. But I think that leadership position had sort of been lost in the last few years under Bob as a result of his severe frustration over dealing with labor. As a result of the strategic plan to stop growing—which I agreed with at the time—I think the company lost something. We allowed our leadership role to slip."[5]Carty also consciously sought to change the company's leadership style. "Bob's command orientation was vitally important for American during the transition from regulation to deregulation, and for its dramatic growth thereafter," Carty said. "Bob got things done in a hurry and his style was just as important as his considerable intellect. He pushed people. He made people mad. But they were pushed into doing new and exciting things, and the airline became a leader in just about every category of the business you can name.[6]

"But times had changed. The airline wasn't growing. In fact, I think that's why Bob was unhappy his last couple of years as CEO."Carty wanted a more collaborative culture, and knew he couldn't copy Crandall's style. "I'm pretty aggressive, but nothing like him," he said.[7] He also believed that the airline still was "positioned to do some very positive things in our labor relations [given that] pilots were getting frustrated themselves in being unable to grow. They couldn't promote to captain; couldn't promote to bigger planes, and therefore couldn't get big raises. Throwing the company into neutral was beginning to have the impact that Bob and the rest of us thought it would have. But that was beginning just around the time Bob left. He wasn't going to get the benefit of that. I thought I was."[8] Carty soon detected a thaw in management's relationship with the flight attendants' union as well as a fairly dramatic improvement in management's ability to work with the Transport Workers. But that period of positive labor relations did not last long.

In November 1998, six months after he moved into Crandall's old office, Carty announced the purchase of Reno Air for $124 million. He saw it as a small, cautious, tactical move that would feed more traffic to American's existing network, and therefore benefit pilots and other employees whose careers had begun to stall under the transition plan. APA saw it differently. Just before announcing the Reno Air purchase, Carty called APA president Rich LaVoy to give him a heads-up. Carty maintained that LaVoy expressed no objections. In any case, by the time the deal closed on December 23, APA leadership was strongly opposed. LaVoy was telling management and the news media that the union's contract did not allow Reno Air pilots to fly, even temporarily, under their own contract. Therefore, he argued, American was violating the contract every time Reno Air pilots flew after December 23. By early February the number of pilots on American's daily "sick list" had risen to medically and historically unexplainable highs. Then hundreds called in sick on February 6, 1999. Management's initial reaction was to wait for the pilots to calm down.

When the numbers calling in sick continued to rise, management publicly warned pilots that its patience was exhausted. On February 10, four days into the "sickout," American sought relief in federal court. The case was assigned to a no-nonsense, tough-talking, former beat-cop-turned-securities-and-contracts-attorney named Joe Kendall. The APA couldn't possibly have drawn a federal district judge who was more intellectually prepared to handle that particular case or more unfriendly to its legal position. Kendall ordered American's pilots to return to work and union leaders to make sure they did. But the next day, the number of pilots on the sick list rose dramatically, and it stayed high for two more days. Kendall was not amused. In a second hearing, he found the union corporately—and its elected officers personally—in contempt. He gave LaVoy and Vice President Brian Mayhew a courtroom tongue-lashing. Kendall was particularly angry at LaVoy for having made a telephone hotline recording advising pilots that while Kendall had ordered them back to work, FAA regulations said that only a pilot had the authority to determine whether he or she was well enough to fly. Kendall saw that as a thinly veiled order from the union president to continue with the sickout in contravention of a federal court order. He ordered the union to post $10 million in an escrow account as a down payment toward damages suffered by American as a result of the sickout. LaVoy and Mayhew were hit with $10,000 and $5,000 fines, respectively. Eventually he ordered the union to pay American $45.5 million in damages. (Management later forgave the union's debt as a sign of good will.)

So Carty won a showdown with American's pilots. But he'd never intended for it to happen, and the price he paid was extraordinarily high, especially considering that the Reno Air acquisition never generated the hoped-for market share gains or profits. Months later, the CEO who came into office hoping to build better relations with American's labor unions found himself involved in a bizarre and bitter labor war after less than a year on the job. During post-sickout contract negotiations at a rustic inn on Orcas Island, Washington, Carty's relationship with the pilots' leaders was permanently damaged. "Once we got to Orcas Island the talks were brutal," he said. "We made some progress and eventually got a deal done, but my relationship with the APA's officers and board members took a big hit. That's where they finally figured out they weren't going to get anything close to what they'd been asking for. They had to swallow a deal they didn't like. And I was the bad guy in the eyes of some of them. My relationship with them was never really as good as I'd wanted it be from that point on."[9]

In the spring of 2000, Carty heard that United and US Airways were discussing a merger. American decided it needed to either squelch the deal or match it. Carty had scheduled a meeting with John Dasburg, CEO of Northwest Airlines, and Gary Wilson, Northwest's vice chairman. The three were already talking when United's $4.3 billion acquisition was announced. In the following weeks, Dasburg, Wilson and a team of associates made a full presentation to American's management. But Wilson, in particular, had what Carty called a "very elevated opinion of Northwest's value," and the parties never could come close to agreement on a price even though they all agreed that adding Northwest's dominant transpacific and Asian flight network to American's powerhouse domestic, transatlantic and Latin American route network would create a carrier capable of dominating global competition. "I heard later that after our meeting where we made it clear we would not pay anything close to what they were asking, Wilson and his partner, Al Checchi, whom he had teamed up with to buy Northwest year earlier, were disappointed that they had asked way too much," Carty said. "They really missed out on an opportunity there because eventually they had to take [Northwest] into bankruptcy and they lost a lot of money."[10]

With the possibility of a Northwest deal eliminated, American looked at other options, none of which seemed very appealing. That fall, as Thanksgiving approached, US Airways CEO Stephen Wolf called Carty with an idea. He was concerned that antitrust regulators in Washington would reject United's acquisition of US Airways. So he, with United's blessing, proposed selling half of US Airways' profitable Boston–New York–Washington shuttle division to American and half to United, with the two carriers then operating the shuttle as a joint venture. Wolf also said US Airways planned to spin off the regional jet operations at its Washington National hub to DC Air, a new company being formed by Bob Johnson, founder of Black Entertainment Television and a US Airways board member. Johnson wanted American to be a 49 percent stakeholder in DC Air, since some DC Air passengers would connect to the joint-venture shuttle. Also, Wolf said, United wanted American to agree to operate significant amounts of service between United hubs in order to appease the antitrust regulators. The goal of the complicated arrangement was to enable the US Airways breakup to get past antitrust regulators who had signaled their opposition to allowing United to buy so many assets. Carty thought the deal sounded good—though not great—for American, at least in part because it would advance the cause of industry consolidation and would eliminate a weak carrier prone to undermining the industry's pricing system. But he and his staff deliberately dragged out the negotiations with United because they didn't want United to catch wind of a second deal they were working on.[11]

American was also talking with the management of bankrupt TWA about acquiring most of its assets and employees. By itself, that deal would have made American a bigger, more formidable competitor than United would become after closing its US Airways deal. By pulling off both the TWA acquisition and the deal to buy some US Airways assets, American would open a big gap between itself and United. On January 9, 2001, Carty announced both deals in a grand setting, the American Airlines Theater on Broadway in New York City. Carty and Tom Horton, American's CFO at the time, sought to convince analysts and reporters that the twin deals were a great step for American. Not everybody bought their pitch, but there was no denying it was a brassy and important move. Things looked great for a month. Then, suddenly, ticket sales

TWA CEO Bill Compton (left) with Don Carty, who met at TWA's Kansas City maintenance base to celebrate the merger of TWA and American early in 2001 (courtesy American Airlines).

began to slump and the sales department was warning that the airline's biggest corporate clients were signaling dramatic reductions in 2001 flying because a recession was fast approaching. By Easter, a market bubble in technology stocks—a bubble that had been propelling Wall Street on a rocket ship trajectory for five years—was bursting, and the economy was weakening dramatically. Additionally, United was making it plain in its dealings with Washington regulators that it no longer was keen to buy US Airways. American, however, was still on the hook for TWA. By the time the deal closed in April 2001, the nation was in a recession. Additionally, American's employees, weary of the career stagnation caused by the transition plan, weren't happy about adding more than 20,000 mostly very senior TWA employees to American's ranks.

Then came the September 11 terrorist attacks, which had a particularly dramatic impact on American. AA Flight 11 was the first of two planes deliberately flown into the World Trade Center in New York by radical Islamic terrorists, and Flight 77 was the terrorist-hijacked flight that slammed into the Pentagon. For three days, no commercial planes flew in the United States. And when they did return to the skies, they did so with few passengers. TWA's St. Louis hub was supposed to have been a relief valve for American's overcrowded Chicago and DFW hubs, but it turned into a massive money-loser due to the huge drop in passenger traffic that resulted from the recession and subsequently from the massive slowdown in air travel following September 11.

"I'd told my wife early on [as CEO] that I wanted to manage the company in such a way that I would never have to lay anyone off," Carty recalled. "I didn't tell anyone else. I just told her. I wanted to make sure we didn't rush so far ahead during the good times that when the bad times came we had to lay people off. Of course, 9/11 blew up on us and I announced the biggest single layoff in airline industry history. So much for achieving my noble private goals. But we had no choice. The company would not have survived and everyone would have lost their jobs if we hadn't done that. It was the single biggest disappointment of my career."[12] Carty's career at American never recovered from the twin blows of the recession and the attacks. Even before the two events, he and his senior staff had diagnosed that American needed to trim a whopping $2 billion from its annual costs. "Then 9/11 happened and it quickly became apparent to us that our five-year window for cutting $2 billion out of the company had been cut to 18 months," he said.[13] Carty continued,

A lot of people in the company were advocating that we go ahead and file [for Chapter 11 bankruptcy] as early as the fall of 2002. Several senior people on my team made that argument: just file and let's get on with the process of restructuring. It was tempting. And I certainly had bankruptcy counsel preparing a filing as a backup plan. But I asked my team, "Whose lot in life are we trying to improve by filing for bankruptcy?" Shareholders? No. They'd get wiped out. Creditors? No. They'd take big haircuts. Employees? No. There would be lots of layoffs and pay cuts and benefits cuts. Customers? No. We would be reducing service and our service quality probably would go down. So that meant that we in management would be the only ones whose lot in life would improve if we filed. We would just be filing to make our jobs easier, because I can guarantee you that it was not easy trying to manage a huge carrier in those lousy economic conditions with the kind of huge cost problems we had.[14]

Management quietly began to poll employees, going around its union leaders, to see how open workers were to the kind of radical cost cutting that was needed. It also asked the unions to renegotiate their contracts. The three major unions reluctantly agreed. But, they weren't going to make things easy on management, and they especially weren't going to make things easy on Carty.

Then Carty handed labor a huge stick with which to batter him. By early 2002, some were portraying Carty and his management team as self-serving bunglers whose TWA deal had left American especially vulnerable by the time of September 11. Not surprisingly, a handful of senior and fast-rising, star mid-level executives decided that the winter of 2001–02 was a good time to leave the company. Airline executive salaries had never been all that great compared with the pay that executives earned in other industries. Executives typically stayed in the airline industry for the combination of personal and family travel benefits, interesting intellectual and managerial challenges, and an addiction to the fast-moving, rough-and-tumble industry. But after September 11, American executives not only had their sense of economic and career security shattered, but also had had their pay cut 30 percent and were being harshly criticized by labor. Most notable among those who left was CFO Tom Horton, who accepted a much higher-paying job as CFO at AT&T. In response, American's board set up a retention bonus system to help keep valued officers from leaving at a time when it needed the best minds available. The terms of the bonuses varied, but the most senior officers, including Carty, would have received, among other benefits, bonuses equal to twice their salaries if they remained at American until at least 2005. When employees, who already had voted on accepting $1.8 billion in pay and benefits cuts, learned of the officers' retention bonus plan, they were outraged. Union leaders immediately said they would throw out the results of the vote, an act that American's board had made clear would trigger a Chapter 11 bankruptcy filing. "It was obvious that they'd made me the bad guy," Carty said. "I'd told the union leaders in 2002 what I was going to do. I didn't go into details but I told them I was going to have to do something to retain my best executives who were leaving for higher paying jobs. I knew they wouldn't like it because we were asking for big cuts from labor. But I told them I had to do it to keep the people I needed to guide the company through a very difficult time. I didn't go into details but they knew I was doing something. And they didn't make a big deal of it at the time."[15]

While Carty wasn't surprised that labor targeted him, he had not expected that the retention bonuses would become the centerpiece of their campaign against him. "But as with the Reno Air issue, if it wasn't that issue, it would have been something else,' he said. "They needed something to aim their displeasure at and I was the obvious choice."[16] In his last act as CEO, Carty convinced leaders of the APA and the TWU not to put the concessions back out for a revote. The airline's board, he told them, had already made the decision that if any of the three unions rejected the deal by a deadline set for the next morning, it would put the airline into Chapter 11 bankruptcy. To seal the deal, Carty tied his own resignation—which was probably inevitable at that point anyway—to the two unions' abiding by the members' initial vote to accept concessions. However, APFA leaders would not cancel their revote on the concessionary contract. Carty's replacement, Gerard Arpey, was given less than a day to change their minds. As Arpey negotiated, Gary Kennedy, the company's general counsel, and a troop of bankruptcy attorneys were at the federal courthouse in New York City, waiting for a call telling them to push the company's Chapter 11 bankruptcy petition through the court's mail drop.

That call never came.

15

A Moral Man Loses a Battle

Paul Harral leaned over to ask his dinner partner, American Airlines' executive vice president for finance and planning, Don Carty, what seemed to him to be the most intriguing question of the evening. "I know most of the members of your party are here tonight," Harral said. "But who, again, is that young fellow over there?" "That," replied Carty, "is Gerard Arpey. And the only thing between him and the corner office is me."[1] It was 1993 and this every-other-year pow-wow between leaders of the *Fort Worth Star-Telegram* and American Airlines was being hosted by the *Star-Telegram* at Fort Worth's toney City Club as a way to keep the paper in touch with the leaders of the city's—and Texas'—largest employer. Harral, the paper's vice president and editorial director, had attended such dinners before, yet he'd never seen, heard of, or even read about the boyish-looking 35-year-old who, obviously, had become part of CEO Bob Crandall's inner circle. But based on Carty's intriguing answer, the confident and intelligent way Arpey comported himself at dinner, and the obvious deference paid him by other senior American leaders, it became obvious to Harral—and to the rest of the *Star-Telegram* contingent—that this young man was American's rising star.

Arpey joined American in 1982 straight out of the University of Texas. The airline was running on financial fumes that year, trying to skirt bankruptcy in the midst of a cash-draining fare war. Crandall had imposed a rock-hard headquarters hiring freeze, a freeze he waived only three times. One of those waivers enabled the hiring of Arpey, who was quickly assigned to the team analyzing the two-tier wage scale that Crandall was considering proposing to the airline's unions. Once the unions agreed in 1983, Arpey quickly became a central figure in the data and financial analysis work that went into deciding what planes should be bought to serve each route. "Things weren't going well for American in 1982," Arpey recalled years later. "But that whole situation gave me an opportunity. Within a month or so, I was sitting in on important strategy sessions—albeit as the most junior guy in the room."[2] In 1989, at age 30, Arpey was promoted to vice president of financial planning analysis. Three years later he was bumped up to senior vice president of planning. On the surface, it appeared to have been a battlefield promotion that Crandall awarded after pushing out another executive. But Carty's revealing answer to Harral made clear that Arpey was more than just the next guy in line.

If anyone was ever born to be an airline CEO, it probably was Gerard Arpey. His father, Jim, had been an executive at several carriers. The younger Arpey recalls hanging out as a child at the Manhattan headquarters of TWA, where his dad was a vice president. When the family moved to Houston, where Jim Arpey became senior vice president of operations and technical services at Continental, a teenage Gerard learned about the airline business from adults who ran it. "Gerard was used to socializing with people like Frank Lorenzo, PeopleExpress founder Don Burr, [former Frontier Chairman] Al Feldman and [former American and TWA President] George Warde," Jim Arpey said in a 1996 interview. "And out of that, I think my son gained a level of comfort in dealing with such people that helped him early on in his career. In that regard, he takes after his mother, who has yet to meet the first person who has intimidated her."[3]

It came as no surprise that when Gerard headed off to the University of Texas, he chose to major in business, or that when he stayed on to earn his MBA, he wrapped up his academic career with a thesis on the then–still burning policy debate over airline deregulation. Nor was it surprising when Arpey began to work summers in Houston for Delta Air Lines, loading and unloading bags and cargo in the sweltering 120-degree-plus bellies of jets. Jim Arpey credits hard work and mentors at American for his son's success. "He may have gotten a head start because of his background, but he's learned far more from those guys than he ever did from me. And he's worked very hard to achieve what he has," Jim Arpey said.[4] In fact, the reputation Gerard Arpey earned for himself in his early years at American was as a brilliant analyst, a soft-spoken but confident thinker and strategist, and an extraordinarily hard worker. It wouldn't be accurate to say that Arpey had no social life during his early years at American, when he was still single. But in

Gerard Arpey spent three decades at American. When he left, he turned down a severance package (courtesy American Airlines).

those early years, Arpey outworked all of the many hotshot MBA grads Crandall stock-piled. "You had to be willing to put in the hours. I was," Arpey shrugged.[5]

In 1995, after Carty was promoted to president, Arpey was bumped up again, this time to chief financial officer. For the next 15-plus years he was a central figure in every decision of even modest significance at American. Although the carrier soared to record profits in 1997 and 1998, largely on the strength of a booming U.S. and global economy, those were still stressful, tough years. Crandall's frustration with labor and the airline's inability to achieve his grander goals because of its stubbornly high labor costs had caused him—with the agreement of Arpey, Carty and the rest of the management team—to throw American's growth plans into reverse. They called it the Transition Plan, but it was obvious to everyone that, in fact, the airline was shrinking ever so slowly. Labor relations only grew worse, and they continued to fester even after Crandall retired.

In 2000, Carty took what he expected would be the final step in grooming Arpey. With the exception of his summer jobs loading bags at Delta, Arpey had never worked in operations. To be a truly effective CEO, Carty believed, Arpey needed significant hands-on operational experience. And fate provided an opportunity to make that happen. Executive Vice President of Operations Bob Baker, who had effectively run the

In American's system operations control center, located in Fort Worth near the airport, dozens of technical and operations specialists manage the carrier's operations. On Sept. 11, 2001, Gerard Arpey came here to shut the airline down (courtesy American Airlines).

airline's day-to-day operations with very little input from either Crandall or Carty since 1985, suffered a recurrence of the cancer that already had cost him a couple of pieces of his lungs. Baker previously had lost the gentlemanly competition with Carty to become Crandall's replacement at CEO, but he had remained a loyal and valuable contributor. Like most senior American executives, Baker had been trained in finance, but he became known as Crandall's top hands-on manager, capable of fixing any problem in any department.

As head of the airline's operations for 15 years, Baker had made himself an expert on virtually every technical aspect of the business. Additionally, he led a panel of industry experts who worked with the FAA to dramatically change the nation's air traffic control system, increasing capacity and enhancing safety. Baker was certain he would beat his cancer, as he had twice before, but its return meant he would have to cut back on his work schedule. Carty elevated Baker to vice chairman, enabling him to continue to represent the company and the industry on technical matters in Washington, and promoted Arpey to replace him as executive vice president of operations. The move not only honored Baker for his long, meaningful contributions to the airline and retained his valuable services, but also afforded Arpey that last bit of seasoning.

Arpey arrived at his office early on September 11, 2001. About 7:15 a.m. Central Time, word reached him that American Flight 11 out of Boston had been hijacked. After a few seconds of stunned silence, he raced to his car and over to the airline's huge systems operations control (SOC) center to take personal command of the crisis response. Repeated efforts to reach Carty, who that morning was answering e-mails from his home office 15 miles away in Dallas, failed. By the time Arpey arrived at the SOC, operations managers had learned that a second American jet, Flight 77 from Washington's Dulles International Airport, also had been hijacked. They also were hearing unconfirmed reports that one, maybe two, United planes had been hijacked as well. Arpey didn't know exactly what was happening, but he instinctively understood that some sort of orchestrated attack on U.S. commercial aviation was under way. At 7:46 a.m. Fort Worth time, Flight 11 crashed into the north tower of the World Trade Center in lower Manhattan. A few minutes later, Flight 77 would go dark on American's controllers' screens. That meant whoever was flying it had switched off the transponder relaying the plane's position to ground tracking stations. Then, at 8:03 a.m. Central Time, a United plane flew into the south tower of the World Trade Center.

Upon confirming that TV footage of the second impact was not a replay of video of the first crash, Arpey issued the most dramatic order in American's—or any carrier's—history. He ordered every plane to land immediately at the nearest airport; no exceptions. Hundreds of American jets were in the air at that moment. Nothing like that had ever been done. But Arpey wanted them all on the ground immediately, before any more could be hijacked. Arpey's order, which Carty affirmed upon his arrival at the SOC, preceded by more than a half hour a similar order from the FAA grounding all non-military aircraft. Ultimately, American Flight 77 would be deliberately crashed by its hijackers into the Pentagon. American's remaining aircraft—like all other commercial jets in the United States—would be stranded for three days wherever they happened to land. When they did return to the air, they carried extraordinarily sparse passenger loads—for weeks. Most people were too frightened to fly. That greatly exacerbated the downward financial pull of a recession that began early in 2001, just as American was completing its acquisition of TWA.

American's situation was made even worse two months later, on November 12, when Flight 587, an Airbus A300–600 with 260 passengers and crew bound for San Juan, Puerto Rico, crashed into the Belle Harbor neighborhood of Queens shortly after taking off from John F. Kennedy International Airport. All those aboard, plus 5 people on the ground, were killed. The National Transportation Safety Board determined that the crash resulted from the plane flying through the turbulent wake of a preceding widebody, and from the pilots' overuse of the plane's rudder in response. That caused the tail fin to snap off, an event from which the pilots could not recover. It was a terrible accident, but at least it was unrelated to terrorism.

By January 2002, Carty and his team determined that American needed to trim approximately $2 billion of annual operating costs to stay out of bankruptcy. The ensuing battle with labor over management's demand for $1.6 billion to $1.8 billion in labor cost savings climaxed in April 2003 when Carty tied his own resignation to the union's acceptance of the concessions. While two unions reluctantly bought the deal, the flight attendants balked, reflecting their outrage over Carty's late disclosure of a valuable executive retention bonus plan. That night American's board named Arpey CEO, but gave him only until the next morning to get a deal. Without one, they would put American into bankruptcy. Arpey met with APFA president John Ward late into the night on April 24, 2003, trying to figure a way to make the concessions palatable to the APFA's enraged board members. Some tweaks to the deal proved sufficient, and the union's board approved the package the next morning. "Everybody thinks that bankruptcy was discussed only during that one moment of the Carty kerfuffle in the spring of 2003," Arpey later recalled.[6] "No. It was every board meeting for five years, from before that time until way past that time." At each meeting the board wrestled with the question of whether to pull "the emergency handle now or continue the fight."[7] That boardroom debate continued well into 2005.

Although American and AMR dodged bankruptcy in 2003, problems remained, and they became Arpey's problems. Arpey had to continue to reduce costs, find new ways to generate revenue and win back the trust and support of the airline's completely alienated and angry employees. He launched a corporate culture repair effort, bringing in outside corporate relationship counselors to guide a formal reconciliation process between top executives and their union counterparts. He met at least once a month, and sometimes more frequently, with union leaders for long, free-flowing discussions that touched not only on management's plans but also on any subject that any of the leaders wanted to bring up. Arpey also began what became a semi-regular pattern of taking cuts to his own pay or rejecting some (though not all) pay raises and stock awards given to him by his board. John Darrah, president of the pilots' union at the time, said, "You couldn't be any more transparent than Gerard has been with us." He went on to laud Arpey as "absolutely the right man" to lead American at that time.[8]

Within weeks of taking command, Arpey began rolling out what he dubbed the Turnaround Plan. It had four tenets: lower costs to compete; fly smart—give customers what they want; pull together, win together and build a foundation for the future. They represented Arpey's best intentions for American. But as sincere and noble as they appeared to be, they failed to inspire labor support for the additional concessions Arpey repeatedly sought. Rather, the airline continued to falter under uncompetitive labor costs, skyrocketing fuel costs, troubled economic times, intense pressure from fast-growing discount carriers, and renewed competition from conventional carriers that had passed through the financial car wash of bankruptcy.

Arpey revived the microscopic attention to cost detail for which American had been known in Crandall's early years. Between 2001 and 2004, American cut $2 billion in non-labor annual operating costs. The carrier reduced the price it paid for engine air filters from $31.70 each to $1.25. It saved $570,000 annually by acquiring plastic dining utensils through an Internet auction process. It lowered the price it paid for items called "engine spacers"—small washers made to withstand the intense heat inside jet engines—to $9 each from $49 each.[9] Arpey downsized and eventually closed the St. Louis and San Juan hubs, while the Chicago and DFW hubs were rescheduled to reduce costs without sacrificing revenue. Arpey also took unpopular steps to increase American's revenue generating capacity. He reversed Carty's marketing scheme that had seen American remove at least one row from every plane to provide a couple inches of extra leg room for passengers. Travelers appreciated the extra inches, but proved unwilling to pay the slightly higher average fare that American needed to make up for the lost revenue. In February 2008, United began to charge for a passenger's second checked bag; the following June, American implemented a first-bag fee. American subsequently became a leader in the industry push to generate ancillary revenue.

Still, American was losing the battle. It lost nearly $6.8 billion between 2000 and 2004. By 2005, "We recognized that we had done a lot to move us in the right direction, but with virtually everyone else using the bankruptcy courts to cut labor costs, we knew we were going to need to do a lot more," Arpey said. "We wanted to do an orderly restructuring. But we did not think it was right to use bankruptcy merely as a tool to achieve that."[10] In 2006, Arpey recruited his friend Tom Horton to return to the airline. At AT&T, Horton had engineered the partial reconstruction of the old Bell empire through combinations with Cingular and SBC. Though Horton had been promoted to vice chairman at AT&T, his work there was done. He was evaluating several attractive opportunities to lead major companies when his buddy Arpey called. "I basically twisted Tom's arm to come back and help me," Arpey said. "It was asking for a lot from a friend. I know he had some really good opportunities."[11] For Horton, who had grown up in Texas and had earned degrees from both Baylor and SMU, a return to American meant going home.

"Yeah, I had some other opportunities, but I love this company. I believe in the people of American, and what we were trying to do," Horton said. "Gerard called and really wanted me to come back and help. I did have some other opportunities ... but coming back here was the right thing for me to do."[12] Working together, and with help from the modest economic recovery after the long post–9/11 recession, the pair led American to what seemed a significant turnaround. Parent AMR had lost $857 million in 2005. In 2006, the carrier reported a net profit of $231 million—tiny in terms of return on investment and as a percentage of revenue, but still a profit. That year, the operating profit was $1 billion, compared with a 2005 operating loss of $89 million, despite unprecedentedly high oil prices. In 2007, profits totaled $504 million and operating profits were $965 million. Still, Arpey and Horton did not allow themselves to see the improved financial performance as anything more than a temporary reprieve. They understood that American's cost problems would intensify at an accelerating rate. In late 2005, Arpey declared that American needed to trim another $1 billion in costs just to keep 2006 expenses level with 2005's, due to rising oil prices and built-in labor cost increases. American put together a plan to trim $700 million in non-labor costs, including fuel conservation efforts, and began talks with labor about ways to modify inefficient, uncompetitive work rules.

By mid–2006, Arpey and Horton were piecing together a long-term financial and strategic plan. It would require dramatic changes to the financial structure and fleet, changes in American's domestic and international route networks, more aggressive exploitation of the Oneworld global alliance and, ultimately, big labor cost reductions. The plan assumed that labor cost savings eventually could be negotiated and that, if not, at least the airline would be positioned for a successful turnaround in Chapter 11. That mindset gave them a small head start on handling the crisis that crippled the industry in 2008, when oil shot to previously unthinkable prices, peaking at just over $133 a barrel. In response, Arpey and Horton shrank the airline as fast as they could. By the fourth quarter American's operations were 8 percent smaller than they had been in the fourth quarter of 2007—the second-biggest schedule reduction in the carrier's history.

Also in 2008, all 300 of American's workhorse MD-80s were grounded by the FAA in a display of bureaucratic pique after the embarrassing discovery that Southwest had failed to carry out an airworthiness directive on its Boeing 737 fleet. When FAA field inspectors, under pressure from agency big wheels in Washington, weren't satisfied by American's response to another airworthiness directive to check every MD-80 in the nation overnight, FAA headquarters ordered the carrier's MD-80s grounded immediately. The grounding was attributed to the discovery of a seemingly minor deviation from the formally approved method for binding wire bundles that pass through the MD-80's main landing gear wheel wells. It took American days to get its MD-80s back

147

into the air. Hundreds of thousands of travelers' trips were severely disrupted. Ultimately 2008 turned out to be the worst year in American's history. Despite record revenues of $23.8 billion, AMR's net loss was a staggering $2.1 billion and its operating loss was $1.9 billion. In 2009, AMR reported a net loss of $1.5 billion, and a $1 billion operating loss, on a 16.6 percent drop in revenues, to $20 billion. Both Arpey and Horton spent a good chunk of the year shuttling between Fort Worth and Tokyo in a desperate attempt to keep American's bankrupt-but-still-key Oneworld partner, Japan Air Lines, from switching to the Delta-led SkyTeam global alliance. Such a move would have stripped American of nearly all its access to Asian markets beyond Tokyo, leaving it in an uncompetitive position in the world's fastest-growing air travel market. Arpey eventually played the key role in keeping JAL in Oneworld by cultivating a close, personal and trusting relationship with JAL's new chairman, Kazuo Inamori.

Arpey and Horton even explored more radical solutions. According to sources involved in the process, they at some point approached archrival United about merging. To address antitrust concerns, they were prepared to sell American's Chicago hub to discount carrier AirTran. Initially, all sides were excited by the idea, but then concerns mounted. AirTran ran the numbers and decided it would lose money, said a source, who added that AirTran then asked to be paid to take the assets—an arrangement American and United could not stomach. Meanwhile, both of those airlines came to recognize that even making the deal (and retaining United's Chicago hub), would not have been enough to get antitrust clearance for an American-United merger.

In the summer of 2011, Horton had another idea. He approached US Airways CEO Doug Parker about a deal at a gathering of the aviation industry leaders' not-so-secret club called El Conquistadors del Cielo at the club's ranch in Wyoming. "It was right on the back of our big airplane order," Horton said. "But we couldn't make a deal with our pilots and they couldn't make a deal with their pilots. It became a sad time. We knew then we had to do the restructuring. Gerard wanted to do it outside of bankruptcy, and I agreed. But we knew we had to do the restructuring one way or the other."[13]

Arpey made clear his adamant opposition to filing bankruptcy, largely on moral grounds. In a 2010 interview with *TheStreet,* his commitment to principle came through plainly. "This company stands for something, more than just any old company," he declared. "Gradually, it will emerge as a successful company that honored its commitments and its pension obligations and that was guided by principles of doing what's right. The path we have taken has created cost challenges for us. But I believe there is something misguided about how we measure success, if success is bankruptcy, giving pension obligations to taxpayers and not paying back creditors. By that measure, we have failed."[14]

Arpey's position was questioned often, and sometimes in insulting ways, by Wall Streeters, the media, and industry insiders. Some viewed him as a Pollyanna. His board members' impatience steadily grew. Still, Arpey remained resolute that American could be restructured without bankruptcy. The key, he said, was getting the labor cost savings to fund growth. In return, labor would be rewarded through promotions, increased job security and preserved pensions. In short, he was proposing an updated version of Crandall's Growth Plan, which he had worked on nearly 30 years earlier. "The rest of the industry had been through bankruptcy. We were operating at a $1.2 billion to $1.4 billion cost disadvantage," Arpey said. "We wanted to grow. And we needed to grow."[15]Horton was tasked with putting together the financial building blocks of the restructuring plan. Both men worked hard on wooing labor leaders, while Arpey sought to keep AMR's board members on board. "We kept trying to convince our board that we didn't need to get all the way to the United or Delta deals" with their unions, which were made in bankruptcy court, Arpey said. "I believed, if we made more modest changes that would support a growth plan, our labor costs would eventually converge with Delta and United," he said. "We had already put in place all the other strategic pieces of the puzzle."[16]

The survival plan had several key pieces. American rescheduled its network to maximize revenue benefits from its DFW, Chicago and Miami hubs, and from its international gateway operations in New York and Los Angeles. Those five locations were called the "cornerstones." Also Oneworld was strengthened in 2010 when American

(Left to right) AMR President Tom Horton, Airbus CEO Tom Enders, AMR CEO Gerard Arpey and Boeing Commercial Airlines CEO Jim Albaugh with thumbs up at 2013 announcement of American's $38 billion order for 460 narrowbody aircraft (courtesy American Airlines).

and British Airways and three partners secured antitrust approval to form a cost-saving, revenue-maximizing joint venture for their combined transatlantic operations. American and BA had applied for such immunity three times since 1998, and had been effectively turned down twice. But finally, American gained the same transatlantic advantage that Delta and United had enjoyed since the 1990s. Later in 2010, American and JAL won antitrust approval for a transpacific joint venture. The third element of the survival plan called for a massive fleet renewal program, announced in July 2010. It showed the vision Arpey and Horton had to restore American's grandeur. The largest order in commercial aviation history included firm orders for 460 narrow-body aircraft from both Boeing and Airbus, along with 465 options through 2025. Additionally, in September 2009, American signed deals with airplane finance company GE Capital Aviation Services, and CitiGroup, whose Citibank unit issues American's AAdvantage credit cards, that raised $2.9 billion in new liquidity. That deal ultimately enabled American to enter Chapter 11 bankruptcy in November 2011 without a need for an expensive debtor-in-possession loan. The fourth part of the survival plan was familiar: lower costs, particularly lower labor costs.

Throughout the years 2008–2011, Arpey continued to believe he and Horton could somehow convince labor to provide the cost savings needed to avoid Chapter 11 and to launch a new growth plan. "I sincerely believed that our airplane deal would be the catalyst to make a deal with our pilots, and that the TWU and flight attendants would follow," he said.[17] Arpey still bristles at the criticism he endured for opposing bankruptcy. Every step taken during his last three years as CEO of American was made, he said, with an eye toward putting in place the right strategic foundation and keeping both options—bankruptcy and out-of-court restructuring—alive. But while Arpey remained publicly focused on avoiding bankruptcy, behind the scenes Horton and the company's legal advisors were preparing a contingency bankruptcy plan. And they set an automatic trigger for filing it. "We had what we called the MCT—minimum cash threshold," Arpey said. "After 9/11 we came up with that. We knew we never again wanted to be in a liquidity squeeze, so we figured out what that number should be. And we adjusted it from time to time based on economic circumstances. It was meant to be a thoughtful calculation of what the company's true liquidity position needed to be to operate normally. And we never intended to go below that number. We kept the MCT in mind as we paid our debts, funded our pensions, paid all our bills and laid the strategic foundation for long term success. I'm proud that we did all of that for all those years and never crossed the MCT line. And I'm proud to say that what we did was the right thing to do."[18]

In the second half of 2011, as American approached the climax of union contract negotiations, Arpey remained publicly calm. Behind the scenes, though, he and Horton were anxiously pressing labor. "We made it very clear to our union leaders what their options were." he said. "Tom would say right in front of them, 'One way or another we are going to have a competitive cost structure, whether it's through agreement or through bankruptcy. And in the meantime we're going to run the company on the assumption that we are going to have a competitive cost structure.' But I don't think our union leaders believed our board would ever pull the trigger on bankruptcy. Or if they did, they couldn't convince their boards of it."[19] American's board pulled that trigger on November 28, and asked Arpey to stay on to help shepherd the company through the bankruptcy process. But he declined, resigned and turned down a severance package. At the time he also fully expected that his thousands of unexercised stock options and shares granted to him over the years would become worthless in bankruptcy. Horton was named to replace his friend as CEO. AMR Corporation and American Airlines filed Chapter 11 bankruptcy petitions the next day in New York. And true to Gerard Arpey's word, his signature did not appear on those documents.

16

Labor Takes the Lead

From the day Continental filed for bankruptcy protection in 1983 to the American Airlines filing in 2011, the role of labor in airline bankruptcies evolved dramatically. Labor seemed a victim in the first case, when Frank Lorenzo established what would become a template that every other legacy airline followed, using the bankruptcy code to reduce unsustainable labor costs. But two decades later, labor became a key participant in shaping the American bankruptcy, likely to be the last major step in the airline industry's consolidation. Labor ascended within the airline industry even as its influence diminished nationally, as U.S. union membership declined from 35 percent in 1954 to about 11 percent in 2011. In fact, the US Airways–American merger effort, undertaken hand-in-hand with labor, was probably one of the most successful ventures in the recent history of the labor movement because unions used their influence to fashion an outcome that benefited their members as well as airlines and investors.

In the 1983 Continental filing, as well as in the 1989 filing by Eastern Air Lines, Lorenzo, the top executive at both carriers, showed some of the vision that enabled him to emerge as the primary architect of the modern U.S. airline industry. Lorenzo built big carriers from little carriers through mergers; he began the buildup of the Newark operation that became the industry's most profitable hub, and he was the first to offer redesigned airline fares, introducing both low "peanuts fares" and restrictive, nonrefundable fares. But Lorenzo is best known for his ability to use bankruptcy to his advantage, and for the enmity he incurred for doing so. Lorenzo realized early that under the bankruptcy code he could avoid much of the give-and-take of contract negotiations and instead negotiate with a clear deadline and the requirement for just a single vote, by a bankruptcy court judge, to implement a contract. Bankruptcy law favors companies because it is intended to enable them to survive as viable businesses, not only freed of burdensome contracts, leases and unsecured debt, but also given the ability to raise operating capital by issuing new stock.

Nevertheless, it cannot be said that the Eastern bankruptcy, strike and shutdown represented a defeat for labor. The verdict is more complex. Eastern's shutdown resulted in thousands of lost union jobs, but it also reinforced the view that an airline has little if any chance to survive a long strike by a major union, particularly if a strike is supported by other unions on the property. Three unions struck Eastern in March 1989. The carrier filed for bankruptcy protection that same month. Thousands of employees crossed picket lines and the airline hobbled along for nearly two years, enabled by a permissive bankruptcy court judge to use its remaining funds to keep flying. Finally in January 1991, in its 65th year of operations, Eastern shut down, primarily as a victim of high oil prices, which soared from $16 a barrel in July 1990 to $40 a barrel in September. During the bankruptcy, unions sought alternate management, and eventually Judge Burton Lifland selected Martin Shugrue, a labor-friendly former Pan Am executive, to run the airline as trustee. But in general, labor and other creditors were adversaries throughout the process, with the unions seen as primarily interested in thwarting Lorenzo's plans.

Miami labor attorney Mark Richard was involved in both the Eastern case, where he represented flight attendants, and the American case, where he represented the Transport Workers Union. In the American case, Richard said, "Instead of going around the mulberry bush, the unions took a business approach, using strategy and bargaining."[1] The outcome was an airline that emerged from bankruptcy with higher labor costs than had been foreseen and with executives who appeared to be labor-friendly. Certainly, they owed a debt to labor.

Throughout the bankruptcy and the merger negotiations that accompanied it, the three largest American labor unions—Allied Pilots Association, Association of Professional Flight Attendants and Transport Workers Union—stuck together, even though their strategies varied. "The interaction and coordination between APFA, APA and TWU was extraordinary," said Dave Bates, APA president during the critical two years before and just after the bankruptcy filing. "We were all in favor of the merger, and we were all going in the same direction. There were never any significant bumps in the road between us. As the effort picked up, we were having daily conferences. Whenever I was in Washington, I made a point of visiting with the leaders of the other unions, Laura Glading, John Conley and Jim Little, and I feel they are some of the greatest people I have known."[2] During the various negotiating sessions and meetings, meanwhile, the union attorneys and advisers "were calling each other or texting five or six times a day,"[3] Richard said.

It remains to be seen whether the merger's labor-friendly image will endure. By the time it occurred, many US Airways employees had lost faith in the America West team, not surprisingly, since two of the three major US Airways unions failed to escape their bankruptcy contracts during the seven years between the 2005 merger with America West and the 2013 merger with American. A third, the International Association of Machinists, the largest union at US Airways, sat out the push for a merger because of a long delay in contract negotiations. But the American labor leaders exalted in their ability to use their influence in a way that seemed to better the lives of their members. APFA president Laura Glading had heard the warnings that US Airways executives were wolves in sheep's clothing, but she largely dismissed it. "I always say, I am not going to judge my relationships with somebody based on somebody else's experience," Glading said.

> They have been very honest with me, very easy to work with. When people ask me if I trust them, I say, "I trust them to do everything they need to do to have the most successful airline in the world." Will that conflict with what flight attendants want? I am sure it will. Will we go to battle? I am sure we will. But I certainly feel as though there is a willingness and understanding with Doug Parker and Scott Kirby that I never experienced at American. We needed a culture change, because the culture had gotten to the point where it was impossible to get anything done.[4]

Glading in fact emerged as one of the most important leaders in the merger; Richard called her "the most powerful [labor] force with the creditors committee."[5] Another attorney involved in the case, who asked not to be named, said that Glading and Jack Butler, a Skadden Arps partner who represented American's creditors, played the most prominent roles in getting the creditors to back the deal. This is not to minimize the early involvement of Dave Bates and TWU president Jim Little. Pilots are always the biggest labor players at an airline, and US Airways was fortunate that Bates was an early, committed supporter, even though his union was fractured and he was eventually ousted. Little also backed the merger, although the TWU always took the approach that it wanted first and foremost to preserve jobs for its members, no matter what management team survived. In the end, the critical elements were that the three unions worked together; they sometimes played the two carriers off against one another, and they took the lead in convincing American creditors that the US Airways bid could be viable.

Glading had been elected APFA president in April 2008, 30 years after she joined American following her graduation from St. John's College. On taking office, she immediately began to participate religiously in the quarterly meetings between American executives and labor leaders. By 2011, she said,

> I knew that things were going south financially. Gerard Arpey was trying desperately not to go to bankruptcy, and it seemed that if [American] could get what they wanted from the pilots, they could kick the can down the road a little farther. But they were expecting more from pilots than I thought the pilots would give, and I didn't think they had a viable business plan. So that summer, I went around making base visits, and I said I thought the company was going to file bankruptcy. I knew that would make some people angry, because some people don't like to hear bad news, but I felt I had a responsibility to do it. I just didn't think it would be so soon.[6]

At the time American filed, Glading was in the midst of trying to decide whether to run again for president, a demanding job that detracted immensely from her time with her husband and son. The filing convinced her to run again. "I said I could live with the fact that the flight attendants didn't want me back, but I didn't want to face, ten months down the line, knowing that I had walked away."[7]

Little, who was born in Glasgow, Scotland, in 1951, emigrated to the United States with his family when he was 13. He learned to be an aircraft mechanic in the air force and he joined American in 1971 as a fleet service worker at New York's Kennedy Airport. Later, working as a dispatcher in Dallas, he became active in the union. He went through the 2003 brinkmanship as a union leader, and over the ensuing years he could see that the constant drama of management efforts to reduce costs had not succeeded in fixing the company or in removing the bankruptcy threat. A turning point came in 2009, when John Donnelly, appointed that June to be the union's research director, told Little that American was bumping up against its minimum cash threshold and appeared bankruptcy-prone. "I said, 'Let's hope it doesn't happen,' but I didn't want to be caught short," Little said. "We started looking around for a bankruptcy attorney."[8] Richard

Laura Glading, president of the Association of Professional Flight Attendants, was a leading advocate for a merger (courtesy APFA).

recommended Sharon Levine, a veteran labor and bankruptcy attorney. Little hired her in 2009, an act of forethought. Still, in the fall of 2011 the TWU was in the final stages in two sets of negotiations. A contract with fleet service and dispatch workers had been sent out for ratification, and negotiations on a mechanics contract were nearing a conclusion.

Little also provided one of the most striking quotations during American's bankruptcy, after Reuters reported that the carrier owned a five-bedroom town house in London's ritzy Kensington district that was valued as high as $30 million. In the Reuters story, published about two weeks after the bankruptcy filing, Little was quoted as saying, "This would have been Marie Antoinette's favorite airline." TWU spokesman Jamie Horwitz said the union wanted to be sure that "Tom Horton had no honeymoon"[9] when he took over as AMR CEO on November 29, 2011, the day the company entered bankruptcy. Kyle Peterson, the reporter who covered the bankruptcy from Reuters' Chicago bureau, said a Reuters reporter in Europe saw the address listed in the filing and "knew it to be in a wealthy London neighborhood."[10] A reporter from Reuters' London bureau subsequently visited the townhouse. "TWU was eager to comment," Peterson said, "and the 'Marie Antoinette' quote was really potent. It got a lot of attention."[11] Said Horwitz, "We thought it was symbolic of what was going on with the airline, that they would hang onto a $30 million house for the executives to occupy."[12]

Dave Bates had been president of the Allied Pilots Association for less than two years when serious merger chatter began. In 2010, Bates—then a 55-year-old Miami-based 777 captain—was elected to succeed a confrontational predecessor. At the time, Bates was one of a new breed of pilot union leaders who followed a model established by Lee Moak, the Delta pilot union chairman who was elected in 2010 to be president of the Air Line Pilots Association. Moak believed that for pilots to succeed the airline must succeed as well. It was not a concessionary position, but rather a vision of shared success. However, it went against a more combative view held by a segment of pilots at every airline, particularly at airlines where labor had been forced into concessions by bankruptcy filings. Pilots, the highest-paid work group, invariably made the biggest concessions.

In American's case, labor had already made concessions in 2003, and many pilots felt that was enough, even if their concessions were not at the same level as the ones pilots made at other airlines. Bates initially took the view that he could work with American management to secure a mutually beneficial contract. In an interview two months after taking office, he declared: "We are going to do things significantly differently going forward. I am very much invested in this airline. All of our pilots are. We want to see the airline grow and succeed. We've signaled to management that we want an entirely different business relationship, and our overtures to management have been well received."[13] At the time, Bates praised CEO Gerard Arpey as "a moral guy who is sincere in wanting to protect the pensions of employees of American Airlines."[14]

But despite continuing contract talks, Bates and his team could never reach a deal with the company, which was losing money and spiraling toward bankruptcy. In October 2011, American publicly announced its contract offer, perhaps thinking it could circumvent union leadership and appeal directly to the rank and file. The chance of approval was so slight that the union did not even call for a vote. As *Dallas Morning News* American beat reporter Terry Maxon wrote at the time, "We may be at the point now where management has gone as far as it can with a deal that doesn't go nearly far enough for the pilots to approve."[15] Said Bates: "It was increasingly obvious that the airline was failing and had not found a way to be profitable."[16] The airline's executives belatedly acknowledged the same conclusion. On October 27, the airline hired Rothschild, Inc., to begin working on a possible restructuring, then-treasurer Beverly Goulet later revealed in bankruptcy court testimony. Until late October, American had embraced "a limp-along strategy that would allow us to continue down the path we were on, with the hope that things would line up in such a manner than we would stave things off," Goulet said in court.[17] The strategy was very obviously failing, however, and Bates started to look for alternatives.

His search led him to the Yucaipa Companies, the Los Angeles–based investment company headed by billionaire Ron Burkle, who had a history of labor-friendly investments, as well as a history of financial relationships with Bill and Hillary Clinton. Discussions between leaders of the Allied Pilots Association and Yucaipa began that October. "I had a number of meetings with Ron himself and some top executives representing him," Bates said.[18] The primary executive was Jonathan Ornstein, a veteran aviation executive who at the time headed Mesa Airlines and had had a mixed relationship with labor over the years. Ornstein "likes putting deals together," Bates said. "He is very creative, very high-energy, and his idea was to help Ron, working as a white knight, to participate in a rebirth of American Airlines."[19]

The exact methodology was not clear, Bates said, but with American's stock trading in the single digits because of rampant bankruptcy fears, a hostile takeover seemed a realistic threat. A payoff for the investment could be envisioned because the historically unprofitable airline industry was beginning to show signs of change. "Like a number of people, I was becoming aware that after so many decades of carnage, the airline industry was finally beginning to get its act together, and could very well become a good investment over the next five years," Bates said.[20] During the time they worked together, Ornstein and Bates developed a close relationship. "I felt the pilots were in such a strong position to lead a deal themselves that I told them, 'If you can act dispassionately and do a transaction from a financial perspective, you can end up owning a very successful company,'" Ornstein said. "I'm not generally known as a labor guy, obviously, but I have worked closely with unions in the past in these types of situations."[21] As American approached bankruptcy, Bates, Burkle and Ornstein envisioned a scenario where Yucaipa would provide post-bankruptcy financing and APA would have a big say in how the post-bankruptcy carrier would be run. The plan became so likely that a press release was drawn up to announce a deal. But hopes diminished when American filed with about $4 billion in cash, enough to finance its bankruptcy without outside help.

American filed for bankruptcy protection on November 29, 2011. Although bankruptcy speculation was intense, the timing was a surprise to nearly everyone. The day before, Laura Glading was on a flight from JFK to Dallas. "The crew asked me when we would file, and I said, 'Not until February,'" Glading recalled.[22] Nevertheless, within five minutes of the filing, the TWU had posted bankruptcy information on its website and sent e-mails to its members referring them to the site. "We had press releases written in advance, and past bankruptcies had been studied by our advisers," said Jamie Horwitz. "The TWU leadership said, 'We hope they don't go bankruptcy and we don't think they need to,' but for two years TWU was in intensive bankruptcy preparation." Horwitz recalled that TWU had an agreement with American management that it would get advance notice about a filing, "but when it was about to happen, they gave us one minute."[23] The bankruptcy plan had three principal components: It would boost revenue, largely because a new fleet would enable it to serve more markets with newer airplanes. AA would rid itself of restrictive scope provisions in the pilot contract, so that it could operate more regional jets and engage in more codesharing, particularly with JetBlue at New York Kennedy Airport. And it would reduce labor costs through 13,000 layoffs—including 9,000 among TWU workers. Combined, the improvements were valued at $3 billion by 2017, including $1.25 billion in employee cost savings, resulting from a 20 percent reduction in costs for each work group.

On the day American filed, Jack Butler was having lunch at the Helmsley Park Lane Hotel in midtown Manhattan. His companions were Harvey Miller, American's bankruptcy attorney, and David Resnick, a high-profile investment banker who was being honored at the luncheon for his contributions to the restructuring community. Unlike Miller and Resnick, Butler did not know that American would file for Chapter 11 protection later that afternoon. "That filing caught everyone by surprise," he said. "That night, I went home and thought about the airline where I had been a frequent flyer loyalist since 1986. I said to myself, 'I have four million miles and Bob Crandall was one of the most innovative guys in the history of this industry and American was at the top of the heap. Now it's fourth in domestic air traffic and has awful labor relations and real questions about its future.' I said, 'There's got to be a way our firm can make a contribution,' and we decided to go after the creditors' committee."[24] The nine committee members included three banks; Boeing and Hewlett-Packard, both major American vendors; the Pension Benefit Guaranty Corporation; and the big three American unions. "Some of the committee members were more often on opposite sides of the table," Butler said. "The pitch we made to them was that if you want to succeed here and be really influential, you have to stick together. You have to realize that all your issues will be resolved, but sequentially, and we have to be involved in the mix and to find the best deal for everyone."[25]

Miami labor attorney Mark Richard represented the TWU before and during the American bankruptcy. He represented flight attendants during the Eastern bankruptcy (courtesy Mark Richard).

Soon after American filed, it called union representatives

together in Dallas to introduce its restructuring plan. "It was a shallow plan, little more than lie-flat seats in the planes and getting more business travelers and more flying," Richard said. "It was like putting cushions in Burger King. There was not a sustainable business plan. None of the metrics added up. When people walked out in the hallways and bathrooms, they were saying, 'This is unbelievable—American doesn't really have a plan.'"[26] Bates' impression was similar. "They didn't really have a business plan," he said. "They were just looking for draconian cuts. This was a phony bankruptcy, all about coming after labor. American did not have a liquidity crisis, nor did we see one coming. They talked about competitive labor costs, but we knew that in some areas we were higher and in some we were lower. In bankruptcy, they were looking for a massive cost advantage over competition, not competitive labor costs. Once we saw the 1113, I don't think anyone with a union card had much use for American management."[27] Section 1113 of the bankruptcy code allows a debtor to reject a collective bargaining agreement or to reach a consensual agreement with a union to modify the agreement.

The airline's approach meant that when the US Airways bid began to surface, labor was primed to hear more about it. At the same time, however, labor harbored deep concerns about Parker's management team because of its mixed history of labor relations and doubts that it was sufficiently competent to oversee the world's biggest airlines. "There was no US Airways in the lexicon," Richard said:

> Labor and management always had a tough relationship there, and we had no reason to think it would change. Everybody was saying, "These guys have a curse: are we just trading one guy for another? Are we even allowed legally to talk to them?" There was enormous trepidation, at the beginning, over how to do this. And there was fear over whether they could even close a deal, given this history. Did they have the firepower to pull this off? Did they even have a business plan that worked, or would the unions just look to the creditors like they were tilting at windmills? Labor needed to show the creditors and both airlines that we understood that they wanted a viable airline and that we were business-savvy. We didn't want to seem to bring them a laughingstock idea.[28]

The creditors committee had its first meeting on December 6, 2011, a week after American filed. Out of 17 firms that bid to represent the committee, Skadden Arps was selected, with Butler and his partner Jay Goffman as the lead attorneys. Although the firm had been involved in nearly every major airline bankruptcy since the 1980s, it was Butler's first time to represent a creditors' committee. One of the first things the committee's professionals did, Butler said, was to meet individually with each of the groups so they could fully understand each one's concerns. "We started to build rapport with people," he said.[29] One result: Throughout the process, the creditors had only minimal disagreement, vastly increasing their effectiveness.

At the first meeting, Glading gave a presentation, telling committee members that flight attendants provided the primary interaction with an airline's customers. "I told them that American Airlines will not be successful unless you have the buy-in of the flight attendants," she said. "I told them, 'We can make this work but we want something in return.'"[30] She also discussed the airline's decline since the Crandall days. "I talked about the pride we used to have when I was hired, how we would wear our uniforms into the grocery store on our way home because we were so proud of them," she said. "But the last time we had new uniform [designs] was in the mid–1980s. I said we want to work for a great company and we want the company to succeed, but we need to feel we are treated fairly." Glading did not rest her case on rhetoric, because she knew that she could add value only if she could work together with the other creditors. "You can go in there all principled and saying, 'This is outrageous and obscene—the labor unions make sacrifices and the lawyers get rich,' or you can go in and try to work with people. And I bonded with everybody, because I went in there thinking I have to know what their interests are too. We needed something where we could all work together, so I tried to recognize their interests and get closer to them." Over time, Glading said, she got to know the members of the creditors' committee besides the union representatives. "What was great was watching the transformation as they came to understand the employees' role," she said. "At first, they had us in a box as labor unions."[31]

After the first creditors' committee meeting, Glading sat down with APFA leaders and attorneys. Given that the pilots had Lazard Freres as a financial adviser and the creditors had two financial advisory firms, Glading wanted to hire a blue-chip firm to represent flight attendants:

> I noticed that all of these advisers and lawyers and investment bankers knew each other. They all worked at the same firms and they would move from firm to firm, and they had all worked on bankruptcies together. So I said I want us to have one of these guys too, I want somebody who has lunch with these guys that we saw at the meeting. My advisers told me that it was too expensive, but I said we had to do it if we wanted to be a player. So we hired Jefferies as our financial adviser. It was one of the best moves I made. These guys were amazing. They had never represented a labor union before, but they went in with passion, and they even came on base visits so they could really understand our situation. Also, they could pick up the phone and talk to the other financial advisers. It was important that we had somebody who knew them and could speak their language."[32]

Jefferies representatives convinced the creditors that including an early out provision in the contract, allowing senior flight attendants to be paid to retire early, would in the end save money for the airline. About 2,200 flight attendants elected to take the early outs. Over time, the APFA spent about $9 million to pay its advisers and expenses; most of the money was repaid from the airline's payment to the creditors' committee members.

Initially, despite her intense involvement in the creditors' committee, Glading did not know how long she would be a member. That depended on whether she was re-elected as union president. In February 2012, she won a narrow victory, claiming 4,434 votes or 50.9 percent of the total and beating her opponent, Liz Geiss, by 150 votes. Geiss had led in the first round of voting, and members of Geiss' slate were elected to be vice president and treasurer. Glading began her second term on April 1. It was only after the election that she could fully embrace the task that became her most important contribution to the merger and that is likely to define her legacy, becoming labor's primary representative on the creditors' committee, which took the lead in advocating for a merger that American strongly opposed. Glading was the only union leader to attend every meeting, and she forged relationships while there. "I spoke with Lee Moak and others who had been through bankruptcy, asking them what worked and what didn't work, and everybody talked about getting a seat on the creditors' committee, having a vote, and having a say," she said. "After that, I went to every meeting, and I never shut up."[33]

The creditors committee was adamantly opposed to termination of the employee pension plans. As Butler told its members: "If you terminate, you create a $10 billion to $12 billion unsecured claim which swamps all the other claims, PBGC becomes the controlling creditor, and you deep-six the rest of the committee." The right answer, he said, was to adopt an idea that the pilots' union's advisers had been exploring to freeze rather than terminate the plan. The liability would then be capped and absorbed by the airline, which would continue to fund the plan over time. Early on, American agreed to the creditors' demand. Freezing the plan, Butler said, was "the cornerstone" of the creditor committee's strategy. The next step, he said, was to convince American not to immediately go after the labor contracts, which gave everyone more time to consider options.[34]

17

Let's Meet for Dinner

Early in 2012, the America West team began to once again actively pursue the dream it had envisioned for nine years, a merger with a major airline. This time the target was American, the third of the big three U.S. carriers to enter bankruptcy, and the only one it had not publicly pursued. It is hard to imagine that America did not represent the ultimate prize for the team, since Parker and others had joined the industry at a time when American was viewed as the world's leading carrier, and in fact had worked there under Crandall. As a merger partner, American suffered due to its lack of presence in Asia, but it largely compensated for that with first-rate hubs in Dallas and Miami; a hub in Chicago, diminished only because United had a bigger Chicago hub; dominance of the number one U.S. international route, linking New York Kennedy and London Heathrow; and supremacy in Latin America as a result of Crandall's having bought the Miami hub from Eastern.

American's bankruptcy filing rang the bell for the America West team to begin actively talking to analysts and potential investors. In January, the team gathered partners including investment bank Barclays and restructuring experts Millstein and Company. Another step occurred on January 27, when US Airways and the Association of Flight Attendants announced they had reached a tentative contract deal after five years of talks, removing a barrier to a merger. "It's very easy for them to explain in a merger effort why they don't have a deal with pilots," said Mike Flores, president of the US Airways chapter. "But there's no explanation for why they don't have with flight attendants, other than they were being cheapskates."[1] Among its components, the deal created a single contract for the America West and US Airways work groups. In an interview a few days before the announcement, Glading had declared: "There is always some skepticism because [US Airways] hasn't successfully merged east and west, so how is it that they think they can make this [merger] work?"[2]

While the tentative deal was an important marker of the airline's commitment to clearing out the roadblocks to a merger, flight attendants did not approve it until a year later, on February 28, 2013, in a third contract vote, which took place after Flores had been recalled because some local union leaders felt he was advocating too strongly for the contract. Following Flores' recall, the union prevailed upon local leaders to more enthusiastically support the contract and also negotiated a few changes—primarily, specifying a $40,000 buyout payment and paying a $1,700 signing bonus to partially compensate flight attendants for the delay in gaining approval, which, when it came, was by an 80 percent margin.

Early on, US Airways executives spoke to the professionals representing American's creditors' committee about their interest in a merger. But the committee balked, saying it was too early to consider a bid. The committee counseled patience. "We said we can't do a merger deal or consider alternatives if we don't have a base plan from American," Butler said. "We had to get labor deals, we had to get the pension frozen and not terminated, and we had to work on fleet restructuring."[3] American, meanwhile, wanted to move quickly to complete the bankruptcy and then, from a position of strength, explore alternatives such as a merger. At a dinner with American executives in February, the committee's lead advisors—from Skadden, investment banker Moelis and Company and financial advisor Mesirow Financial—said that would not be acceptable. Delta and United had both completed mergers only after they emerged from bankruptcy, and in those cases, "the value of the merger went to future management and investors, not to the bankruptcy stakeholders," Butler said. "So we told them we wanted a robust plan, and then we wanted to compare alternatives. They were not on board."[4]

In January, Dave Bates recalled, "a senior AMR manager called me and said that US Airways was looking at a takeover and that I should come out against it."[5] Bates declined to make such a commitment: the decision was not difficult. "American was seeking draconian pay cuts and had shown so much arrogance and also, frankly, I had little confidence in their reorganization plan," he said. Bates had always found it difficult to negotiate with American, a pattern that continued after the filing. "They had layers of analysts and bean counters, every decision had to be processed through different parties, and they could not respond to proposals in real time," he said. "There were few changes after Horton took over." So Bates continued on his own path, which included continued shopping for new management. The effort led him to Palm City, Florida, a wealthy enclave about a hundred miles north of Miami on Florida's east coast, the winter home of Bob Crandall. "Crandall knew how to run an airline," Bates said. "We didn't like the guy when he was CEO, but we were glad he was on our side and some of the potential partners in a new American had floated his name."[6]

On February 12, 2012, the two met in Crandall's home. "It was a very good meeting, very cordial and productive," Bates said. "We covered a lot of ground, and got to know each other. I got his feelings about American and the industry and where American had gone wrong. He had a lot of pride in the company, and he was deeply distressed at the turn of events and the condition American was in—it was heartbreaking to him." Bates suggested that potentially Crandall might return to the airline to run it again. It was a "very exploratory" discussion, Bates said, but Crandall "seemed willing to do it, to come back under the right set of circumstances. We never negotiated any details, but he said he would do it. We had a number of talks, and he had a team picked out that was ready to take over."[7] Although both parties realized that Crandall's return would be controversial, they would have been willing to take the next step, which would have been floating Crandall's name. But they never got there, and until the publication of this book, the talks with Crandall were not been publicly disclosed. "Over the years, many people have asked me if I would return," Crandall said. "I have always said that I would do so if asked—but of course, the board never asked."[8]

Meanwhile, in late February US Airways began to interact with the leaders of American's labor unions. A day after her election on February 24, Glading was informed by advisor Dan Aiken that Scott Kirby wanted to speak with her. "Dan said somebody was asking him to ask me to call Scott Kirby," she said. When she called, Kirby said he wanted to meet with her in New York. Glading had a relationship with US Airways because Tom Weir, the airline's treasurer, was her cousin. American executives suspected that the relationship provided an avenue for back channel negotiations, Glading said, but in fact she and Weir maintained an arm's length relationship throughout the merger discussions.

As president of the Allied Pilots Association, Dave Bates was a key early advocate for a merger with US Airways (courtesy Dave Bates).

Meanwhile, by late February Bates was also preparing to initiate contact with US Airways. "They knew support from labor was critical," Bates said. "They had learned that from their Delta and United [merger efforts]. I suspected they would eventually reach out to us, but I wasn't sure when, and for my part I wasn't going to sit around and wait."[9] Bates had two avenues for reaching out to US Airways. First, APA had retained Lazard as an advisor, and Lazard had a February meeting with US Airways. Additionally, Jonathan Ornstein was a business associate and friend of Scott Kirby's. That month, Bates said, "I had a conversation with Jonathan Ornstein and we talked about the different possibilities and it was becoming clear that the best path forward was the potential for getting involved with US Airways."[10] At that point Bates asked Ornstein to set up a meeting with

Kirby. Ornstein called Kirby, Kirby called Bates, and the two agreed to meet in New York on Monday, March 12, the day before the 2012 JP Morgan Transportation Conference. Bates and Kirby had met for the first time ten months early, at the 2011 Wolfe Trahan Transportation Conference at Fordham University in the Bronx. There, they chatted for a couple of minutes.

During the week of March 12, Transport Workers Union president Jim Little was at the AFL-CIO annual meeting in Orlando when Sharon Levine, the bankruptcy attorney retained by the union, called and told him that US Airways was actively pursuing American. "I already knew Doug Parker from America West, where we had the fleet service workers and the dispatchers," Little said. "I thought he was a pretty sincere CEO. He was always up-front with us. He didn't come across as a stuffed shirt; he came across as a guy you would like to have a beer with. So I went to a hotel room and called Doug Parker and he called back. I asked, 'Are you making a run at American? Is this for real or are you just a spoiler?' He said it was serious, but he didn't want to talk about it on the phone. He said, 'I would like you to come out and meet with Robert Isom and Scott Kirby and me in Phoenix, and I would like to share with you our vision for American Airlines."[11] On March 22, Little flew to Phoenix for the meeting. "We talked about the structure and he went into details and finances and what he thought the business plan would look like, and I was very impressed," Little said. "When I got back to New York, I called Dave Bates and Laura Glading. I told them I had been to Phoenix. I said it looks like this could be very serious."[12] The three unions were all on the same page; they were put off by American's restructuring plan and willing to consider putting aside doubts and aligning with the America West team.

One of the most famous restaurant meetings in the history of the airline industry occurred in the spring of 1985 in the Cherokee Sirloin Room, a neighborhood steak place in St. Paul, Minnesota. There Republic Airlines CEO Stephen Wolf met with Northwest Airlines chairman Steven Rothmeier and negotiated the sale of Republic to Northwest. That meeting came fairly early in the consolidation of the U.S. airline industry, while the landmark restaurant meeting on Monday, March 12, 2012, came at the end of the cycle. This one brought together Bates, Kirby, and Dennis Tajer, a pilot and APA spokesman. It occurred in a room beside the kitchen in the Oceana Restaurant, on West 49th Street between Sixth and Seventh avenues. "We wanted a private dining room because you don't want to have those discussions in public," Bates recalled. "So they put us in a room where they had staff meetings. It had glass windows and you could watch all the action in the kitchen."[13] The meeting started with small talk between Kirby and Tajer, both of whom had been in the air force. The trio ordered oysters from a menu that included eastern oysters and western oysters, and somebody made the joke, "Here we are, already talking about 'east' and 'west,'" the warring groups of US Airways pilots.

As might be expected, the three discussed the synergies between the two airlines' networks, the possibility for a better contract than American was offering, and the key point that US Airways would make repeatedly throughout its push for a merger: the combined carriers could move from domestic weakness on their own to combined domestic strength as the biggest airline in the eastern third of the country, the biggest in the center of the country and the third biggest in the west. At the end of the dinner, Bates and Kirby began discussions on the framework for a collective bargaining agreement, one that was far better than what American had been seeking. "I outlined some of our major concerns and was intrigued by Kirby's responses," Bates said. "He said, 'What next?' and I said, 'I want to see you and Doug Parker as soon as possible.'"[14] After the dinner, Bates and Kirby began exchanging text messages.

At a follow up meeting on March 22 in Phoenix, Parker and Kirby joined Bates and union vice president Tony Chapman. By then, Parker and Kirby had talked with all three of the key American unions, who were working in concert to make the merger happen. The day after the meeting, Kirby spoke to the JP Morgan conference. Asked what lessons US Airways had learned from its failed 2006 effort to acquire Delta, he responded that if you want to do a merger in the airline business, "It's important to have allies," particularly labor allies. "One thing we learned is we can't do it alone," Kirby said. "In an ideal world, it's important to have the constituents of bankruptcy, particularly labor, on your side. An outright hostile transaction won't work."[15] Two weeks later, at US Airways media day in Tempe, Parker was generally tightlipped about merger possibilities, but he did tell reporters: "You can't do it on value—you have to have the employees on your side."[16]

Evidently, Kirby liked the food at Oceana. On March 19, a week after he had met with Bates and Tajer, he met there with Glading and her advisor Dan Aiken. Glading, who had told few people about the planned meeting, feared that somebody would see her with Kirby. But "the only person who saw us was Dr. Ruth, [who] came back to check out the room where we were eating," Glading said. "We recognized her, and we said hello."[17] At the meeting, Kirby said that Tom Weir had told him that Glading was "like a sponge; she really listens." Kirby laid out his hopes for a merger, just as he had with the pilots. Glading was interested, but wouldn't commit to anything more than a trip to Phoenix on March 31. There she had dinner with Parker, Kirby, Weir, and two of her advisors. "I sat next to Doug," she said. "He said, 'I want a deal, I want you to do this, but I don't want you to just use our agreement to get more in the 1113 negotiations. I want you to decide that you really want it. I want you to decide that you really want it.' He didn't want us to play both sides, and I made the commitment that if I was really going to do it, I would be all in." After dinner, Glading called the AFA's US Airways negotiating team and asked them to fly to Phoenix in order to discuss the US Airways proposal. "I knew that if I signed that deal, it was not just a possible contract," she said. "It was a commitment to do whatever I could to bring about a merger. For me, it was about who was going to give us job security and a better company. It was going to be all or nothing." Glading was fortunate, she said, that despite the close election for the top union positions, her entire board backed the merger. "My board was 100 percent unified," she said. "They could not have been more solid."[18]

Once the three unions indicated they were interested in talking with US Airways, Kirby was assigned to work with the flight attendants and pilots, while Isom was assigned to work with the TWU groups. At this point, the unions' differences were becoming more apparent. The APFA gave up on American early on, as Glading became convinced that US Airways provided the flight attendants' best hope for the future. The APA had to deal with its internal problems and could not fully commit to backing a merger. Meanwhile, the TWU, unlike the other two unions, initially faced the prospect of thousands of job losses and had the burden of eleven separate contracts with American, including four at American Eagle, while the other unions had single contracts with the carrier. "We didn't put all of our eggs in one basket," Little said. "The other groups were more focused on a merger being the only option. They thought a merger was the holy grail. But we weren't sure this deal with US Airways was going to happen, so we were still hammering away with American."[19]

On April 3, teams from the TWU and the carrier began to work out details of a term sheet in talks in Dallas. "It was tough to do because a lot of the information they needed was proprietary," Little said. "I couldn't share all the information I had because it was confidential. I deal with a lot of carriers and I cannot share confidential information."[20] Little told Isom that he wanted a better deal from US Airways than the heavily concessionary contract American was seeking: in particular, he wanted to preserve jobs in Fort Worth, Tulsa and elsewhere. For fleet service workers, this meant reducing the number of cities—on a list of about two dozen—where American wanted to turn over their work to outside vendors. For mechanics, saving jobs meant maintaining the amount of in-house maintenance work done by TWU mechanics. "My concern was that US Airways farms out 54 percent of overhaul work," Little said. "We spent a lot of time on that. In Tulsa we do a lot of our own work, and we do it more quickly than other places. I am proud of that. Also, at American we do a lot of the component work in-house, where US Airways farms that out; I couldn't provide a lot of the specifics, but I assured [Isom] that we could save a lot of money doing that."[21] The airline's team agreed to limit fleet service outsourcing and to maintain Tulsa employment levels at 90 percent for at least two years, while it reviewed whether the cost benefit was as high as TWU said it was. But Little could not convince US Airways to scrap American's plan to close the Fort Worth Alliance maintenance base, partly, he said, because there was not sufficient time for US Airways to review the facility's operating costs.

Richard said the TWU asked American for two things. One was a sustainable business plan and the other was flexibility in setting terms, particularly in the area of retaining jobs. "When a 55-year-old mechanic is laid off in Tulsa, his next job is working at Pep Boys," Richard said. "That is disrespectful."[22] If the TWU failed, Little said repeatedly, "That would mean 6,000 or 7,000 moms and dads who didn't have a job."[23] Richard said TWU operated under the assumption that Judge Sean Lane would rule in favor of American in its bid to abrogate labor contracts because precedent showed that companies nearly always succeed in that effort. "Other unions thought they had better chances, but we felt it was never going to be won," he said. So the union focused on Section 1113 negotiations with American and on making sure that whatever American offered, US Airways offered something better. "The TWU strategy was to ride two horses and never get on one until the moment where we had to make a choice," Richard said. "We put our heart and soul into an American deal and we put our heart and soul into a US Airways deal, and we told everybody that was exactly what we were doing. It became clear that US Airways was using the labor piece as an asset on their balance sheet, saying, 'we can get a deal where American cannot.' It was not that they loved labor, but for them labor peace was a selling point. They were using the unions and the unions were using them."[24]

As the negotiations continued, Richard said, US Airways made clear that it was willing to maintain wage levels and, by continuing to in-source work, to save some TWU jobs. For months, he said, American's position continued to be a "scorched earth, you-have-no-choice contract."[25] But at a certain point, American began to realize that US Airways was gaining traction, first with the unions and then with the creditors. And suddenly, he said, American became more flexible. "They moved to slightly less intransigent," he said:

> We showed them how to be more efficient—they walked through shop floors and hangars with our guys, and we were having a legitimate dialogue on how to save jobs. Then we would run to US Airways, and say this is what we need. US Airways had no appetite for in-sourcing, but we got them to agree to in-source more jobs. And every time US Airways got a step closer to home plate, another scintilla of flexibility would be shown by American. They decided to give more to TWU than they ever had thought. The way US Airways operated was that they wanted to be personally popular and to connect with us, like frat boys. Horton and American Airlines wanted to be able to spike the ball in the end zone. This became a testosterone thing for him and for American. American was smart enough to try to react, but it was too late, because every week the Parker team got smarter and smarter. At first they were smart with labor, but eventually they became smart with the creditors as well, and they were able to make deals to win over the creditors committee. So American got the 1113 it wanted with the pilots, but it lost out on Wall Street, with the marble counters.[26]

Little would shuttle between the two sets of talks, using the terms of one deal to get better results in the other deal. American had started out with plans to lay off 13,000 workers: in the end, the merger contract included only a few hundred layoffs, along with early-out packages for about 1,500 workers. When US Airways agreed to reduce the concessionary impact by $300 million, Little got the same deal from American. Eventually, American matched the US Airways wage and benefit offer, providing an immediate 4.3 percent increase on signing for every TWU work group, and cut back on its layoff target. Additionally, the TWU got "me too" provisions that assured parity with the contract gains the other work groups negotiated. Additionally, the TWU, like the other unions, was engaged with the Pension Benefit Guarantee Corporation in negotiating American's agreement to freeze rather than terminate the pension plan. "We managed to get all the pieces we thought were necessary," Little said. "I kept saying, 'Don't get married to any of these things, they are just place holders.' We were on two tracks."[27] Nevertheless, Little preferred the merger, which he felt would restore American to its place as the number one airline, which would provide more job security for his members. "When I saw the US Airways business plan, I thought it was a breath of fresh air," he said.[28]

What did Little get for his work in negotiations? Not much. In August 2013, Little announced he would not seek another term as union president, a post he had held since 2006. The concessions involved in negotiating a contract in bankruptcy, following the 2003 concessions (at that time Little was director of the TWU's air transport division), were too much for a candidacy to bear, despite the favorable comparison to the contract American originally offered. "We got everything we could possibly get from a bad situation—the benefits clearly outweigh the negatives," he said;

> but morale was at an all-time low at American. Members were unhappy with management and with the union—they blamed us for the bankruptcy. I've gotten a lot of heat on that, and it's extremely disappointing for me. You put your heart and soul into trying to preserve a standard of living for your members—that's my job—and I know we did all we could. But there are no accolades. I'm not ready to retire, but I never wanted to be an impediment. I've always said two things: if labor unions don't evolve, they dissolve. And no good deed goes unpunished.[29]

Progress on the pilot contract continued. In the first week of April, Bates returned to Phoenix with his hand-picked team to work on a tentative deal. It was, of course, unusual to construct a labor agreement between a company and a group of workers employed by a competing company, but no one saw that as much of an impediment. "You can call what we negotiated 'a term sheet,'" Bates said. "It was pretty bare bones."[30] Bates brought about a dozen people to Phoenix, including bankruptcy lawyers; representatives from Lazard, the union's general counsel; and union subject matter experts. "We met with the entire senior management team at US Airways," he said. "We watched the way the interacted: they obviously worked very well together. The chemistry was nothing like what we saw at American. I came to think that Doug Parker is an excellent leader who knows how to motivate people and to inspire teamwork." During that week, teams from both the APA and the APFA were in Phoenix negotiating simultaneously with US Airways teams, both headed by Scott Kirby, while the team from the Transport Workers Union was in Dallas negotiating with Robert Isom. In Tempe, negotiations took place at a motel near the airline's headquarters. "We were using breakout rooms next to each other, and Kirby would pop in on both [groups]," Bates said. "A lot of the talks between Kirby and me took place outdoors under a palm tree."[31] The APA team went back to Dallas on April 8, but talks continued over the phone.

Bates still wanted a meeting where remaining APA officers could meet with Parker and Kirby. That meeting was set for April 10 at the Arlington Hilton, which was five miles south of the union's headquarters. Bates picked up Parker and Kirby at the DFW business aviation center on the airport's northeast side—they had flown in on a private plane to escape detection—and drove them to the hotel. To preserve secrecy, Bates had union leaders, manned with walkie-talkies, covering all of the hotel exits. But for some reason, the pilot manning the back door did not recognize Terry Maxon, the airlines reporter for the *Dallas Morning News*. Rather, the pilot told Bates, "I wonder who the funny guy with the mustache is."[32] Maxon had been tipped off that the US Airways executives would meet with the union leaders at the hotel. As he waited for them to arrive, he munched on a club sandwich from a nearby convenience store.

As Bates pulled into a parking space near the back door, he recognized Maxon and uttered a curse. "I thought Terry looked straight at us, but he didn't see us," Bates said. "Because of the way the sun was coming down, there was glare on the windows. Also, like all union bosses, I have tinted windows. I did a missed approached and tore out of there. I told all the security guys to bring everybody back to [union] headquarters, and poor Terry missed out on the scoop."[33] While Maxon remained at the back door, the APA contingent fled out the front door. "After the time for the execs to arrive had come and gone, I went inside and found that the union's conference room had been emptied," Maxon said later. "I waited in the lobby for several hours, figuring they had either gone upstairs or relocated elsewhere. But I never saw the people inside the SUV and couldn't confirm that they had arrived."[34] Later, ensconced and undetected at union headquarters, Parker and Kirby met with the APA's board of directors. After they departed, the two sides negotiated for three days, closing the deal on April 13.

18

Hey, What About Us?

As it negotiated union contracts following the merger with US Airways, the America West team took a hare-and-tortoise approach. The hare was the talks with American unions, which seemed to proceed at breakneck speed. The tortoise was talks with its own unions. Their pace was languid. The seniority battle between east and west pilots enabled management to delay for years making improvements in two contracts that were both close to the bottom in the industry. The delay in pilot talks enabled delay in flight attendant talks, because the practice had always been to get a pilot contract first. Meanwhile, the airline's biggest union, the International Association of Machinists, got contracts covering mechanics and flight attendants in 2009, four years after the merger. Those contracts became amendable at the start of 2012. Talks began a year before that date but moved slowly, especially after the International Brotherhood of Teamsters launched a raid on the US Airways mechanics. The raid caused a suspension of the talks, one more indication that the America West management team, as it sought delay in order to keep costs down and appearances up, was blessed with immense good fortune.

Regarding the talks on new contracts for American workers, the approach was to leave the US Airways unions in the dark. That lasted as long as it could, but in April 2012 it could last no longer. For Dave Bates, once a deal was reached, the next logical step was to reach out to his equivalent at US Airways, because any contract that American pilots had at a combined airline would eventually apply also to US Airways pilots. However, Bates said, "USAir preferred that I hold off a few days until Gary Hummel took office" as the new president of the U.S. Airline Pilots Association.[1] Not only had relations soured with Mike Cleary, USAPA president at the time, but also the airline was concerned with leaks. Some details of the American pilots' term sheet had already appeared in US Airways pilot chat rooms. "A lot of buzz was taking place, but US Airways wasn't quite ready to introduce this to their employees," Bates said.[2]

The first report that the airline had agreements with the three unions appeared in a story, attributed to sources, that was posted by *TheStreet* around noon on April 19. "US Airways has been successfully gathering union support for its effort to merge with bankrupt AMR and could unveil a union-backed bid as early as next week," *TheStreet* reported.[3] Immediately, US Airways shares began to rise, closing up 16 percent for the day. "The story's appearance caused us to move forward our joint announcement, which was made the following day," Bates said.[4] On April 20, US Airways and the unions jointly announced that new contracts would preserve 6,200 of the 13,000 jobs that AMR had planned to eliminate and "would provide competitive, industry-standard compensation and benefits, as well as improved job security and advancement opportunities for all employees of the combined airline."[5] American management was so indignant that high-level communication between American and its unions immediately ceased, Bates said.

Within hours after the April 20 announcement, the IAM issued a statement saying it would "oppose any merger that would take place at the expense of workers, the flying public, and the communities served by these two airlines," Looking ahead, the union said it would "fight for the fair treatment of all employees at US Airways and American Airlines."[6] Later, Local 1725 president Bill Wise said of Parker: "I don't recall the last time he was in the maintenance base. It's sad that he's out wooing other labor groups without settling contracts here at US Airways."[7] Months later, in an e-mail to members entitled "US Airways, American Airlines Announce Back-Room Deal," Sito Pantoja, IAM general vice president, declared: "US Airways needs to get serious about coming to contract terms with its own employees instead of bribing American's employees to support its merger dreams."[8]

On April 17, 2012, the day before he took office as USAPA's third and last president, Gary Hummel had gotten a couple of surprises. "I got a call from Doug Parker who told me that they were waiting until my term began to make an announcement about the merger [effort]," Hummel said.[9] He also got a call from Bates, who said, "I gave him a full briefing on everything."[10] It was a sudden initiation for Hummel, then 56, a Philadelphia-based Airbus A320 captain who had joined USAir in 1984. The calls provided an early indication of the potential for surprise and stress that the new job presented. In Hummel's case, the stress level was so high that within a year he would find that it would actually endanger his life.

Mike Cleary was a belligerent if sometimes misunderstood leader whose relationship with the airline hit bottom after he presided over a 2011 safety slowdown. (Because pilots have broad discretion in determining whether an aircraft is safe to fly, they are easily able to delay an airline's operations, although the tactic not only represents a contract violation if it can be proven but also runs the risk of antagonizing not just management and passengers but also the remainder of the airline's work force.) Cleary was not told of the discussions with the American unions. In his campaign for the union presidency, Hummel made it clear he was not going to follow the path Cleary had set. He called himself a "peacemaker"[11] and promised to end the conflicts between the two pilot groups as well as between the pilots and the airline.

"I think the [America West] pilots, as well as the company, are looking forward to having a peacemaker, and my role in life has always been that," Hummel said.[12] Afterward, he reflected: "Management was hopeful there would be a traditional honeymoon period with a new group at USAPA and perhaps they could start over on a firmer footing. They were waiting for the administration at USAPA to change, because obviously the history had been one of antagonism."[13] Hummel of course welcomed the possibility that a new contract would enable the US Airways pilots to shed the bankruptcy contract they had signed in 2004. "It was our opportunity to inject ourselves into the process in order to ensure that the membership in USAPA gained the same working conditions and pay benefits as the American pilots," he said. "My first steps were to call my first board meeting to notify the board of the situation and what was to come, and to begin communicating with Dave Bates."[14]

As president of the US Airline Pilots Association, Gary Hummel saw a merger as a way to secure major contract gains for his members (courtesy USAPA).

On April 18, Hummel took office. On April 30, he presided as Bates and Neil Roghair, the APA's negotiating chairman, met with USAPA leadership in Charlotte. "At first we were met with a pretty icy reception, but later on I think most of USAPA's leadership came to realize the benefits a merger would bring to both pilot groups," Bates said.[15] A few days later, Hummel flew to Phoenix to meet with Parker and reiterated his initial thought, that "the only way we would proceed with this in a friendly manner was if USAPA pilots were guaranteed the same pay benefits and working conditions as American pilots on day one," he said. "Immediately thereafter, we proposed a memorandum of understanding which did just that. It was a separate agreement between USAPA and US Airways, just as APA had a separate agreement, but ours was a memorandum of understanding, rather than a term sheet, because we already had a contract."[16]

In many ways, the memorandum of understanding represented the pot of gold at the end of the rainbow for US Airways pilots, both east and west, who had made sacrifices since September 11, 2001, to keep their airlines in business. In the case of the east pilots, the sacrifices included working under some of the industry's lowest pay rates for nine years and having their pensions taken over by the federal government, which resulted in lower-than-anticipated payouts. Over six years, the memorandum of understanding would bring US Airways pilots $1.6 billion of benefits, including pay raises of 13 percent to 35 percent over existing rates, substantial increases beyond that, and lump sum payments of $10,000 each. A brief skirmish within the union leadership involved the date when the pay raises would take effect, but in January USAPA's board of pilot representatives endorsed the MOU in an 11–0 vote. In February 2013, pilots approved the contract by a 75 percent margin, with margins ranging from 56 percent at the Philadelphia pilot base to 98 percent at the Phoenix base.

In a sense, once the MOU was signed, Hummel had succeeded in completing the most important task of his tenure. But his work did not stop, as the job of overseeing the details of an airline merger was just beginning. Like any pilot union president, Hummel faced opposition no matter what he did, and he was constantly called upon to explain himself to various parts of his constituency. This included east pilots who felt he was too conciliatory toward both management and the America West pilots, as well as west pilots who nearly unanimously continued to oppose the very existence of USAPA. For the west pilots, in fact, the elimination of USAPA was in some ways the best part of the merger, although of course the pay improvements were also welcome. In the view of the west pilots, USAPA's existence represented a direct challenge to the seniority that an impartial arbitrator had awarded them in binding arbitration. "I think I speak for all AWA pilots when I say, we are happy to call ourselves American Airlines," said a former America West pilot, who asked not to be named. "We look forward, quickly please, to joining the APA and ridding ourselves of what we consider a true form of cancer—USAPA."[17]

Bates meanwhile had another hurdle to jump. Even though he had agreed to a term sheet with US Airways, he still had to secure a bankruptcy contract with American. "It wasn't something I had high expectations for, but was told by our advisers that we had to fill this square," he said.[18] Early in June 2012, he went to New York to negotiate, with a bankruptcy judge from another circuit acting as mediator. In Section 1113 negotiations, the deck is always stacked against the union, but Bates was committed to getting the best possible deal for American pilots. Negotiations began June 4. "Our advisors and US Airways' advisers were adamant that the only way we could get the creditors to consider a merger was to finish the labor issues," Bates said.

> The creditors did not want to evaluate that until there was closure on labor agreements. We agreed that the best avenue was to get these negotiations out of the way, even though we knew the outcome wouldn't be very good. But when we went in there, American had a new generosity. They knew every word of our collective labor agreement with US Airways; someone had provided that to them. They never came close to what we achieved overall with US Airways, but on some items AMR matched. One of my highest priorities was to achieve parity with Delta and United as soon as we could. This would essentially provide for a 100 percent snapback to the industry standard and not serve to drag it down. During my initial discussions with USAirways, I was getting regular briefings from the Delta pilot leadership who were negotiating for a new contract, and I felt they would come up with a good deal.[19]

From the first time he saw the term sheet in April, Gary Hummel had strong feelings about the length of time before pilots at the new American reached parity with

Delta and United pilots. "One of the immediately apparent deficiencies was that it had to be a three-year review," Hummel said. "They were talking about six years, and we said, 'no way.' No way would we give them a six-year pass."[20] Bates agreed fully. The Delta pilot deal was negotiated in May and approved in June. "After the Delta deal was announced, I knew it was a total game-changer, an opportunity that I was not going to let pass," Bates said. Initially, the best deal Bates could get from US Airways had been an agreement that it would match Delta/United in five years. But once the Delta deal was negotiated, Bates went to Kirby and said he needed an equivalent contract in three years. "He said go to AMR and get it from them and I'll match it," Bates said.[21]

Although the initial offer from American was for a six-year contract with no snap-backs, eventually Bates' team succeeded in negotiating a three-year match as well as a 13.5 percent pilot stake in the reorganized company, both items that would transition to the USAirways agreement. Bates felt good about those negotiating victories. After all, in the 2003 contract negotiations, APA had agreed to major concessions with no snapback at all. But when Bates brought the American offer back to APA's board of directors, he could not get the board's endorsement. "The opposition argued that it would empower Horton and we would have to live under it for up to 10 years—arguments that have now been clearly shown to be without merit," Bates said. "I agreed it was a bad agreement, but in the context of bankruptcy you always get a bad agreement. There was considerable risk that in a rejection scenario the court could abrogate our agreement and deny our 13.5 percent claim. In addition, our deal was far better than what any of the other large pilot groups had ever gotten in bankruptcy: We all got pay raises, but more importantly I stressed that the offer should be viewed as a temporary bridge agreement to get us to the far better one that we had negotiated with USAirways."[22]

The board sent the proposal to the members for a vote, but would not endorse it. The opposition was vocal and well organized, and a private conversation between some top executives and some pilots at a Los Angeles–area restaurant in late July heavily influenced the outcome. One of the pilots who attended the meeting wrote a long message, widely distributed among the pilots, quoting a senior executive as saying that the airline needed a contract and would return to the negotiating table if the tentative agreement was rejected. Within days, hundreds of pilots called union offices to ask how they could change their "yes" vote to "no." In the final count, 60 percent of the members voted to reject the contract. Then some pilots started an effort to recall the board members who voted in favor of the offer. Some board members had significant doubts about a merger. Additionally, "A failed vote is a very destructive event in any union," said one pilot leader, who asked not to be named. A fact of life at the APA is that its presidents tend to have ever-worsening relationships with their boards during the presidents' three-year terms, part of the eternal bickering about whether the national officers or the board members—who are local leaders—are running the union. Under pressure, Bates stepped down on August 8, a few hours after the contract was

US Airways aircraft stacked up at the gates at Charlotte Douglas International Airport on September 11, 2011 (Patrick Schneider, courtesy *Charlotte Observer*).

rejected. "I felt I could have survived a recall election, but the last thing I wanted to do was to put the union in a state of turmoil at a critical time, so I reluctantly agreed to take the bullet," Bates said. "When the board said they planned to bring in Keith Wilson, I knew he was a good solid stand-up guy who would pick up the baton and see this thing through."[23]

It wasn't just the pilots who needed to sign an 1113 contract with American. The flight attendants were in the same boat. Like Dave Bates, Glading did not like the contract but knew that it needed to be approved for the sake of the bankruptcy process that was the best path to a merger. "I had to go on the road," Glading said. "It was hard. I negotiated the best contract in 2001, then I had to negotiate concessions in 2003, and then in 2012 I had to get people to give up 17 percent. I had to beg them. I guaranteed a merger if they ratified it. I said I have not lied to you yet; this merger can happen, but you have to do this first."[24] When the pilots' contract vote failed, Glading was worried. "I thought ours would tank too," she said. But in August 2012, flight attendants supported the contract by a 60 percent margin, reflecting the unanimity in their leadership, who had backed it 16–0. "When I got elected it was with a mixed slate that included two people I didn't run with," Glading said. "They had to

Tom Horton (left) and Doug Parker posed at the December 9, 2013, celebration of American's emergence from bankruptcy and merger with US Airways (courtesy American Airlines).

get behind it. They understood."[25] The strong backing Glading found is rare in the union movement.

On May 12, 2013, Mother's Day, Gary Hummel was in Philadelphia International Airport preparing to captain a flight to Phoenix, where he planned to attend a Tuesday court hearing in the lingering dispute over the Nicolau award. In addition to being union president, Hummel maintained a regular flying schedule, a dual responsibility that all three USAPA presidents had attempted to meet. "I hate going out there [to Phoenix] because the three-hour time change means that I can't get home the same day and I have to spend the night," Hummel recalled. "But I felt lucky that I could pick up a trip out of Philly to Phoenix."[26]

Hummel felt ill after arriving at the airport. He imagined he had food poisoning, having just finished lunch, and he went to a bathroom in Terminal B and threw up. After that, he sat down to rest, took off his jacket, loosened his tie, and rolled up his sleeves. "Then it hit me," he said. "I felt like I was in a scene in a bad movie. Luckily, I saw another pilot going downstairs in the elevator, and I followed him," he said. On the airport's lower level, Hummel made it to the US Airways chief pilot's office. There, assistant chief pilot Dennis Horn caught a glimpse of him and immediately called an ambulance. "If he hadn't done that, I don't think I'd be talking to you today," Hummel said. The ambulance arrived quickly and medics wheeled in Hummel, who was having a heart attack. "By then I was in and out of consciousness," he said.

> But when I came to in the ambulance, there was an EMT over me, a young man, and he was screaming at me, "Stay with me." I looked down and noticed that I was in uniform. I looked around and saw a fire extinguisher, a crash ax, consoles and buttons, and the only thing in my mind was that I was in an A330 over the North Atlantic and I had passed out and someone was trying to revive me. So I looked up at him and said, "If you'd stop screaming at me and tell me what's wrong with the airplane, I'll fix it." By the time I got to the operating table, the doctors had heard this story, and one of them said to me, "You pilots are all alike, you're always trying to take control of the situation," and I said, "No problem, that's why they give us four stripes."[27]

The surgery was successful, but by October a stent in Hummel's chest had scarred over. That month, he was walking across the mall in Washington after meeting with the National Mediation Board when he felt discomfort. He called his doctor in Pittsburgh, who said he should get to the hospital in Pittsburgh. On the way Hummel made a detour to Charlotte, where he met the next morning with newly elected leaders of the Charlotte local. The next morning he flew to Pittsburgh, and the morning after that he had heart surgery. The Charlotte meeting had been cordial, but it did not lead to a particularly compatible ongoing relationship. "I made sure the Charlotte reps and I got off on the right foot," Hummel said later. "But then they tried to recall me."[28] In a January 2014 recall election, backed by nine of the 11 members of USAPA's governing board, Hummel survived, winning 51 percent of the vote.

A week after winning the recall election, Hummel got more good news when a U.S. District Court judge in Phoenix ruled in USAPA's favor in the union's continuing courtroom battle with its minority constituents, the former America West pilots. Judge Roslyn Silver stated repeatedly in her opinion that she didn't care much for USAPA's courtroom tactics. But she also said that the union had not breached its duty to fairly represent the west pilots and that the west pilots need not be separately represented in seniority discussions with the American pilots. Given the west pilots' assertion afterwards that they would continue to pursue their case, the ruling did not bring an end to the seniority battle, but for the moment at least it put the ruling and its backers on the defensive.

19

Breaking Down the Doors

Once Doug Parker decided to actively pursue American Airlines, he faced strong resistance from two quarters. First, the American Airlines management team preferred to stay in place, and later the Justice Department opposed the merger. While Parker's team brilliantly managed the first battle, it seemed to completely miscalculate what might happen in the second one. The team badly misjudged what the antitrust division might do, exactly as it had done in pursuing the merger with Delta in 2006, seemingly reflecting a willful lack of understanding concerning the regulatory consequences. As a result, the Justice Department's opposition came as a surprise. The department announced on August 13, 2013, that it would sue to block the merger, which it found anti-competitive. When Parker briefed union leaders about the case on a conference call the next day, "he sounded like he was blindsided," said Roger Holmin, president of the US Airways chapter of the Association of Flight Attendants. At the same time, Holmin said, "He was confident that we as a company will prevail in court."[1] In the end, the confidence was justified, although the case never made it to court.

The successful outcome of the battle for the creditors' committee support was announced on Valentine's Day, 2013, when the two airlines shook hands and said they planned to merge with Parker at the helm. American's board had approved the merger the preceding night. Although it had been widely assumed in the media and the analyst community that Parker would be CEO of the combined airline, deal insiders did not necessarily share that assumption. "The larger airline was American, and Tom Horton had just presided over the best reorganization in the history of the airline business," Jack Butler said. "His management team did a terrific job on fleet restructuring and many business issues, and the directors of American were anticipating that the management of the much larger airline would continue to run the business. That's a normal expectation and American Airlines had exclusivity [to propose a reorganization plan]."

Of course, some American stakeholders, especially the labor unions, believed Parker should be at the helm, and Laura Glading lobbied constantly to be sure that view was accepted. In general, in the early stages, the committee deferred the "social issues," such as who would run the post-bankruptcy airline, and focused on sorting through the comparative economics of American's standalone plan and other alternatives including a merger. The process also involved a second creditors' group, known as the ad hoc com-

Tom Horton (left, coatless) and Doug Parker (right) conduct a joint conference call with analysts and media on February 14, 2013, to announce agreement on a merger (courtesy American Airlines.)

mittee of AMR creditors, who held $2 billion in bonds, notes, claims and other debt issued by the company. Its members were pleased that the resolution of the case was going to provide them not only with a good return on the debt, but also with value for the equity that many of them had acquired. Normally, outstanding common shares in a bankrupt company decline to zero and are canceled on emergence from bankruptcy so that the company can issue new stock. However, the American case was a rare exception.

Many of the members of the ad hoc creditors' committee, including various hedge funds, had purchased their holdings post-bankruptcy. "Anyone who bought into AMR after the bankruptcy bought at a steep discount and made money," said a source who was told of the ad hoc committee's deliberations. "So they were in a good spot, in a position where they were willing to negotiate and [wanted] a quick deal. There is always a big risk that you will stay in bankruptcy for a long time and the company will fall apart. This case was unique in that the [unions] went behind management's back and, when AMR figured that out, they had to think about doing a deal quickly." The creditors' desire for a quick and certain resolution of American's reorganization case through the merger with US Airways resulted in the creditors' committee and ad hoc committee negotiating a settlement agreement that created a framework for how the estimated $11 billion value of the merger would be distributed—including the guaranteed distribution, sought by American's board and management team, of at least 3.5 percent of American's share of the merger to holders of existing equity. Ultimately, the determining factors in the American board's approval of a merger with Parker as CEO would be the unified support for Parker on the creditors' and ad hoc committees as well as the guaranteed return for American's equity holders.

Kevin Starke, an analyst for CRT Capital Group, was the first to report that the shares might have value. In a report issued December 7, 2012, Starke wrote that an equity recovery "cannot be ruled out." Some of the members of the ad hoc bondholders group had "substantial holdings in the common stock"[2] and might support a reorganization plan that benefitted equity holders and bondholders, Starke wrote. His reports triggered a sharp climb in the value of the American shares, which had been trading as a penny stock. Eventually, the stock would trade in the mid–20s and rise to almost $40 a share. The share price did so well that some American equity holders made billions, with a lot going to institutional investors. Ultimately it would turn out that holders of American equity would own about a quarter of the merged airline going forward—an unprecedented return for bankruptcy equities. All of the prospective value on the table made the selection of the CEO a lot less important to economic stakeholders, so they deferred to what US Airways had demanded in its merger proposal and what the American unions wanted, agreeing that Parker would become CEO and Horton would have a short-term supporting role as non-executive chairman.

For both of its battles, US Airways developed public relations strategies that involved securing broad-based support, particularly from labor and the media. A particular example came on July 17, 2012, when Parker took the stage before the National Press Club in Washington, D.C., to promote the merger. For US Airways, which had long relied on Parker's communications skills to make its case to everyone from employees to reporters to government officials, getting him in front of the National Press Club represented a valuable opportunity. The opportunity was supported by the TWU, which has its communications office in Washington. "We pitched that to the press club, to have Parker talk about the merger and the industry," said TWU spokesman Jamie Horwitz. "We wanted to have him go there and go on record as saying he would do this in conjunction with the unions; an appearance would give us public validation that was what he wanted to do. Initially, the newsmaker committee of the press club was going to sponsor it, but there was such interest that it was elevated to the National Press Club luncheon. It became a big deal: there were a lot of reporters in the room, and it sent a strong message that the media and labor were supportive."[3]

At the session, Parker displayed his common-man appeal. To show the merger's inevitability, he quoted Bob Dylan as saying, "You don't need a weatherman to know which way the wind blows," adding, "Analysis just complicates the situation. You don't need all of that to tell you what you already know. You already know what the right answer is. Everyone on Wall Street knows it." He isolated American management as the merger's only opponent, and said, "I don't want to guess as to why it is they don't support it."[4] When the questions from the reporters, many from outside the airline industry, veered toward dissatisfaction with airline service, Parker improvised. Asked whether he had ever tried to reach a real person on US Airways' customer service phone number, he began to take his cell phone out of his pocket before thinking better of it—saying it might not work.

Besides Parker's easy informality on a national stage, two things stood out that day. First, while the leaders of the three American unions were on the podium, US Airways union leaders were not. Parker "dumped his steady and took the new girl in town to the prom," said USAPA spokesman James Ray. "Even though he needed to show that he was labor friendly, it was apparent that his own employees weren't important in the process to him."[5] Secondly, it wasn't just US Airways that had a media strategy. American had one too. Its executives spoke frequently to airlines reporters, touting the repeatedly successful monthly results that American achieved. American's public relations staff was kept busy issuing positive statements and setting up interviews to point out their successes, even as the ground was sinking around them. On the morning of Parker's press club appearance, AMR chief financial officer Bella Goren conducted several interviews as American reported a second-quarter profit of $95 million as well as its best quarterly revenue ever. Goren told *TheStreet* that the results "reflect only a fraction of our restructuring process"[6] and that even better results were coming. Parker

Doug Parker advocates for American merger while visiting Charlotte on March 17, 2013 (John D. Simmons, courtesy *Charlotte Observer*).

spoke in the early afternoon. Within minutes of the conclusion of his remarks, AMR released a statement declaring, "Today's excellent results demonstrate that the new American is performing extremely well," and noting that its merger evaluation "will be a disciplined process guided by the facts and will not be influenced by baseless rhetoric."[7]

Later, Horton recalled that on November 29, 2011, the day American filed for bankruptcy protection, he called Parker. "I made a mistake and called his house instead of office," Horton said:

> I got his wife, Gwen, and we talked for a while about family and things, catching up. I knew Doug and his family well from his days here, and we'd stayed in touch over the years. Afterwards, I called Doug at the office. I said there's still a deal to be done but we've got to get our house in order first—and it'll be a very successful restructuring. Next thing I know, USAirways is running a campaign in favor of a merger. On April 20, 2012, Doug calls and says he's got a deal with our pilots to support a merger and that he thought he had the support of a significant chunk of our creditors for a deal. What he proposed was a 51/49 split with USAirways being the fifty-one. I told him that was ridiculous since we were more than twice their size. Yeah, I was a little mad about it. I thought it best for us to stay in control of our own future through the bankruptcy and then do the deal from a position of strength. But I got over it pretty quickly. Really from that point on my mission was to make sure we got the very best merger outcome for the owners of American, for the creditors, and for our people.[8]

I think that approach worked rather well for us. This ended up as 72/28 in favor of American, with a chunk of equity set aside for the old AMR equity holders." In the end, the AMR creditors will receive full recovery of their claims, which were valued around 20 cents on the dollar when American filed for bankruptcy. And the shareholders, who are typically wiped out in a bankruptcy, will receive equity in the new American valued at around $12 billion—an outcome without precedent."[9]

Once the deal was worked out between the airlines and American's creditors, the focus shifted to the Justice Department. Here Parker's team underperformed. It argued that American and US Airways should not have to give up any slots in a merger. Slots are assigned takeoff and landing times that enable airlines to operate at congested airports including Washington National, long dominated by US Airways. Parker laid out his case to retain all the slots in various venues, including a June 19 hearing before the Senate aviation subcommittee. There, he said that while the new American would have about two-thirds of the slots at National without divesting any, it would have just 50 percent of the seats because it allocated so many of its slots to serving small cities with smaller aircraft. If other airlines were given the slots, he said, they would likely fly to larger cities that already had service.[10] At the hearing, Susan Kurland, Transportation Department assistant secretary for aviation and international affairs, said, "Service to smaller communities is important to DOT." She said that if the Justice Department seeks divestiture, the DOT would seek to ensure that "the merged carrier would have a slot portfolio sufficient to serve small communities as well."[11]

Meanwhile, Parker pointed out that when US Airways and Delta were required to divest National slots in 2011, in order to enable a trade of slots at New York LaGuardia for slots at National, JetBlue used the slots it purchased to add three daily Boston flights, increasing the overall number of National-Boston flights to 25, as well as to add flights to Fort Lauderdale, Orlando, and Tampa, all of which had at least a half-dozen daily flights. In other words, JetBlue simply added service to cities that already had service. Parker also said that US Airways could be forced to eliminate its least profitable flights from National. "If it is a choice to ask us to divest slots and give them to another carrier, we by definition with a scarce resource will continue to [serve markets] that are most lucrative," he said. "We'll reduce service to small and mid-sized communities, and the carriers that get those slots will fly to large communities."[12] While the argument was compelling, it may have backfired in two ways. For one thing, the DOT apparently had a different view of JetBlue's slot use at National. In a March 10, 2014, filing, the agency noted that after JetBlue entered the Reagan National to Boston route in 2010, average fares dropped by 39 percent while the number of passengers nearly doubled. Additionally, it appears that the people most convinced by the argument were Parker and his team. The DOJ's lawsuit came as a major shock to US Airways executives. After all, they had been assured by US Airways' antitrust attorneys that the deal would clear antitrust review. Nevertheless, during a press conference on August 14, the attorneys assured reporters that no one should have been surprised by the lawsuit.[13] This raised the question: Why hadn't they shared that view with their clients?

In any case, once the Justice Department announced it would oppose the merger, US Airways management once again called on labor to rally support. In September, employees from both carriers blitzed Washington, calling on members of Congress and staging a rally. One group of union leaders, including Laura Glading, met with Bill Baer, head of the Justice Department's antitrust division. Additionally, on September 18, about 350 employees gathered for the rally outside the U.S. Capitol building. Five members of Congress from North Carolina, Pennsylvania and Texas spoke in support of the merger, as did a half-dozen union leaders. "It was a beautiful day with perfect blue skies and all of us from two companies coming together with one goal in mind: Let us compete together," said US Airways spokeswoman Michelle Mohr. "We were just getting our voices out there."[14]

At the rally, Glading described a 45-minute meeting between union leaders, Baer, and a deputy attorney general. "The regulators were very, very attentive; they asked a lot of questions," Glading said. "I think it was a great opportunity for us to get our stories out, because it's our story that got us here today."[15] Two weeks later, Texas attorney general Greg Abbott, a key backer of the Justice Department lawsuit, withdrew his support. In October, the mayors of seven hub cities—Charlotte, Chicago, Dallas, Fort Worth, Miami, Philadelphia and Phoenix—sent a letter to Attorney General Eric Holder, asking him "to reconsider this ill-conceived lawsuit."[16] Most prominent among the mayors was Rahm Emanuel of Chicago, who was President Obama's chief of staff from 2008 to 2010.

Eventually, on November 12, 2013, the Justice Department and the airlines announced a settlement—primarily involving divestitures of slots at National—that enabled all parties to declare victory. On a media conference call with Baer, a reporter suggested that the department didn't get much more than the airlines had originally offered. "You're dead wrong," Baer responded. "There was nothing close to this that was ever on the table until recently. There just was not."[17] Baer, meanwhile, noted that the divestiture package in total, which also included 19 slots at New York LaGuardia and gates at five other airports, was "the largest ever in an airline merger."[18] On the airlines' conference call, Horton was asked whether the carriers recently made substantial movement in negotiations. "I don't think the settlement is terribly different from what I would have anticipated early on," Horton responded. "I think it's a reasonable settlement. It allows us to go build the world's best global network."[19] Meanwhile, asked about the toughest concession in the settlement package, Parker responded: "The most painful is the slots at Reagan."[20] Afterwards, online commentator Joe Brancatelli tweeted: "It seems to me DOJ got a good settlement for a lawsuit that airline apologists said had no basis in fact."[21]

Why did the Justice Department agree to settle? A source familiar with the negotiations cited three factors. First, "the folks in the trenches at Justice had trouble delivering to senior management at Justice what they had promised," he said. "As expert reports were exchanged, they began to see weakness in their case, which was not as strong as they had thought." Secondly, the source said, the public relations campaign was successful, despite the antitrust division's strong tradition of being unresponsive to public pressure and even though Baer said on the conference call that labor lobbying—the only unique piece of the lobbying campaign—had no impact. Baer conceded, however, that he and his deputy "had a terrific meeting" with labor leaders. "We pay attention to the fact that people have concerns [and] we understand them [but] our decisions have to be made based on competition and what's good for consumers," he said.[22] On the airlines' conference call, Parker cited the labor support as a major factor in assuring a settlement.[23] "All of those people who came out in favor of the merger over a period of time established a drumbeat," the source said. "That created an environment where I believe people started looking for an opportunity to settle." And thirdly, the source said, "Bill Baer got what he wanted. You can never tell exactly what's on peoples' minds when they file lawsuits, but Bill Baer and the attorney general were very focused on trying to make sure there was improved access for low lost carriers at Reagan and the other airports, and they largely achieved what they sought to achieve."

For the America West team, the long march to presiding over a major airline came on December 9, 2013, at American Airlines headquarters, site of a ceremony where NASDAQ officials welcomed American Airlines Group to the exchange and Parker rang the opening bell. Hundreds of employees attended, and a NASDAQ executive told

American Airlines and US Airways merged on February 9, 2014, in what may be the final major step in the consolidation of the U.S. airline industry (courtesy American Airlines).

them that the louder they cheered, the higher the stock price would go. On the first day of trading, the shares gained 2.7 percent to close at $24.60. The weather outside was icy, prompting Terry Maxon to write, for the *Dallas Morning News* aviation blog, "Those who said it would be a cold day in hell before American Airlines and US Airways would merge got the weather right but the location wrong."[24] The attendees included Bob Crandall, who voiced his support for the merger and the new management team, and embodied the hope that the airline might once again rise to the level it achieved when he was in charge. On the podium, Crandall stood beside Parker and Horton. Said Parker: "We are taking the best of both US Airways and American Airlines to create a formidable competitor, better positioned to deliver for all of our stakeholders. We look forward to integrating our companies quickly and efficiently so the significant benefits of the merger can be realized."[25] Parker also said the biggest challenge would be operational integration, with full integration of the two carriers expected to take 18 to 24 months.

Besides inviting Crandall, a symbol of American's past success, to the event, Parker provided two other signs that his tenure at the airline would be different. In a newsletter, he said he asked to have his compensation set at least 15 percent below that of his peers at Delta and United. "I won't be paid as much as my peers at Delta and United until you are," he said in the newsletter.[26] The airline also said that Parker had eliminated reserved parking spaces for top executives at headquarters as well as security guards for the executive offices. A week later, Parker embraced American's heritage, announcing that the airline would fly a TWA-themed legacy aircraft and an aircraft painted with American's 1968 livery. They would join the four US Airways heritage aircraft, honoring Allegheny, America West, Piedmont and PSA, as well as a newly painted aircraft with the US Airways 2005 paint scheme. Also, employees were asked to vote to select the paint scheme for the combined fleet of 964 aircraft.

Still, an imbalance in the new management team was on display when, on January 28, 2014, at the start of the first earnings call for the new American, eight executives were identified as being available to speak. Of those, seven had been most recently employed at US Airways, and six previously worked at America West. Just one, Bev Goulet, chief integration officer, came from American, a far larger airline. While success has its rewards, it has never been shown that a lack of inclusiveness is the best way to ensure that it continues. Additionally, for the new American, the problems would be far different than those that faced America West and US Airways. The America West team, now running the world's biggest airline, would be looking down at smaller rivals rather than up at bigger ones. It would have, for the first time, preeminent hubs in Dallas and Miami and, for the first time, a hub at Chicago O'Hare that was equal in size to United's. Nevertheless, American did not have the strongest hand or even the second-strongest hand. Rather, it had its New York hub in Philadelphia and its West Coast hub in Phoenix. It badly trailed its two rivals in Asia. And at Chicago O'Hare, for the first time ever, the America West team would be competing with a major global airline operating a hub at the same airport.

In eight-and-a-half years, the team had come a long way from Tempe. Starting out in Dallas, it still had a long way to go.

Chapter Notes

Chapter 1

1. Ed Colodny interview, December 21, 2012.
2. Ed Colodny, quoted in Viewpoint, page 7, in "Fifty Years of Flying High" USAir in-flight magazine, May 1989.
3. Ibid., page 77.
4. Ed Colony interview, December 21, 2012.
5. John Goglia interview, May 15, 2013.
6. David Castelveter interview, May 15, 2013.
7. Ed Colodny interview, December 21, 2012.
8. Ibid.
9. Ibid.
10. Ibid.
11. Ibid.
12. Frank Lorenzo interview, February 12, 2013.
13. Ed Colodny interview, February 7, 2013.
14. Ibid.
15. Ibid.
16. Ed Colodny interview, December 21, 2012.
17. Ibid.
18. Mike Flores interview, June 27, 2013.
19. Ibid.
20. Ibid.
21. Ed Colodny interview, February 7, 2013.
22. Ed Colodny interview, December 21, 2012.
23. Jerry Orr, quoted by Ted Reed in "US Airways' Charlotte Hub Grows Up," *TheStreet*, November 22, 2007.
24. Ed Colodny interview, December 21, 2012.
25. Mike Flores interview, June 27, 2013.
26. Ed Colodny interview, December 21, 2012.
27. Ed Colodny interview, February 7, 2013.
28. Ibid.
29. Ibid.
30. Ibid.
31. Ibid.
32. Warren Buffett, quoted by Antoine Gara in "Buffett: Planes, Trains and Investment Pains," *TheStreet,* May 6, 2013.
33. Ed Colodny interview, February 7, 2013.

Chapter 2

1. David Castelveter interview, May 24, 2013.
2. James Ray interview, July 5, 2013.

3. Ibid.
4. Mike Flores interview, June 27, 2013.
5. Seth Schofield interview, June 7, 2013.
6. Ibid.
7. Ibid.
8. Ibid.
9. David Castelveter interview, May 24, 2013.
10. Seth Schofield interview, June 7, 2013.
11. Ibid.
12. John Goglia interview, May 15, 2013.
13. National Transportation Safety Board report issued July 3, 1990. http://www.ntsb.gov/aviation query/index.aspx.
14. John Goglia interview, May 15, 2013.
15. National Transportation Safety Board report issued October 22, 1991. http://www.ntsb.gov/avia tionquery/index.aspx.
16. John Goglia interview, May 15, 2013.
17. David Castelveter interview, May 24, 2013.
18. Nation Transportation Safety Board report issued February 17, 1993. http://www.ntsb.gov/avia tionquery/index.aspx.
19. John Goglia interview, May 15, 2013.
20. National Transportation Safety Board report issued April 4, 1995. http://www.ntsb.gov/aviation query/index.aspx.
21. John Goglia interview, May 15, 2013.
22. Ibid.
23. David Castelveter interview, May 24, 2013.
24. National Transportation Safety Board report issued March 24, 1999. http://www.ntsb.gov/avia tionquery/index.aspx.
25. John Goglia interview, May 15, 2013.
26. David Castelveter interview, May 24, 2013.
27. John Goglia interview, May 15, 2013.
28. Ibid.
29. Seth Schofield interview, June 7, 2013.

Chapter 3

1. Dan Reed, *The American Eagle: The Ascent of Bob Crandall and American Airlines* (New York: St. Martin's, 1993), page 44.
2. Ibid., pages 89–90.
3. Ibid., page 19.
4. Ibid., pages 20–21.

5. Ibid., page 23.
6. Ibid., pages 25–27.
7. Dave Frailey interview, 1991, Dallas.
8. Dan Reed, *The American Eagle*, pages 31–32.

Chapter 4

1. Dan Reed, *The American Eagle: The Ascent of Bob Crandall and American Airlines* (New York: St. Martin's, 1993), pages 33–37.
2. Al Casey interview, 1991, Dallas, Texas.
3. Ibid.
4. Ibid.
5. Dan Reed, *American Eagle*, page 55.
6. Ibid., pages 166–169.
7. Ibid., page 56.
8. Al Casey interview, 1991, Dallas, Texas.
9. Dan Reed, *American Eagle*, pages 127–140.
10. Al Casey interview, 1991, Dallas, Texas.
11. Dan Reed, *American Eagle*, page 106.
12. Tom Plaskett interview, 1992, Irving, Texas.
13. Al Casey interview, 1991, Dallas, Texas.
14. Ibid.
15. Dan Reed, *American Eagle*, pages 185–191.
16. Ibid., pages 205–208.

Chapter 5

1. Terry Maxon, e-mail to author, September 23, 2013.
2. Dan Reed, *The American Eagle: The Ascent of Bob Crandall and American Airlines* (New York: St. Martin's, 1993), page 17.
3. Bob Crandall interview, April 4, 2013.
4. Ibid.
5. Ibid.
6. Ibid.
7. Ibid.
8. Ibid.
9. Ibid.
10. Ibid.
11. Ibid.
12. Ibid.
13. Ibid.
14. Ibid.
15. Ibid.
16. Ibid.
17. Ibid.

Chapter 6

1. Bob Crandall, quoted by Dan Reed in *The American Eagle: The Ascent of Bob Crandall and American Airlines* (New York: St. Martin's, 1993), page 78.

Chapter 7

1. Ed Beauvais interview, March 5, 2013.
2. Michael Roach interview, February 27, 2013.
3. Ibid.
4. Mike Conway interview, November 11, 2013.
5. Michael Roach interview, February 27, 2013.
6. Ed Beauvais interview, March 5, 2013.
7. Mike Conway interview, November 11, 2013.
8. Michael Roach interview, February 27, 2013.
9. Ed Beauvais interview, March 5, 2013.
10. Bob McAdoo interview, March 12, 2013.
11. Mike Conway interview, November 11, 2013.
12. Ibid.
13. Ed Beauvais interview, March 5, 2013.
14. Ibid.
15. Mike Conway interview, November 11, 2013.
16. Ibid.
17. Ibid.
18. Ibid.
19. Ed Beauvais interview, March 5, 2013.
20. Mike Conway interview, November 11, 2013.
21. Bill Franke interview, March 7, 2013.
22. Ibid.
23. Ibid.
24. Mike Conway interview, November 11, 2013.
25. Ibid.
26. Ibid.
27. Ed Beauvais interview, March 5, 2013.
28. Ibid.
29. Mike Conway interview, January 27, 2014.
30. Jonathan Ornstein interview, January 24, 2014.
31. Ibid.
32. Ibid.
33. Bill Franke interview, March 7, 2013.
34. Ibid.
35. Ibid.
36. Ibid.
37. Ibid.

Chapter 8

1. Jerry Orr, quoted by Ted Reed in "US Airways: Nod to Charlotte," *TheStreet*, December 23, 2009.
2. Tom Davis, quoted by Ted Reed in "Under His Wing," *Charlotte Observer*, June 15, 1997.
3. Ibid.
4. Bill McGee, quoted by Ted Reed in "Under His Wing," *Charlotte Observer*, June 15, 1997.
5. George Batchelor, quoted by Ted Reed in "Under His Wing," *Charlotte Observer*, June 15, 1997.
6. Tom Davis, quoted in "Under His Wing," *The Charlotte Observer*, June 15, 1997.
7. Gordon Bethune, quoted by Ted Reed in "Flying High in Houston," *Charlotte Observer*, December 1, 1997.

8. Ibid.

9. Tom Davis, quoted in "Fifty Years of Flying High," *USAir* inflight magazine, May 1989, page 88.

10. George Mason, quoted by Ted Reed in "Jerry Orr's Airport," *Charlotte Observer*, October 11, 1999.

11. Tom Davis, quoted in "Under His Wing," *Charlotte Observer*, June 15, 1997.

12. Jerry Orr, quoted by Ted Reed in "How US Airways' Charlotte Hub Became Deregulation's Biggest Winner," *TheStreet*, April 17, 2013.

13. Sandy Rederer interview, July 14, 2013.

14. Colleen Fields, quoted by Ted Reed in "Piedmont Founder's Day: Airline's First Flight Took Off 50 Years Ago," *Charlotte Observer*, February 21, 1998.

15. Nigel Adams, quoted by Ted Reed in "Piedmont Founder's Day."

16. Tom Davis, quoted by Ted Reed in "Piedmont Founder's Day."

17. J.B. Simpson, quoted by Ted Reed in "Piedmont Founder's Day."

18. Bill McGee, quoted by Ted Reed in "Piedmont Founder's Day."

19. Bill Wise, interview, July 12, 2013.

20. Ibid.

21. Ibid.

22. George Mason, quoted in "Flying High in Houston," *Charlotte Observer*, December 1, 1997.

23. Gordon Bethune, quoted in "Flying High in Houston."

24. Teddy Xidas, quoted by Ted Reed in "1 Union, 2 Visions," *Charlotte Observer*, March 21, 2004.

25. Ibid.

26. Terri Pope, quoted in by Ted Reed in "1 Union, 2 Visions."

27. Jerry Orr, quoted in "How US Airways' Charlotte Hub Became Deregulation's Biggest Winner," *TheStreet*, April 17, 2013.

28. Ibid.

29. Ibid.

30. Doug Parker, quoted by Ted Reed in "Seven Hot Topics in the US Airways and American Merger," *TheStreet*, March 25, 2013.

31. Dave Barger, quoted by Ted Reed in "Charlotte Airport Boss: Why Would Houston Airports Battle Each Other?" *TheStreet*, May 24, 2012.

32. Terri Pope, quoted by Ted Reed in "Head of the Hub: Passengers Want Their Flights to Run on Time. Terri Pope Works Hard to Make That Happen," *Charlotte Observer*, May 28, 2001.

33. Terri Pope, quoted by Ted Reed in "American Comes to Charlotte, the Heart and Soul of US Airways," *TheStreet*, December 10, 2013.

34. Jerry Orr, quoted by Ted Reed in "North Carolina's Latest Disgrace: Iconic Airport Chief Fired at 72," *TheStreet*, September 23, 2013.

35. Doug Parker, on US Airways earnings call, October 23, 2013.

Chapter 9

1. Stephen Wolf, quoted by Ted Reed in "US Airways Execs Decline Incentives Worth Millions," *Charlotte Observer*, May 20, 1999.

2. Danny Carter, quoted by Ted Reed in "US Airways Execs Decline Incentives Worth Millions," *Charlotte Observer*, May 20, 1999.

3. Stephen Wolf, quoted by Ted Reed in "US Airways Execs Decline Incentives Worth Millions," *Charlotte Observer*, May 20, 1999..

4. Stephen Wolf, quoted by Ted Reed in "Building an Airline the Wolf Way," *Charlotte Observer*, August 25, 1997.

5. Ibid.

6. Al Topping, quoted by Ted Reed in "Building an Airline the Wolf Way," *Charlotte Observer*, August 25, 1997.

7. Stephen Wolf, quoted by Ted Reed in "Building an Airline the Wolf Way," *Charlotte Observer*, August 25, 1997..

8. Stephen Rothmeier, quoted by Ted Reed in "Building an Airline the Wolf Way," *Charlotte Observer*, August 25, 1997.

9. Rahsaan Johnson, e-mail to Ted Reed, February 26, 2014.

10. Jerry Grinstein, quoted by Ted Reed in "Larry Nagin Had a Hand in Airline Makeovers," *TheStreet*, February 2, 2009.

11. David Morrow, quoted by Ted Reed in "Building an Airline the Wolf Way," *Charlotte Observer*, August 25, 1997.

12. Stephen Wolf, quoted by Ted Reed in "Building an Airline the Wolf Way," *Charlotte Observer*, August 25, 1997.

13. Wendy Morse, quoted by Ted Reed in "Pilots Union Wants to Work with United," *TheStreet*, January 7, 2010.

14. Stephen Wolf, quoted by Ted Reed in "The Challenge at Hand," *Charlotte Observer*, November 14, 1996.

15. Stephen Wolf, quoted by Ted Reed in "Wolf Keeps Pressure on Pilots Union," *Charlotte Observer*, May 22, 1997.

16. Rakesh Gangwal, quoted by Ted Reed in "The Challenge at Hand," *Charlotte Observer*, November 14, 1996.

17. Stephen Wolf, quoted by Ted Reed in "US-Airways Still Stumbling Over Baggage of Merger Legacy," *Charlotte Observer*, April 21, 1997.

18. Ibid.

19. Bob McAdoo interview, March 12, 3013.

20. Details from "United-US Airways Deal Largest in Airline History," by Ted Reed and Audrey Williams, *Charlotte Observer*, May 24, 2000.

Chapter 10

1. Statistics provided by Alliance Capital analyst Vivian Lee, quoted by Ted Reed in "US Airways

Falls Below $3 a share," *Charlotte Observer*, May 14, 2002.

2. Ted Reed, "Labor Blasts Airline CEO's Statement: US Airways Leader Says 'Parity Plus One' Pay Not Feasible, Wants to End It," *Charlotte Observer*, March 26, 2002.

3. Ibid.

4. Bill Wise interview, January 31, 2014.

5. Ibid.

6. David Bronner, quoted by Ted Reed in "High-Flying Bet Losing Altitude," *Charlotte Observer*, May 28, 2004.

7. Jerry Grinstein, quoted by Ted Reed in "Delta: US Airways Sets Bad Example," *Charlotte Observer*, January 15, 2004.

8. Ibid.

9. David Siegel, quoted by Ted Reed in "US Airways: More Cuts Coming," *Charlotte Observer*, March 25, 2004.

10. Ibid.

11. Fred Coors, quoted by Ted Reed in "US Airways: More Cuts Coming," *Charlotte Observer*, March 25, 2004.

12. Jack Stephan interview, April 6, 2013.

13. David Castelveter interview, June 1, 2013.

14. Ibid.

15. Bill Wise, quoted by Ted Reed in "CEO of Struggling US Airways Resigns: CEO Weathered Bankruptcy but Faced Mounting Union Opposition." *Charlotte Observer*, April 20, 2004.

16. Mike Flores interview, June 27, 2013.

17. David Siegel, quoted by Ted Reed in "Firm Hands Reaping Applause at USAir," *TheStreet*, August 8, 2006.

18. Ibid.

19. Stan Choe and Ted Reed, "Airline Expected to File Today," *Charlotte Observer*, September 12, 2004.

20. Ibid.

21. Mike Flores, quoted in "Airline Expected to File Today," *Charlotte Observer*, September 12, 2004.

22. Bruce Lakefield, quoted by Ted Reed in "Firm Hands Reaping Applause at USAir," *TheStreet*, August 8, 2006.

23. Doug Parker, quoted by Ted Reed in "Firm Hands Reaping Applause at USAir," *TheStreet*, August 8, 2006.

24. Jonathan Ornstein interview, January 10, 2014.

25. Bill Pollock, quoted by Ted Reed in How US Airways Was Saved, *The Street*, February 23, 2006.

26. Ibid.

27. Mike Flores interview, June 27, 2013.

28. David Castelveter interview, June 1, 2013.

29. Ibid.

Chapter 11

1. Jeff Smisek, quoted by Ted Reed in "US Airways: Who Are You Calling Ugly?" *TheStreet*, May 5, 2010.

2. Tom Horton, quoted by Ted Reed in "AMR CEO on US Airways Bid: "What's in the Water in Phoenix," *TheStreet*, February 3, 2012.

3. Ibid.

4. Tom Horton, quoted by Ted Reed in "AMR CEO Makes Case for Independence," *TheStreet*, April 23, 2012.

5. Tom Horton, quoted by Ted Reed in "US Airways and American Shake Hanks," *TheStreet*, February 14, 2013.

6. Bob McAdoo interview, March 12, 2013.

7. "US Airways Executive Vice President and Chief Administrative Officer Jeffrey McClelland Passes Away," US Airways press release, Sept. 11, 2006.

8. Doug Parker, quoted by Ted Reed in "US Airways CEO: How 9/11 Changed Our Airline," *TheStreet*, September 6, 2011.

9. Ibid.

10. Doug Parker, quoted by Ted Reed in "Assessing US Airways' Doug Parker's Legacy," *TheStreet*, May 13, 2013.

11. Ibid.

12. Bob Mann, quoted by Ted Reed in "US Airways CEO Parker Pulls It All Together," *TheStreet*, May 15, 2008.

13. Doug Parker, quoted by Ted Reed in "Parker Keeps His Promise," *TheStreet*, December 1, 2006.

14. Dawn Gilbertson, quoted by Ted Reed in "Can US Airways, After 7 Years of Practice, Pull Off an AMR Merger?" *TheStreet*, January 3, 2013.

15. David Castelveter interview, August 12, 2013.

16. Doug Parker, quoted by Ted Reed in "Firm Hands Reaping Applause at USAir," *TheStreet*, August 8, 2006.

17. Bill McKee interview, February 4, 2013.

18. Ibid.

19. Ibid.

20. Ibid.

21. Doug Parker, quoted by Ted Reed in "US Airways Flying High," *TheStreet*, May 9, 2006.

22. Scott Kirby, quoted by Ted Reed in "US Airways Flying High," *TheStreet*, May 9, 2006.

Chapter 12

1. Doug Parker, quoted by Ted Reed in "US Air Goes After Delta," *TheStreet*, November 15, 2006.

2. Jerry Grinstein, quoted by Ted Reed in "US Air Goes After Delta," *TheStreet*, November 15, 2006.

3. Doug Parker, quoted by Ted Reed in "US Air Goes After Delta," *TheStreet*, November 15, 2006.

4. Ibid.

5. Scott Kirby, quoted by Ted Reed in "US Air Goes After Delta," *TheStreet*, November 15, 2006.

6. Ibid.

7. Jerry Grinstein, quoted by Ted Reed in "Senate Skeptical of Airline Deals," *TheStreet*, January 24, 2007.

8. Trent Lott, quoted by Ted Reed in "US Airways Merger Hopes Dim," *TheStreet*, January 29, 2007.

9. Claire McCaskill, quoted by Ted Reed in "US Airways Merger Hopes Dim," *TheStreet*, January 29, 2007.

10. Jerry Grinstein, quoted by Ted Reed in "US Airways Merger Hopes Dim," *TheStreet*, January 29, 2007.

11. Robert Roach, quoted by Ted Reed in "US Airways Merger Hopes Dim," *TheStreet*, January 29, 2007.

12. Lee Moak, quoted by Ted Reed in "US Airways Merger Hopes Dim," *TheStreet*, January 29, 2007.

13. Bill Baer, quoted by Ted Reed in "Why Doug Parker's Legacy Hangs on a US Airways/American Merger," *TheStreet*, August 29, 2013.

14. Bill Baer, speaking during Department of Justice media conference call, November 12, 2013.

15. Delta creditors' committee, quoted by Ted Reed in "US Airways Drops Delta Bid," *TheStreet*, January 31, 2007.

16. Doug Parker, quoted by Ted Reed in "US Airways Drops Delta Bid," TheStreet, January 31, 2007.

17. Doug Parker, quoted in the *Arizona Republic* and in "Doug Parker a Bit Too Human," *TheStreet*, February 12, 2007.

18. Doug Parker, quoted in "Doug Parker a Bit Too Human," *TheStreet*, February 12, 2007.

19. Doug Parker, quoted in "US Airways Releases Statement Regarding Alleged DUI Incident," February 9, 2007.

20. Jonathan Ornstein interview, August 14, 2013.

21. Ibid.

22. Doug Parker, quoted by Ted Reed in "United, US Airways Call Off Merger Talks," *TheStreet*, May 30, 2008.

23. Glen Tilton, quoted by Ted Reed in "United, US Airways Call Off Merger Talks," *TheStreet*, May 30, 2008.

24. Sources quoted by Ted Reed in "Why the US Airways/United Merger Collapsed," *TheStreet*, April 23, 2010.

25. Doug Parker, quoted by Ted Reed in "Parker Hinted at United/US Airways Merger," *TheStreet*, April 8, 2010.

26. Scott Kirby, quoted by Ted Reed in "Making the Case for an AMR/US Airways Merger," *TheStreet*, March 23, 2012.

27. Scott Kirby, quoted by Ted Reed in "US Airways' Merger Probability Is High," *TheStreet*, June 1, 2010.

28. Ibid.

29. Ibid.

Chapter 13

1. Mike Flores, quoted by Ted Reed in "US Airways Pilots Bothered by List," *The Street*, September 22, 2009.

2. Bill McKee interview, February 4, 2013.

3. Jack Stephan interview, April 5, 2013.

4. George Nicolau, writing in ALPA Arbitration Board opinion and award in the matter of the seniority integration of the pilots of US Airways, Inc., and the pilots of America West, Inc., May 1, 2007, pages 4 and 5.

5. Ibid., page 6.

6. Ibid. page 25.

7. Ibid., page 27.

8. Ibid., pages 29 and 30.

9. Jack Stephan interview, April 5, 2013.

10. Ibid.

11. George Nicolau, writing in ALPA Arbitration Board opinion and award in the matter of the seniority integration of the pilots of US Airways, Inc., and the pilots of America West, Inc., May 1, 2007, page 14.

12. Jack Stephan interview, April 5, 2013.

13. Ibid.

14. Ibid.

15. Ibid.

16. Ibid.

17. Jack Stephan writing in "MEC Chairman's Message to Pilots, February 8, 2008."

18. Ibid.

19. Mark King, quoted by Ted Reed in "US Airways Pilots Vote for New Union," *TheStreet*, April 17, 2008.

20. Pete Janhunen quoted by Ted Reed in "US Airways Pilots Vote for New Union," *TheStreet*, April 17, 2008.

Chapter 14

1. Quoted by Dan Reed in *The American Eagle: The Ascent of Bob Crandall and American Airlines* (New York: St. Martin's, 1993), page 136.

2. Ibid., page 155.

3. Ibid., page 166–167.

4. Ibid., page 156.

5. Don Carty interview with Dan Reed, November 18, 2013, Dallas.

6. Ibid.

7. Ibid.

8. Ibid.

9. Ibid.

10. Ibid.

11. Ibid.

12. Ibid.

13. Ibid.

14. Ibid.

15. Ibid.

16. Ibid.

Chapter 15

1. Paul Harral, personal conversation with Dan Reed, 1993.

2. Gerard Arpey, quoted by Dan Reed, in "Gerard Arpey Grew Up in the Airline Business," *Fort Worth Star-Telegram*, June 3, 1996

3. Jim Arpey, quoted by Dan Reed in "Gerard Arpey Grew Up in the Airline Business."

4. Ibid.

5. Gerard Arpey interview with Dan Reed, Irving, Texas, November 20, 2013

6. Gerard Arpey telephone interview with Dan Reed, March 5, 2014

7. Ibid.

8. John Darrah, quoted by Dan Reed in "American Strains to Find Footing After Shaky Year," *USA Today*, April 21, 2004.

9. Figures from Dan Reed, "American Strains to Find Footing."

10. Gerard Arpey interview with Dan Reed, March 5, 2014.

11. Ibid.

12. Tom Horton interview with Dan Reed, November 26, 2013.

13. Ibid.

14. Gerard Arpey, quoted by Ted Reed in "American Airlines CEO: How We Do Things Differently," *TheStreet*, September 7, 2010.

15. Gerard Arpey interview with Dan Reed, March 5, 2014.

16. Ibid.

17. Gerard Arpey interview with Dan Reed, November 20, 2013.

18. Ibid.

19. Ibid.

Chapter 16

1. Mark Richard interview, August 22, 2013.

2. Dave Bates interview, August 14, 2013.

3. Mark Richard interview, August 22, 2013.

4. Laura Glading interview, December 2, 2013.

5. Mark Richard, e-mail to author, November 18, 2013.

6. Laura Glading interview, December 2, 2013.

7. Ibid.

8. Jim Little interview, August 2, 2013.

9. Jamie Horwitz interview, December 4, 2013.

10. Kyle Peterson, e-mail to author, January 21, 2014.

11. Ibid.

12. Jamie Horowitz interview, December 4, 2013.

13. Dave Bates, quoted by Ted Reed in "American Pilots Change the Flight Plan," *TheStreet*, September 6, 2010.

14. Dave Bates, quoted by Ted Reed in "American Airlines CEO: How We Do Things Differently," *TheStreet*, September 7, 2010.

15. Terry Maxon in "American Shares Drop Below 2 in Early Trading Tuesday," *Dallas Morning News* Airline Biz blog, November 15, 2011.

16. Dave Bates interview, August 14, 2013.

17. Beverly Goulet, testimony in U.S. Bankruptcy Court in New York, April 24, 2012.

18. Dave Bates interview, August 14, 2013.

19. Ibid.

20. Ibid.

21. Jonathan Ornstein interview, August 14, 2013.

22. Laura Glading interview, December 2, 2013.

23. Jamie Horwitz interview, December 4, 2013.

24. Jack Butler interview, November 14, 2013.

25. Ibid.

26. Mark Richard interview, August 22, 2013.

27. Dave Bates interview, August 14, 2013.

28. Mark Richard interview, August 22, 2013.

29. Jack Butler interview, November 14, 2013.

30. Laura Glading interview, December 2, 2013.

31. Ibid.

32. Ibid.

33. Ibid.

34. Jack Butler interview, November 14, 2013.

Chapter 17

1. Mike Flores, quoted by Ted Reed in "US Airways Flight Attendants Deal Raises Pay, Protects in Merger," *TheStreet*, February 3, 2012.

2. Laura Glading, quoted by Ted Reed in "US Airways Flight Attendant Deal Could Help Merger Effort," *TheStreet,* January 27, 2012.

3. Jack Butler interview, November 14, 2013.

4. Ibid.

5. Dave Bates interview, August 14, 2013.

6. Ibid.

7. Ibid.

8. Bob Crandall, e-mail to Ted Reed, October 13, 2013.

9. Dave Bates interview, August 14, 2013.

10. Ibid.

11. Jim Little interview, August 2, 2013.

12. Ibid.

13. Dave Bates interview, August 14, 2013.

14. Ibid.

15. Scott Kirby, quoted by Ted Reed in "US Airways Exec: Labor Support Needed for Takeover Bid," *TheStreet*, March 13, 2012.

16. Doug Parker, quoted by Ted Reed in "Making the Case for an AMR/US Airways Merger," *TheStreet*, March 23, 2012.

17. Laura Glading interview, December 2, 2013.

18. Ibid.

19. Jim Little interview, August 2, 2013.

20. Ibid.

21. Ibid.

22. Mark Richard interview, August 22, 2013.

23. Jim Little interview, August 2, 2013.

24. Mark Richard interview, August 22, 2013.

25. Ibid.

26. Ibid.

27. Jim Little interview, August 2, 2013.

28. Ibid.

29. Ibid.
30. Dave Bates interview, August 14, 2013.
31. Ibid.
32. Ibid.
33. Ibid.
34. Terry Maxon, email to Ted Reed, August 19, 2013.

Chapter 18

1. Dave Bates interview, August 14, 2013.
2. Ibid.
3. Ted Reed, "US Airways Has Labor Backing for AMR Takeover: Sources," *TheStreet*, April 19, 2012.
4. Dave Bates interview, August 14, 2013.
5. Doug Parker, message to employees, April 20, 2012.
6. International Association of Machinists press release, quoted by Ted Reed in "US Airways Unions on Merger: Don't Forget About Us," *TheStreet*, April 20, 2013.
7. Bill Wise, quoted by Ted Reed in "US Airways Merger Edge: Its CEO Is 'One of Us,'" *TheStreet*, July 17, 2012.
8. Sito Pantoja, quoted by Ted Reed in "US Airways Union Assails 'Back Room Deal' with AMR Workers, *TheStreet*, January 29, 2013.
9. Gary Hummel interview, August 8, 2013.
10. Dave Bates interview, August 14, 2013.
11. Gary Hummel, quoted by Ted Reed in "US Airways' New Pilot Leader Calls Himself a 'Peacemaker,'" *TheStreet*, March 27, 2012.
12. Ibid.
13. Gary Hummel interview, August 8, 2013.
14. Ibid.
15. Dave Bates interview, August 14, 2013.
16. Gary Hummel interview, August 8, 2013.
17. Anonymous, e-mail to Ted Reed, December 17, 2013.
18. Dave Bates interview, August 14, 2013.
19. Ibid.
20. Gary Hummel interview, January 10, 2014.
21. Dave Bates interview, August 14, 2013.
22. Ibid.
23. Ibid.
24. Laura Glading interview, December 2, 2013.
25. Ibid.
26. Gary Hummel interview, August 9, 2013.
27. Ibid.
28. Gary Hummel interview, January 10, 2014.

Chapter 19

1. Roger Holmin, quoted by Ted Reed in "Maybe Attorneys Expected DOJ Lawsuit—But Airline Industry Was Shocked," *TheStreet*, August 16, 2013.
2. Kevin Starke, quoted by Ted Reed in "Analyst Was Early to See Possible Value in AMR Shares," *TheStreet*, January 14, 2013.
3. Interview with Jamie Horwitz, December 4, 2013.
4. Doug Parker, quoted by Ted Reed in "US Airways CEO—Everybody Wants a Merger Except for AMR Bosses," *TheStreet*, July 19, 2012.
5. James Ray, e-mail to Ted Reed, March 3, 2014.
6. Bella Goren, quoted by Ted Reed in "American CFO: Just Wait Until Our Cost Savings Kick In," *TheStreet*, July 18, 2012.
7. American Airlines press release, quoted in by Ted Reed in "American CFO."
8. Tom Horton interview with Dan Reed in Fort Worth, November 26, 2013.
9. Ibid.
10. Doug Parker, quoted by Ted Reed in "US Airways CEO Disputes Need for Reagan National Divestitures," *TheStreet*, June 20, 2013.
11. Susan Kurland, quoted by Ted Reed in "US Airways CEO Disputes."
12. Doug Parker, quoted by Ted Reed in "US Airways CEO Disputes."
13. Ted Reed, "Maybe Attorneys Expected DOJ Lawsuit—But Airline Industry Was Shocked," *TheStreet*, August 16, 2013.
14. Michelle Mohr, quoted by Ted Reed in "US Airways/American Workers Merger Blitz Is Unique, Expert Says," *TheStreet*, September 19, 2013.
15. Laura Glading, quoted by Ted Reed in "US Airways/American Workers."
16. Letter to Eric Holder, quoted by Ted Reed in "Pressure Mounts on DOJ to Accept US Airways/American Merger," *TheStreet*, October 24, 2013.
17. Bill Baer, quoted by Ted Reed in "Airline Merger: DOJ Wins Big at National, Loses on Connecting Routes," *TheStreet*, November 15, 2013.
18. Ibid.
19. Tom Horton, quoted by Ted Reed in "Everyone Declares Victory After US Airways/AMR Merger Approval," *TheStreet*, November 13, 2013.
20. Doug Parker, quoted by Ted Reed in "Everyone Declares Victory."
21. Joe Brancatelli, quoted by Ted Reed in "Airline Merger: DOJ Wins Big at National, Loses on Connecting Routes," *TheStreet*, November 15, 2013.
22. Bill Baer, quoted by Ted Reed in "Everyone Declares Victory."
23. Doug Parker, quoted by Ted Reed in "Everyone Declares Victory."
24. Terry Maxon, *Dallas Morning News* aviation blog, December 9, 2013.
25. Doug Parker, quoted in American Airlines press release, "AMR Corporation and US Airways Group Come Together to Build the New American Airlines," December 9, 2013.
26. Doug Parker, quoted in American Airlines Arrivals newsletter, December 9, 2013.

Bibliography

Books

Reed, Dan. *The American Eagle: The Ascent of Bob Crandall and American Airlines.* New York: St. Martin's, 1993.

Interviews

Arpey, Gerard, with Dan Reed. Irving, Texas, November 20, 2013.

Bates, Dave, with Ted Reed. By telephone, August 14, 2013, and subsequent.

Beauvais, Ed, with Ted Reed. By telephone, March 5, 2013.

Butler, Jack, with Ted Reed. By telephone, November 14, 2013 and subsequent.

Carty, Don, with Dan Reed. Dallas, Texas, November 18, 2013.

Castelveter, David, with Ted Reed. By telephone, May 14, 2013, and subsequent.

Colodny, Ed, with Ted Reed. By telephone, February 7, 2013, and subsequent.

Conway, Mike, with Ted Reed. By telephone, November 11, 2013.

Crandall, Bob, with Ted Reed. By telephone, April 4, 2013.

Flores, Mike, with Ted Reed. By telephone, June 27, 2013.

Franke, Bill, with Ted Reed. By telephone, March 7, 2013, and subsequent.

Glading, Laura, with Ted Reed. By telephone, October 22, 2013.

Goglia, John, with Ted Reed. By telephone, May 15, 2013.

Horton, Tom, with Dan Reed. Fort Worth, Texas, November 26, 2013.

Horwitz, Jamie, with Ted Reed. By telephone, December 10, 2013.

Hummel, Gary, with Ted Reed. By telephone, August 8, 2013, and subsequent.

Johnson, Rahsaan, with Ted Reed. By email, February 26, 2014.

Little, James, with Ted Reed. By telephone, August 2, 2013.

Lorenzo, Frank, with Ted Reed. By telephone, February 12, 2013.

Maxon, Terry, with Ted Reed. By email, August 19, 2013, and subsequent.

McAdoo, Bob, with Ted Reed. By telephone, March 12, 2013, and subsequent.

McKee, Bill, with Ted Reed. By telephone, February 4, 2013.

Ornstein, Jonathan, with Ted Reed. By telephone, August 14, 2013, and subsequent.

Peterson, Kyle, with Ted Reed. By email, Dec. 13, 2013.

Ray, James, with Ted Reed. By telephone, July 5, 2013, and subsequent.

Rederer, Sandy, with Ted Reed. By telephone, July 14, 2013.

Richard, Mark, with Ted Reed. By telephone, August 22, 2013.

Roach, Michael, with Ted Reed. By telephone, February 27, 2013.

Schofield, Seth, with Ted Reed. By telephone, June 7, 2013, and subsequent.

Stephan, Jack, with Ted Reed. By telephone, April 5, 2013, and subsequent.

Wise, Bill, with Ted Reed. By telephone, July 12, 2013, and subsequent.

Newspapers and Magazines

The authors have quoted from stories they had written for the *Charlotte Observer*, the *Fort Worth Star-Telegram*, *TheStreet* and *USA Today*.

The USAir in-flight magazine of May 1989 included a lengthy history of the airline entitled "Fifty Years of Flying High."

Index